Praise for *The Change Cookbook*

NO LONGER PR
SEATTLE PUBLI
D1033875

"Healthy food that tastes great"

"Do you want to have more fun in the kitchen?
The Change Cookbook lets you have a ball making
and eating healthy food that tastes great."

–Joel Fuhrman, MD
Six-Time *New York Times* Best-Selling Author
Director of Research, Nutritional Research Foundation

<hr>

"Bursting with soul and taste"

"Milan and Scott have torn it up with *The Change
Cookbook.* Packed with plant-strong recipes bursting
with soul and taste, you definitely want to add
The Change Cookbook to your whole foods
plant-based collection!"

–Rip Esselstyn
Health Activist and Best-Selling Author of *The Engine 2 Diet*

<hr>

"Transformational"

"Dr. Scott Stoll and Milan Ross in their roles respectively
of caregiver and patient have joined their talents to create
a transformational knowledge base and delicious recipes
that will empower the reader to reverse disease, avoid
illness, and achieve lasting well-being."

–Caldwell B. Esselstyn, Jr, MD
Best-Selling Author of *Prevent and Reverse Heart Disease*

---◆◆◆---

"Simple, fun, and delicious"

"*The Change Cookbook* is a beautiful gift to everyone
who has ever wanted to transform their health. It guides
the reader through a delightful culinary adventure,
providing all the essential tools for success.
The advice is sound, and the recipes are sensational—
simple, fun and delicious. This is one resource that will
end up as a constant companion on your health journey."

–Brenda Davis, RD
Dietitian and Best-Selling Co-Author of *Becoming Vegan:*
The Complete Reference to Plant-Based Nutrition

---◆◆◆---

"Life-altering"

"Dr. Scott Stoll's work is changing the way people
look at the connection between clean food and optimum
health. Anyone who has the incredible opportunity
to meet him is presented with compassion, empathy,
and honesty. This life-altering cookbook provides
readers with a chance to meet and—
most important—learn from Dr. Stoll."

–Chad Sarno
Plant-Based Chef, Educator, and Consultant

---◆◆◆---

The Change

COOKBOOK

USING THE POWER OF FOOD TO TRANSFORM YOUR BODY, YOUR HEALTH, AND YOUR LIFE

MILAN ROSS
SCOTT STOLL, MD

SQUAREONE
PUBLISHERS

The information and advice contained in this book are based upon the research of the authors, and are not intended as a substitute for consulting with a licensed healthcare professional. The publisher and authors are not responsible for any adverse effects or consequences resulting from the use of any of the information, suggestions, or recipes presented in the book. All matters pertaining to your physical health, including your diet, should be supervised by a healthcare professional who can provide medical care that is tailored to meet individual needs.

COVER DESIGNER: Jeannie Tudor
TYPESETTER: Gary A. Rosenberg
IN-HOUSE EDITOR: Joanne Abrams

Square One Publishers
115 Herricks Road
Garden City Park, NY 11040
(516) 535-2010 • (877) 900-BOOK
www.squareonepublishers.com

Library of Congress Cataloging-in-Publication Data
Names: Ross, Milan, author. | Stoll, Scott, author.
Title: The change cookbook : using the power of food to transform your body, your health, and your life / Milan Ross, Scott Stoll, MD.
Description: Garden City Park, NY : Square One Publishers, [2018] | Includes index. Identifiers: LCCN 2017021487 (print) | LCCN 2017027761 (ebook) | ISBN 9780757054389 (ebook) | ISBN 9780757004384 (paperback)
Subjects: LCSH: Nutrition. | Vegan cooking. | Self-care, Health. | LCGFT: Cookbooks. Classification: LCC RA784 (ebook) | LCC RA784 .R676 2016 (print) | DDC 641.5/636--dc23 LC record available at https://lccn.loc.gov/2017021487

Copyright © 2018 by Milan Ross and Scott Stoll

All rights reserved. No part of this publication may be reproduced, scanned, uploaded, stored in a retrieval system, or transmitted, in any form or by any means, electronic, mechanical, photocopying, recording, or otherwise, without the prior written permission of the publisher.

Printed in the United States of America

10   9   8   7   6   5   4   3   2   1

Contents

Acknowledgments

MILAN ROSS

I want to start by thanking my best friend, my partner, my wife, Iris. Without her continued love and support, none of this would be possible. I am humbled by your love and grace and grateful that I get to go through this amazing journey called life with you by my side. I love you to the moon and back! Nigel, my son, thank you for inspiring me to be better, do more, and work harder. I am blessed to have you and your new baby sister, Anora, in my life. To my daughter Georgia, I love you more than words can express. Thanks for always reminding me what's important.

Joanette Ross, you were not only an exceptional mother and cook, you were also the person who taught me that food is simply love made visual. I truly hope you are up in heaven smiling as you watch me continue to grow into the man that you and dad (James Ross) raised me to be. I miss both of you like crazy!

To my sisters Barbra, Stephanie, and Jackie, thanks for all the unconditional love and support.

Dr. Scott Stoll, I am honored to call you my friend, business partner, coauthor, and brother. You, Kristen, and the kids are like family to Iris and me. I look forward to all the adventures still to come as we continue our quest to help the world change, one bite at a time.

Chef Vicki Chelf, you are truly a beast in the kitchen! Thank you for all your hard work and support on this project. Scott and I could not have done this without you.

Rudy Shur, you are truly gifted in the world of publishing. Without your vision, direction, and unwavering support, this project would not exist. Thank you for believing in me. Joanne Abrams, you are truly a godsend! Thank you for your attention to detail and for making sure that everything in this book is the absolute best it can be. To the rest of the Square One family, I want to say thank you for all the love and support you continue to give Dr. Stoll and me. We are grateful to have such a wonderful team working with us on this project.

Kristin Irwin, to say that you are amazing would be a huge understatement! You are not only the best attorney and advisor anyone anywhere could ever hope to work with; you are also an incredible person. Thank you for all that you continue to do to help me make my dreams come true.

Kimberly Kirk, you are a blessing! Thank you for always being a source of light and support.

To Mark Koops, Adam Sud, Will Tucker, Tom Dunnam, Wendie Pett, Anthony Harris, Denley Fowlke, and the entire Sunwarrior tribe, thank you for always supporting me!

To everyone out there going through his or her own personal journey, I want you to know that both Dr. Stoll and I support you. You can do this. Just remember that "change" is a verb; you have to supply the action!

DR. SCOTT STOLL

This beautiful book that you hold in your hands is the combined effort of an amazing group of people who have generously contributed their unique gifts and precious time to make this project possible. First, I am eternally grateful for my wife, my partner, my friend Kristen Stoll who is ever my encourager, creative partner in the kitchen, wise sounding board, and champion of simple, delicious food. Milan, it has been a great joy and privilege to work with you on this project. I feel so blessed to have this unique opportunity to bring life-giving change to people in need around the world. Thank you, my brother.

A special thank-you to Vicki Chelf, chef extraordinaire, for all of your assistance and creative ideas that helped make this cookbook a wonderful collection of healthy, delicious meals. A huge thank-you to Rudy Shur and Joanne Abrams for their matchless vision, tenacious persistence, endless patience, and warm kindness through

every step of the creative process. You are both remarkable professionals with integrity that is equaled by your refined and exceptional skills. And a heartfelt thank-you to the entire Square One team for your professional attention to this beautiful book, which will help transform people and families far and wide.

My children have been so patient, supportive, and willing to try new recipes—and even to offer a warm smile and word of encouragement when the recipes were not quite ready for prime time. Thank you, Dawson, Gabriel, Samuel, Joy, Elijah, and Faith.

A special thank-you to all of the people and families that have inspired this cookbook; those who see a healthier, brighter future by changing the food on their plate and have asked for better ways to make wholesome food absolutely delicious. This cookbook and its tempting recipes are for you.

Introduction

MILAN ROSS

Change is not always easy. Sometimes it occurs because of outside influences, and sometimes it comes from within. When I began my own journey of change, I tipped the scales at about 450 pounds. I was fortunate enough to work for a company—Whole Foods Market—that offered a free wellness program to those employees lucky enough to be selected. The program consisted of a week-long stay at a beautiful beach resort. Each morning, participants attended either a lecture or a workshop. The afternoons were free. The doctor in charge of the "Immersion" program, as it was called, was Dr. Scott Stoll. His mission was simple. He would provide those attending the retreat with a working knowledge of why most people get sick and then explain how the disease process could be stopped and even reversed through diet. For one week, all the participants were put on a plant-based meal plan prepared by a top chef.

During the time I was privileged to spend with Scott and his staff, each day was a revelation as I learned about my health—and about myself. I ate meals I would have never have eaten on my own. As the name of the program implies, that week, I was completely immersed in a healthy lifestyle and a flood of truly eye-opening information. This forced me to reevaluate the way I had lived my life up to that point. The more I learned, the more I realized that I had it within myself to control what I consumed. The prediabetes, the high blood pressure, and the aches and pains that came with carrying all that extra weight could disappear if I committed myself to making them disappear. I thought about my wife and young son, and how my size had prevented me from doing so many things with them. By the end of the week, I not only believed that change was possible, but I had also lost an amazing thirty-five pounds.

When I returned home, I had the inspiration and working knowledge needed to alter what I had been eating for decades. Over the next two years, I dropped more than two hundred and twenty-five pounds. And while my week's experience at Dr. Stoll's Immersion was published along with the good doctor's own story in our book *The Change: Transforming Your Yourself and Your Body Into the Person You Want to Be*, I have since discovered a talent for creating amazing dishes that satisfy not only me but also my family and friends. I have found that the principles behind Immersion can easily be applied to the creation of healthful, delicious, satisfying meals. If you've read our book *The Change*, here is a resource that you can use to move forward with your own personal change. If you have not, here is a book of recipes that are sure to delight you, your family, and your guests, and maybe, just maybe, will also set you on the path to better health.

DR. SCOTT STOLL

As a practicing physician, I have been trained to identify health issues and provide my patients with potential solutions. Early in my career, most of the remedies I offered took the form of pills, procedures, or therapies. As my practice grew, I noticed that many of my patients expected to leave my office with a prescription in hand. Whether it was a seasonal cold, back pain, high blood pressure, or a bad headache, they wanted medications to alleviate their symptoms. As time went on, I would see the same patients again and again regarding the same issues. Yes, I could give them further prescriptions for their symptoms, but these prescriptions could not eliminate the underlying causes of their health problems. What was it that I was missing?

As I began to learn more about the foods we eat, the connection between health and diet became crystal clear. I was lucky enough to stand on the shoulders of medical researchers and pioneering physicians who had scientifically shown that poor eating habits have led to an amazing 80 percent of the devastating illnesses that plague our society. But how could I tell my patients that most of their medications would be unnecessary if only they changed the food on their plates? Although I had long talks with many of the people who came to me for help, I learned that old eating habits can be hard to break. And then I was given an opportunity to do something truly extraordinary: I would conduct a week-long immersion program designed to lead participants on a journey to better health. Once they had received both the information and the motivation they needed, and had also experienced the positive effects of a different way of eating, they could make a lasting, sustainable lifestyle change.

Each day, the participants would learn why certain foods were bad for them and other foods were good, and how those foods directly impacted their health. They would also come to grips with the fact that many of the bad foods that people in our society consume every day—refined sugar, for instance—are as addictive as tobacco or even heroin. They would eat only healthy plant-based meals during the week-long Immersion, and to their surprise, they would experience actual withdrawal symptoms, which would disappear in two to three days as their bodies detoxified and healed. But they would also begin to experience greater health, including lower blood pressure and better-controlled blood sugar. The lesson was profound and yet simple: As long as you realize that you have the power to make a choice every day and you know what the best choices are, you can regain your health and change the trajectory of your life.

Among the attendees of the program was Milan Ross. He took all the information we presented to heart. When he returned home, he practiced the dietary principles he had learned, lost a tremendous amount of weight, and overcame his chronic medical conditions. Since then, Milan and I have become good friends as well as coauthors. As you will see, this cookbook is an extension of the program Milan attended, as well as a great collection of tasty kitchen-tested recipes. You will also find a number of interesting facts about foods that will make you stop and think about your health. Remember that your kitchen is the most important room in your home, and the delicious food that you prepare should not only please your palate, but also place you and your loved ones on the road to greater health and a far more satisfying life.

1.

The Basics

Do you want to experience renewed vitality, energy, strength, and health? If so, you'll be happy to learn that greater health is as simple as buying, preparing, and eating wholesome plant-based foods. In fact, your journey to wellness can begin with your next meal.

This chapter was created to start you on your journey by explaining some of the "basics" of plant-based cooking. First, you'll learn why a diet that emphasizes whole plant-based foods is central to a healthy lifestyle. Then you'll learn how to go about stocking your pantry and equipping your kitchen for success. Following this, we guide you in using a handful of simple cooking techniques that will enable you to prepare the delicious dishes presented in this book. Along the way, we provide valuable tips that will smooth your transition from your current way of eating to a diet that will please your palate as you improve your well-being. Let the journey begin!

WHY YOU SHOULD FOLLOW A PLANT-BASED DIET

We designed this cookbook around a whole foods plant-based diet. Studies have shown that the longest-lived, healthiest groups of people on Earth all follow a predominantly plant-based diet containing whole or minimally processed foods and minimal animal foods. Over the past fifty years, extensive scientific research has documented that this diet can prevent at least 80 percent of chronic disease, and in many cases can suspend and reverse serious disorders such as type 2 diabetes and heart disease.

A whole food plant-based diet is beneficial for several reasons. First, because it contains an abundant amount of vegetables, fruits, whole grains, legumes, nuts, and seeds, this diet provides all of the nutrients necessary to maintain your body's optimal function. It offers a wealth of vitamins and minerals, which are required for the billions of chemical reactions that occur every day in your body. It supplies the phytochemicals and antioxidants your body needs to repair DNA damage, reduce inflammation, protect against viruses and bacteria, maintain bone density, and exert a positive hormonal effect throughout the body. And because it is rich in fiber, it supports the beneficial gut bacteria that work to reduce inflammation; strengthen the immune system; control blood sugar; and help prevent cancer, heart disease, arthritis, and many other health disorders.

Some people worry that plant-based diets don't provide enough high-quality protein to meet the body's needs. But according to the American Dietetic Association, as long as you have a varied diet that includes vegetables, beans, grains, nuts, and seeds—all of which contain some protein, and some of which contain a good amount of protein—you will be getting an adequate amount of this important nutrient. In fact, there are more than twice as many grams of protein per calorie in broccoli, kale, and romaine lettuce than there are in a piece of steak. (To learn more about protein, see the inset on page 5.)

A whole food plant-based diet is also beneficial because it does *not* contain the many harmful foods that are usually found in the western diet. The following list presents the foods that feature prominently in the western diet and explains how they can contribute to poor health.

Common Foods on a Standard Western Diet

Refined sugar. These days, more and more information is becoming available on the dangers of sugar, and for good reason. Refined sugar, or table sugar, triggers an acute inflammatory response that contributes to heart disease, diabetes, cancer, and many other disorders. Within hours of eating sugar, there is a measurable increase of inflammation, a constriction of blood vessels, and reduced immune system function that lasts for up to four hours. Sugar also alters the delicate web of microorganisms—called the *microbiome*—that account for 75 percent of the health of your immune system. And, of course, this empty-calorie food causes both blood sugar and insulin levels to spike, and also plays a role in obesity.

Refined flours and other processed foods. These foods have effects similar to those of sugar. They trigger inflammation, cause blood sugar and insulin levels to spike, and affect the body in many other harmful ways. Like sugar, refined flours and processed foods have been linked to the development of many of the disorders that plague our society, including heart disease and cancer.

Animal products. When meat, poultry, and fish constitute more than 10 percent of the total calories in a diet, they can contribute to the development and progression of disease. Research has found that a long list of animal product components can play a role in inflammation, and that cooking over high heat generates carcinogenic chemicals such as HCA, PAHs, and AGEs. The bacteria that live in your gut are sensitive to animal products, and tend to be healthiest in plant eaters. When too many animal products are consumed, there is a measurable shift toward the types of bacteria that produce inflammation. This, in turn, increases the risk of heart disease and many other health problems. Although fish is often recommended as a healthful food because it contains anti-inflammatory omega-3 fatty acids, many fish now also contain high levels of toxins, such as mercury. Also, omega-3 levels can vary widely based upon where the fish are raised. So the toxins found in fish can outweigh any potential benefits. And as you already know, many animal foods provide too much saturated fat and cholesterol.

Processed meats. While all animal foods pose a danger, the greatest risk is associated with processed meats like hot dogs, sausages, sandwich meats, and bacon. Recently, the World Health Organization classified these foods as Group 1 carcinogens, meaning that they are definitely carcinogenic. (For perspective, note that red meats are considered Group 2A carcinogens, meaning that they are *probably* carcinogenic.) Pickled, smoked, and salted foods often contain nitrates and nitrites, which convert to carcinogenic substances during cooking.

Dairy products. Milk and the products made from milk naturally contain high levels of

estrogen, growth hormone, and proteins known as casein and whey. These substances can contribute to systemic inflammation, mucus production, ear infections, acne, polycystic ovarian disease, endometriosis, infertility, intestinal disease, and many cancers, including cancers of the prostate and ovaries.

Salt. Excessive salt consumption can contribute to high blood pressure and heart disease, and increase the risk of stroke, stomach cancer, and osteoporosis. Most Americans consume about 3,300 milligrams of sodium per

Understanding Proteins and Amino Acids

Protein is a vital nutrient. It is present in every cell and tissue—in fact, it is the building block of cells—and is needed for virtually every function the body performs. Since the chief source of protein for non-vegans is animal foods, some people fear that a plant-based diet cannot provide enough protein for good health. But the truth is that a sound plant-based diet includes plenty of this nutrient. To understand why, you have to know a little bit about amino acids.

Proteins are composed of amino acids, which are small organic compounds. There are about twenty amino acids that your body needs to function properly. The body can make some amino acids, but nine of them are termed *essential,* meaning that the body has to get them from the food you eat. In order to be considered a *complete protein,* a food must include all nine of these essential amino acids. Some plant-based foods are complete proteins, including quinoa, buckwheat, hemp seeds, sacha inchi

seeds, and soy-based foods like tofu and tempeh. Many more—most nuts and seeds, legumes, grains, and vegetables—are *incomplete proteins,* meaning that they provide some but not all essential amino acids. But as long as your body gets all of these amino acids over the course of a day, it is able to produce the protein it requires. In fact, when you digest protein, the body breaks it down into amino acids and then reassembles it into the specific forms of protein needed.

The key to getting adequate protein is to eat a variety of whole plant-based foods. If you fill your diet with nutrient-poor processed foods or you eat only a few whole foods—like potatoes and some fruit—it is possible to get insufficient protein. But if you include vegetables, whole grains, legumes, nuts, and seeds in your diet, you'll get all the protein you need, along with many other nutrients that will help your body thrive.

day, which is way above the ideal range of 1,200 to 1,500 milligrams. Although most of the salt in the western diet comes from processed foods rather than the salt shaker, it is best to use minimal amounts of salt in food preparation.

Oil. The oil used in food preparation contains 120 calories per tablespoon, and most vegetable oils are very high in inflammatory omega-6 fatty acids. Even though olive oil is a better choice than many others, it is still high in calories, and these calories can add up quickly. Consider that 4 tablespoons of oil per day—from salad dressings, processed foods, and cooking—would contribute nearly 500 calories! That is why we recommend a minimal use of oil in the kitchen. (For more information on oils, see page 17.)

Soda. Both sugar-sweetened soda and regular soda have been linked to increased appetite and weight gain, as well as a slew of health disorders. You already know the harmful effects of sugar, but switching to diet soda is not recommended. Artificial sweeteners have a long list of potential side effects, including the alteration of the gut microbiome and memory impairment.

You now know why a standard western diet is so damaging to your health and why a whole food plant-based diet is so beneficial. If you are in the process of transitioning to a plant-based food plan, we congratulate you, because you are about to significantly enhance your well-being. But we also urge you to give yourself a little time to move from one way of eating to another. Focus on the basics of your new diet, which should include large helpings of vegetables and fruits, smaller amounts of whole grains and legumes, and a handful or

two of raw seeds and nuts. Eat at least one salad a day so that some of your veggies are raw. Use as little oil, sweeteners, and salt as possible so that you can start appreciating the taste of fresh plant-based foods.

The kitchen-tested, nutritionally sound recipes presented later in this book will make it easy to enjoy a plant-based diet. It's important, though, to take things step by step. Your first step toward a healthy new lifestyle will be to remove the damaging foods from your pantry and stock it with wholesome plant-based foods. The next section is devoted to helping you do just that.

STOCKING YOUR PANTRY FOR SUCCESS

A well-stocked kitchen is one of the most important keys to a whole food plant-based lifestyle. Before you begin stocking up, though, you must thoroughly clean out all of those items that have no place in your new diet. Processed foods—including refined flour, refined sugar, chips, candy, crackers made of refined flours, cookies, and other unhealthy products—have to go. If they remain in your cabinet, refrigerator, and freezer, they will continue to tempt you and your family. People who simply gives up meat, cheese, and eggs while continuing to eat processed empty-calorie foods are sometimes referred to as a "junk food vegans." While they are avoiding the dangers associated with animal foods, they are not eating foods that provide the nutrients needed for good health. With a clean pantry, you won't have to fight the mental battles that inevitably arise when you see junk food on your shelf, and you will start gaining power over your life and your health.

Once you have tossed away all the nutritionally empty products from your kitchen, you'll probably find that you have a lot of open shelf space. That's great, because you'll need room for whole grains, fruits, vegetables, beans, nuts, and all the other foods that you'll be using to create wholesome vegan meals. Below, we discuss some of the most important foods you will be using and provide guidance in choosing them. You will be able to find many of these ingredients in a good supermarket, but for some products, you will probably have to rely on your local natural foods stores. We also urge you to patronize farmers markets, where you'll find in-season produce that's grown locally.

Vegetables and Fruits

While nutrition experts have proposed many different (and in some cases contradictory) diets for better health, all of the experts seem to agree that vegetables and fruits are an essential part of any sound eating plan. Produce is naturally low in calories; rich in vitamins and minerals; packed with fiber; and full of phytochemicals, the health-promoting compounds found only in plants. If that doesn't convince you that fruits and veggies are important, consider that a diet high in produce reduces the risk for heart disease, stroke, and some cancers, and also helps manage body weight when eaten in place of more energy-dense foods, such as cheese, crackers, and chocolates.

We encourage you to give veggies and fruits a starring role in your diet, and to opt for organic produce whenever you can. Organic food is produced without the synthetic herbicides, pesticides, and fungicides that are used on conventionally grown crops; and is also free of genetically modified organisms, or GMOs. Food produced organically has also been shown to contain consistently higher levels of phytochemicals and antioxidants. Of course, organically grown food costs more than conventional crops, so it makes sense to know which foods are highest and lowest in agricultural chemicals so that you can spend your dollars wisely. The Environmental Working Group, or EWG, provides lists of the "Dirty Dozen Plus," which are more likely to be laden with pesticides, and the "Clean Fifteen," which are less likely to contain these harmful chemicals. (See the inset found on page 8.) Both of these lists are updated periodically, so it pays to review them from time to time on the EWG's website (www.ewg.org). Whenever you use conventionally grown fruit, be sure to remove the peel.

Although fresh produce is generally best, in some cases, frozen fruits and vegetables—which are packed at the peak of freshness—are also good choices. As you'll see, our recipes make use of frozen corn, frozen peas, and frozen fruits such as cranberries and pineapple. Our recipes also occasionally use dried fruit, sometimes as a sweetener, and sometimes for its wonderful flavor and bounty of fiber, vitamins, and minerals. When purchasing dried fruit, buy organic so that you avoid sulfites. (Nonorganic fruit is often sprayed with sulfur dioxide to make it look more appealing.) Also try to avoid dried fruits with added sugar. Finally, remember that while dried fruits are packed with nutrients, they are also high in sugar and calories, and should be eaten in moderation, usually to add a touch of sweetness to salads, dressings, baked goods, and other dishes.

The Dirty Dozen Plus and the Clean Fifteen

While it may be ideal to eat only organically grown fruits and vegetables, doing so can be very expensive. Fortunately, the Environmental Working Group, or EWG, publishes a list of the Dirty Dozen Plus (the produce that's most likely to be contaminated by pesticide residues), as well as the Clean Fifteen (the produce that bears few if any pesticide residues). By using the following lists as guides, you can spend your money wisely by paying for organic produce only when it will make a real difference to your health.

The Dirty Dozen Plus

- Strawberries
- Spinach
- Nectarines
- Apples

- Peaches
- Pears
- Cherries

- Grapes
- Celery
- Tomatoes

- Sweet bell peppers
- Potatoes
- Hot peppers

The Clean Fifteen

- Sweet corn
- Avocados
- Pineapples
- Cabbage

- Onions
- Sweet peas (frozen)
- Papayas

- Asparagus
- Mangos
- Eggplant
- Honeydew melon

- Kiwi
- Cantaloupe
- Cauliflower
- Grapefruit

Beans, Peas, and Lentils

Also known as legumes, dried beans, peas, and lentils are an excellent source of protein, minerals such as potassium, and fiber. They are a cornerstone of a plant-based diet and add nutrition, color, texture, and substance to meals while increasing feelings of fullness. Legumes are also one of the best sources of resistant starch, or RS, with about 20 to 30 percent resistant starch by weight. That means that almost half of the starch in raw legumes is resistant to digestion in the small intestine, and instead makes it ways to the large intestine (the colon), where intestinal bacteria ferment. This can benefit us in many ways. It can help us lower blood cholesterol and fats while decreasing the production of new fats. It can help us feel full by triggering the release of hormones that reduce the drive to eat. Because resistant starch doesn't digest into blood sugar, the body doesn't release much insulin in response. In fact, RS may also improve insulin sensitivity. Finally, RS can help feed the good bacteria in your microbiome and reduce inflammation.

As busy families, we have found that a mixture of canned and dried legumes help us stay on schedule and eat well. Ideally, canned beans should be low in sodium and packed in cans that are free of BPA (bisphenol A), a synthetic estrogen found in the epoxy coatings of food cans that can seep into food. (Organic canned beans are usually your best bet.) Before adding the beans to your dish, be sure to rinse and drain them to remove as much salt as possible. Dried beans and lentils are less expensive. They can be purchased in bulk; stored in airtight containers in a cool, dark, dry place; and cooked in a regular pot on a stove top or, if time is an issue, can be prepared in a pressure cooker (see page 24). Always buy them from stores that have a high rate of turnover, so that you can be fairly certain that the legumes are fresh. Old beans and split peas do not cook properly

While many people can enjoy beans without any problems, others sometimes experience digestive complaints, including gas and bloating. If beans cause you discomfort, try one or more of these suggestions for breaking down the compounds that can cause gastric distress:

• Soak your beans for at least eight hours, either overnight or while you're at work during the day. Before cooking, pour off the soaking water and rinse the beans with fresh water.

• Add ¼ to ½ teaspoon of baking soda to the soaking water.

• Cook the beans with a piece of kombu seaweed. Remove the kombu before serving.

• Cook the beans with fennel, ginger, or turmeric.

There is a wide variety of beans and lentils that add different flavors and colors to your dishes. The legumes used most often in this book include the following.

Black beans. Also known as turtle beans, black beans are a long-time staple in Mexican foods, but in recent years have gained in popularity in a range of cuisines because of their distinctive look and taste, and their wonderful creaminess when mashed. Packed with fiber and protein, they are a welcome addition to salads, dips, and main courses. And, of course, they make a luscious soup.

Black-eyed peas. Cream colored with a prominent black spot that resembles an eye, black-eyed peas are actually beans. They are packed with fiber, are a good source of protein, and also provide vitamin A, B vitamins, and potassium. Serve them over rice or use them in soups, casseroles, stews, or chili.

Cannellini beans. These large light-colored beans have a slightly nutty, mild flavor and a creamy interior. They are an excellent source of protein and fiber and also provide antioxidants, iron, vitamin K, and minerals such as copper, calcium, manganese, and potassium. Cannellini beans are widely used in pasta dishes, cold salads, vegetable soups, and stews.

Chickpeas. Also called garbanzo beans and ceci beans, chickpeas are a good source of protein, fiber, and iron. Although they are best known as the principle ingredient in the Middle Eastern spread hummus, they are also used in salads, soups, and stews.

Edamame. Immature green soybeans, edamame are rich in fiber, protein, vitamins, and minerals. The pod itself is not edible; you can eat only the beans within. Available fresh and frozen, they can be boiled or steamed, and can be eaten on their own as a snack, added to your favorite salads, or used to make a delicious green hummus. (See the recipe on page 65. For information on other soy foods, see pages 16 and 17.)

Great Northern beans. Smaller than cannellini beans, these white beans, which resemble white lima beans, have a nutty flavor. Like most legumes, they are low in fat and high in fiber and protein, and they also offer iron and potassium. Great Northern beans are suitable for any number of dishes, including salads, soups, stews, and purées.

Kidney beans. Red, with a distinctive kidney shape and a unique flavor, these beans are rich in fiber and protein, and also offer copper, manganese, phosphorus, vitamin B_1, iron, potassium, and magnesium. They are also loaded with antioxidants. While kidney beans are best known for their use in chili, they are also a welcome addition to casseroles, soups, salads, and many other dishes.

Lentils. These legumes may be tiny, but they pack a big nutritional punch in the form of fiber, protein, and nutrients such as molybdenum, folate, copper, phosphorus, manganese, and iron. They are a favorite in vegan cooking—in all healthy cooking, in fact—because of their wonderful earthy flavor, their versatility, and the fact that they cook so quickly. There are several different types of lentils, including brown, which is the most common type; French green lentils; and red lentils. Use them in soups, salads, stews, meatless burgers, and more.

Lentils can be prepared very quickly in a pot of water. Unlike most other legumes, they do not have to be soaked prior to cooking. However, if you find that they cause digestive issues for you, try soaking them for at least eight hours before cooking. (For other tips on making beans more digestible, see page 9.) This breaks down some of the chemicals that can cause gas and bloating.

Pinto beans. One of the most popular beans in the United States and Mexico, pinto beans provide fiber, protein, folate, vitamin B_1, vitamin B_6, and a number of other nutrients. Like most beans, they are highly versatile, and can be enjoyed as a side dish or included in chilies, burritos, casseroles, salads, and more.

Split peas. Available dried, peeled, and split (they naturally split when the skins are removed), split peas are high in fiber, protein, and various vitamins and minerals, particularly the B vitamins. Although most valued as the main ingredient in split pea soup, they can also be used to make a beautiful green hummus (see page 65) and many other dishes. Green split peas are the best known, but these tasty legumes are also available in yellow and red varieties.

Whole Grains and Flours

For thousands of years, grains have been considered staple foods throughout the world. Whole grains and flours are nutritionally superior to refined grains and flours and the products made from them. Whole grain foods include the following edible parts: the *bran*, or outer layer of the grain, which contains fiber, antioxidants, B vitamins, phytochemicals, and minerals such as iron, copper, zinc, and magnesium; the *endosperm*, which contains mostly carbohydrates, protein, and small amounts of some B vitamins and minerals; and the *germ*, which offers healthy fats, B vitamins, phytochemicals, and antioxidants like vitamin E. When grains are refined, the bran and some germ are removed, along with the majority of the fiber, vitamins, minerals, and other nutrients. For this reason, it is usually best to choose whole grains and whole grain products.

The following grains and flours are used in the recipes in this book. If you do not have celiac disease, gluten sensitivity, or another grain-related sensitivity, we encourage you to enjoy a wide variety of grains. If you do have to avoid gluten or other substances, be sure to choose your grains and grain products with care. Some good gluten-free options include brown rice, buckwheat, millet, quinoa, and teff.

Barley. Barley is a fiber-rich grain with a chewy texture and nutty flavor. It is high in fatty acids and a good source of vitamin E, thiamin, riboflavin, and the essential amino acid lysine. It also contains gluten.

Barley is available in several forms, but in this book we use only pearled barley, which has been processed to remove its inedible hull and its bran. Although in most cases we recommend whole grains, pearled barley is a good choice because it cooks faster and is easier to chew than less-processed forms of the grain. Even though this product is partly refined, it provides 3 grams of fiber in a half-cup serving. That is because barley contains fiber throughout the entire kernel, not just in the bran. Store it in an airtight container in a cool, dark cupboard.

Buckwheat groats. Buckwheat groats are the hulled seeds of the buckwheat plant. A great source of fiber, magnesium, and rutin—a flavonoid that strengthens capillaries—buckwheat is also gluten-free. It can be used untoasted or toasted, in which case, it is sometimes referred to as kasha. It can also be ground into flour. Store whole buckwheat in an airtight container in a cool, dark cupboard, and keep buckwheat flour in an airtight container in the refrigerator or freezer.

Cornmeal. Cornmeal is made from dried field corn, which is starchier than sweet corn. It is a good source of protein and fiber, and also contains vitamin C and the B vitamins. It is gluten-free.

Different grinds of cornmeal are suitable for different dishes. Although you can buy cornmeal labeled "grits" or "polenta," any coarse or medium grind would work for these dishes, while finer grinds are usually used to make cornbread. Because a large percentage of the corn grown in the United States has been genetically modified, it is important to seek out organic brands. Cornmeal can turn rancid quickly, so be sure to store it in an airtight container in the refrigerator or freezer.

Garbanzo flour. Made from dried garbanzo beans, or chickpeas, garbanzo flour lends a sweet, rich flavor to foods. It is a great ingredient for gluten-free baking and can also be used to thicken soups, sauces, or gravies. Store chickpea flour in an airtight container in your refrigerator or freezer.

Millet. Millet's mild-tasting golden grains are high in protein, fiber, B vitamins, iron, and magnesium. Millet is also gluten-free and highly digestible. Use hulled millet—unhulled millet is not suitable for cooking—in place of rice, or grind the uncooked grains into a flour to make pancakes and other dishes. Store whole millet in an airtight container in a cool, dark cupboard. Grind the grains into flour just before using.

Mochi. A Japanese confection, mochi is made from pounded sweet rice that has been formed into a sheet and dried. In this book, we use brown rice mochi—which is made of only brown rice, with no other ingredients—to produce crunchy waffles with a moist interior. (See page 35.) Look for this product in the frozen foods section of your natural foods store, and keep it in the refrigerator for about a week or in the freezer for up to six months.

Oats. Rich in nutrients—including manganese, selenium, tryptophane, phosphorus, magnesium, and thiamin, as well as disease-fighting antioxidants—oats also offer more cholesterol-reducing soluble fiber than any other grain and are a good source of insoluble fiber.

In this book, we use mostly steel-cut oats, which have been steamed, coarsely chopped, and roasted; and old-fashioned rolled oats, which have been steamed and flattened into flakes, enabling them to cook more quickly. In one dessert recipe, we use quick-cooking oats, which have been precooked and dried.

If you have a gluten sensitivity, look for a product that is certified gluten-free. Although oats are naturally gluten-free, they sometimes pick up gluten from other grains during farming, transportation, or storage. Oats should be kept in an airtight container in a cool, dark cupboard.

Quinoa. An ancient Incan favorite, quinoa (pronounced *keen-wah*) contains all nine essential amino acids, making it a complete protein. Loaded with magnesium, potassium, fiber, and antioxidants, it is one of the healthiest grains available and is also gluten-free. It can be found in three common varieties—red, white, and black—and has a very mild earthy taste that lends itself to seasoning with herbs and spices. Store it in an airtight container in a cool, dark cupboard.

Although all grains should ideally be rinsed before you cook them, it is especially important to rinse quinoa, which has a natural bitter coating called saponin. Even if the package states that the quinoa has been pre-rinsed, it's a good idea to run cold water over it to make sure that all the saponin is gone. Use a fine-mesh strainer so that the tiny grains don't disappear down the drain.

Rice. An ancient grain that has been cultivated for centuries, rice is a dietary staple for almost half of the world's population. Gluten- and cholesterol-free with only a bit of fat, rice is an excellent source of complex carbohydrates.

Our recipes use brown rice, which still has the nutritious bran and germ intact; brown basmati rice, which is famous for its aroma and delicate flavor; and wild rice, which is actually a tall aquatic grass native to North America.

When shopping for rice, choose organic products when possible, and store in an airtight container in the cupboard or refrigerator.

Spelt. A nutty tasting ancient grain in the wheat family—and therefore high in gluten—spelt is rich in fiber, protein, and B vitamins. Whole grain spelt flour is sweeter than regular whole wheat flour, and can be used instead of wheat flour in breads, cakes, muffins, cookies, crackers, and pastas. Store the flour in an airtight container in a cool, dark cupboard or in the freezer.

Teff. Native to northern Africa, teff is sweet tasting and a good source of calcium, iron, protein, and fiber. Use this gluten-free grain to make hot breakfast cereal, a side dish, or a creamy pudding. Store the tiny grains in an airtight container in a cool, dark cupboard. When you need teff flour, grind it right before using.

Ingredients for Baking

You've just read about grains and flours, many of which can be used in baking healthful breads and desserts. Sweeteners and some other items used in baking are discussed later in the chapter. In this section, we'll take a brief look at a few more ingredients you will want to have on hand to make the baked goods in this book.

Baking powder. A leavening agent, baking powder lightens texture and increases the volume of baked goods such as muffins, quick breads, and cakes. It works by releasing carbon dioxide bubbles into the wet batter. We recommend choosing an aluminum-free product, as aluminum has been linked to a number of health problems.

Baking soda. Also known as sodium bicarbonate and bicarbonate of soda, this is a leavening agent. Baking soda reacts with acids, such as vinegar, to cause carbon dioxide bubbles. It is sometimes used alone, and sometimes used with baking powder. As all baking soda is free of aluminum, you can purchase the brand you like.

Cocoa and cacao powder. Some recipes in this book allow you to choose either cocoa or cacao powder. What's the difference? Cacao powder is made by cold-pressing unroasted cocoa beans. It contains all of the nutrients found in the beans, including fats, vitamins, minerals, fiber, carbohydrates, protein, and enzymes. Cocoa powder is made from raw cacao that has been roasted at high temperatures. This process reduces both the enzyme content and the overall nutritional value of the product. It also makes the product somewhat sweeter in taste. While both products are nutritious, cacao is the more healthful option. Just be sure to choose a product that contains no added sugar.

Pure vanilla extract. The flavoring agent known as pure vanilla extract is made by macerating vanilla beans in alcohol. The word "pure" means that the vanilla flavor comes only from vanilla beans. Imitation vanilla extract is made from an artificial flavoring known as vanillin, which is extracted from wood pulp. Although some people claim that they can't tell the difference between the two products, you'll get better vanilla flavor—and no bitter aftertaste—when you use the pure product. The difference is especially evident when you make a dish that is not cooked.

Breads and Pastas

Never before has such a wide range of breads and pastas been available in supermarkets. Natural foods stores offer an even greater range of choices, and are especially helpful if you have to avoid certain ingredients due to allergies or intolerances.

Just as we generally recommend using whole grains in breakfast cereals, sides, and other dishes, we urge you to buy whole grain breads and pastas, as they provide the most nourishment. If you have to avoid gluten, though, you'll find an ever-increasing number of gluten-free products for sale. You can also purchase a spiralizer and create your own whole food noodles from vegetables like zucchini, or you can replace grain-based spaghetti with cooked spaghetti squash.

Nuts, Seeds, and Nut Butters

Nuts and seeds are an important part of any sound diet. They are high in protein and fiber, rich in essential fatty acids (good fats), and also offer nutrients such as iron, calcium, vitamin E, and some B vitamins. Just remember that even healthy fats should be eaten in moderation, as they are high in calories. So use nuts and seeds sparingly to add flavor, crunch, and nutrients to salads, veggies, sandwiches, and other dishes.

Buy nuts and seeds in raw, unsalted form, and store in a cool, dry place. If you choose to buy prepared nut butters, look for products that contain only nuts, with no added oil, salt, or sugar. Better yet, make your own nut butters in a high-speed blender. No water, oil, or other ingredients are needed.

Below, you'll find information on the nuts and seeds used in the recipes in this book.

Almonds. Although they are high in fat, almonds boast an impressive nutritional profile, as they are also high in fiber, protein, vitamin E, manganese, and magnesium. Crunchy, with a distinctive flavor, almonds are great in both sweet and savory dishes, from soups to desserts. You can also swirl them in a blender to make a healthy alternative to peanut butter.

Cashews. Although cashews are lower in fiber than most nuts, they are also lower in fat. Plus, they offer significant amounts of protein, copper, manganese, magnesium, phosphorus, iron, selenium, and vitamin B_6. These nuts have always made a healthy snack, but now, they are also used to make dairy alternatives such as cashew milk and cashew-based cheese. In this book, they are the principle ingredient in Basic Cashew Cream (see page 71), a rich cream that can serve as a dip, a spread, a sour cream substitute, and a frosting.

Chia seeds. Edible seeds from a plant native to Mexico, tiny black and white chia seeds provide healthy omega-3 fatty acids, protein, carbohydrates, fiber, antioxidants, calcium, and phosphorus. Because they have a mild flavor, they can be sprinkled on cereals, rice dishes, vegetables, or yogurt; or mixed into drinks and baked goods. As if that wasn't reason enough to add these superfoods to your next shopping list, when stirred into water and left to sit for about fifteen minutes, chia seeds form a gel that can be used to thicken smoothies and juice beverages. Unlike flaxseeds, chia seeds don't require grinding to make their nutrients bioavailable.

Flaxseeds. Sometimes called linseeds, small tan or brown-colored flaxseeds come from flax, one of the world's oldest fiber crops. Flaxseeds are rich in omega-3 essential fatty acids; lignans, which have powerful antioxidant properties; and fiber. Since whole flaxseeds may pass through the intestines undigested, to reap the nutritional benefits of the plant, you should eat flaxseed meal instead of the whole seeds. Because the fat in flaxseeds can quickly spoil once they are ground into meal, always make the meal in your blender or a clean coffee grinder as you need it.

Hemp seeds. Seeds of the plant Cannabis sativa L., hemp seeds are nutritional powerhouses. They provide all twenty amino acids, including the nine essential amino acids, and so are high in complete protein. They also offer more essential fatty acids than tuna, as well as dietary fiber and trace minerals. When pulverized, hemp makes a great thickening agent. In this book, we use hemp seeds to create velvety cream sauces that can be spooned over grains and vegetables. Note that these seeds do not contain the THC found in the leaves of the plant. (To learn about hemp seed milk, turn to page 19.)

Pecans. Richly flavored, pecans are high in monounsaturated fatty acids and are a good source of antioxidants, including ellagic acid, vitamin E, beta-carotene, lutein, and zeaxanthin. They also provide several important B-complex vitamins as well as minerals like manganese, potassium, calcium, iron, magnesium, zinc, and selenium. Use them in salads and baked goods, eat them as a snack, or make pecan butter by processing the nuts in a high-speed blender.

Pine nuts. The edible seed of certain pines, these high-fat nuts—which are also called pignoli—are rich in monounsaturated fatty acids and a good source of vitamin E, B-complex vitamins, manganese, potassium, calcium, iron, magnesium, zinc, and selenium. They are delicious in pasta and rice dishes, in baked goods, and on salads. Because of their high fat content, pine nuts are quite perishable, so buy them in small amounts and store them in airtight containers in the refrigerator.

Poppy seeds. Obtained from the dry pods of the poppy plant, poppy seeds are a good source of fiber; B-complex vitamins; and minerals such as iron, copper, calcium, potassium, manganese, zinc, and magnesium. Although they are most commonly used to top bake goods for visual appeal and crunch, these nutty-tasting nutrient-packed seeds can also be sprinkled on salads and other dishes.

Pumpkin seeds. The edible seeds of the pumpkin, pumpkin seeds—also called pepitas—are rich in protein, monounsaturated fatty acids, vitamin E, B-complex vitamins, and minerals such as copper, manganese, potassium, calcium, iron, magnesium, selenium, and zinc. Crunchy and very flavorful, pumpkin seeds make a great snack and can

What Are Antioxidants?

In this chapter, several discussions of ingredients mention the presence of antioxidants, a term that has become a buzzword in recent years. But what are antioxidants, and why are they considered such a valuable part of a plant-based diet?

Antioxidants are compounds that naturally occur in plant foods. There are thousands of antioxidant compounds, but the ones you've probably heard of are vitamins A (beta-carotene), C, and E; flavonols (found in chocolate); resveratrol (found in red grapes and wine); and lycopene (found in tomatoes). Antioxidants have attracted the attention of health experts because they help prevent or stop the cell damage caused by oxidants, which are harmful particles that are produced by the body, but also result from air pollution, alcohol, and cigarette smoke. When uncontrolled, oxidants can contribute to a number of chronic health conditions, including arthritis, age-related blindness, heart disease, diabetes, and cancer. But when adequate antioxidants are present, your body is better able to prevent the development of these diseases.

What's the best way to get the antioxidants your body needs for good health? Eat a variety of fruits and vegetables, including produce of many different colors, as the colors indicate the presence of different antioxidant compounds. Be aware, too, that dried herbs and spices are a concentrated source of these beneficial substances. What about dietary supplements? While they may be helpful in cases of nutritional deficiency, they simply don't offer the benefits of whole plant-based foods, which provide many antioxidants as well as a wide range of other nutrients.

also be sprinkled on salads, soups, and other dishes.

Sacha inchi seeds. Also called Inca peanuts, sacha inchi seeds come from Peru. Considered "super seeds," they are rich in protein (30 percent protein by weight), and also provide plenty of essential fatty acids—including more anti-inflammatory omega-3 fatty acids than any other seed—as well as vitamin E and fiber. Crisp and nut-like in flavor, they can be used to add flavor and crunch to salads and many other dishes.

Sesame seeds. Obtained from an annual herb that grows in Asia, sesame seeds provide dietary protein, monounsaturated fats, minerals, and vitamins—especially the B-complex vitamins. They are the main ingredients in tahini sauce, and are also used to add crunch and flavor to salads and baked goods.

Sunflower seeds. Found in the seed-studded center of the sunflower, these flavorful morsels are a favorite for snacking and are also highly nutritious. Despite their small size, sunflower seeds are a rich source of vitamins such as E, B_1, and B_6; minerals such as copper, manganese, selenium, phosphorus, and magnesium; essential fatty acids; protein; and fiber. Eat them out of hand or use them to add crunch and nutrition to soups and salads.

Walnuts. A favorite nut for snacking and meal preparation, walnuts are also rich in nutrition. They provide protein, fiber, omega-3 fatty acids, and a slew of minerals, chief among them magnesium and phosphorus. In this book, we include them in hot cereal, granola, and fruit crisp toppings; use them to make crisp vegan crackers; sprinkle them on salads and grain dishes; use them to make a thick gravy, and more.

Soy Foods

Native to East Asia, the soybean plant has been cultivated for well over 13,000 years. Soybeans and products made from soy are valuable in a plant-based diet, as they have a high protein content and are also rich in the B vitamins; calcium and other minerals; and compounds called phytosterols, which have cholesterol-lowering effects. The recipes in this book make use of two types of soy foods—tofu and tempeh.

Tofu. Sometimes called bean curd, tofu is made from soymilk through a process that's similar to cheese making. A staple of Asian diets, it has a mild taste and can absorb the flavors of the other ingredients in your recipe, making it a great addition to a variety of dishes, including soups, stir-fries, sauces, dips, and more. It comes in regular and silken varieties, and each variety comes in soft, firm, and extra-firm consistencies. Depending on the type you buy and how you prepare it, tofu can be smooth and creamy or firm and meaty. It can be eaten without being cooked.

Tofu is sold in vacuum packs or water-filled tubs. It's perishable, so be sure to check the expiration date and to keep it refrigerated once you get it home. Once opened, place it in fresh water and refrigerate it for up to a week, changing the water daily.

Tempeh. This Indonesian staple is made through a fermentation process that binds cooked soybeans together to form a patty. Many commercially available brands add grains such as barley, as well as spices and other flavorings. Unlike tofu, which is bland, tempeh is mildly flavorful, with a nutty taste. Because of its firm texture, it has to be cooked before it is eaten so that it softens up a bit. It is a popular addition to stir-fries, can be crumbled into soups and meatless chili, and makes a delicious meat substitute in sandwiches.

Because tempeh is quite perishable, it is usually found in the frozen foods section of natural foods stores. Keep it in the freezer for up to six months or in the refrigerator for up to a week.

Oils

As you flip through the recipes in this book, you may be surprised to see that oil is not used to cook our dishes, and that even our salad dressings are usually made without oil. Why? Just one tablespoon of oil contains 120 calories, and the average person today consumes five to six tablespoons of oil per day—which means that 30 percent of many people's daily calories come from oil. Oil is a refined food that contains very few micronutrients and does little to improve your health. Most vegetable oils, in fact, are high in inflammatory omega-6 fatty acids. It's far wiser to spend that third of your calories on nutrient-rich foods such as greens, berries, beans, and whole grains. In addition, the heating of oil during cooking has been found to cause toxic substances that can damage your well-being. For that reason, we have developed a number of techniques for cooking without oil. (See page 24.) Once you master these techniques, you will be able to make healthy lower-calorie foods with ease.

That being said, some dishes turn out better if you use just a tiny bit of oil in the form of nonstick cooking spray. This product adds an infinitesimal amount of oil and few calories to your dish. Always choose an organic spray made of only oil, with no additives or hydro-

carbons. Then spray your pot or pan very lightly, or you will add more of the product than is desirable.

Also note that in very few recipes, we add a small amount—a teaspoon or less—of toasted sesame oil to the dish. Very little of this ingredient is needed to richly flavor salads, dressings, and other dishes.

Sweeteners

You have probably already heard this many times, but it's worth repeating: Added sugars—the sugars that are not a natural part of whole foods like fruit—contain no nutrients and therefore provide "empty" calories. As discussed on page 4, sugar is also highly inflammatory, causes blood sugar and insulin levels to rise, and damages the body in many other ways. To make matters worse, sugar is highly addictive, so whenever you have some, you want more.

Because sugar is potentially so damaging to your health, we use no refined sugars in our recipes. Ideally, you should use only whole food sweeteners like dates, but it takes time to get used to a healthy diet that provides only the sweetness found in whole foods. For that reason, we use small amounts of the following sweeteners in our recipes. Note that in each recipe, we use the sweetener that we feel works best in that dish. If you prefer one of the following sweeteners over the others, we encourage you to experiment using it in various recipes and adjusting the amount to taste.

Dates. These small fruits are one of our favorite whole food sweeteners. Rich in dietary fiber; in minerals such as calcium, potassium, manganese, copper, and magnesium; and in antioxidants, dates also boast a caramel flavor that lends itself to many culinary uses. We like to soak Medjool dates in water and process them in a blender or food processor until the mixture is smooth and creamy. (See the recipe for Date Paste on page 45.) The resulting paste can be used as a sweet dessert topping or stirred into baked goods and smoothies for added sweetness and nutrition. It should be recognized that other fruits, too, can be used as natural sweeteners, but dates are especially successful in this role.

Maple syrup. A natural sweetener with a unique flavor, maple syrup is made from the sap of certain maple trees, which is boiled until thick and sweet. Although the syrup is no nutritional powerhouse, it does offer more nutrients than table sugar, and a little goes a long way. That's why we use it to make Maple-Smoked Tempeh BLT (see page 48) and Milan's Guilt-Free Granola (see page 43).

Monk fruit powder. The monk fruit, also known as luo han guo, is a small green gourd that was first cultivated in the southern mountains of China more than eight hundred years ago. The sweetener is made by crushing the fruit and collecting the juice, which is dried to create a powdered extract. Because the juice is twenty times sweeter than other fruit juices and much sweeter than sugar, you need only a little monk fruit powder to add sweetness to a beverage or other recipe. Even better, the extract contains zero calories and is non-glycemic, which means that it does not affect blood sugar levels—a real plus for people with diabetes. Be sure to buy *pure* monk fruit powder. Avoid products that contain fillers or other sweeteners, like dextrose and sugar alcohols.

Stevia. A natural sweetener that comes from the leaves of the Stevia rebaudiana plant, stevia comes in several forms. We recommend whole leaf liquid stevia or dried stevia leaves. Like monk fruit powder, stevia is sweeter than sugar, so only a small amount is needed to enhance beverages such as smoothies. And, like monk fruit powder, stevia does not affect blood sugar levels and is non-caloric.

Vegan Milks

If you drink milk or use it in recipes, changing to a vegan diet means switching from cow's milk to a nondairy alternative. But thanks to the huge selection of nondairy milks on the market, it's not difficult to find something that suits both your tastes and your nutritional needs. In the recipes in this book, we usually give you the choice of using soy, nut, or seed milk. Below, you'll learn a little bit about each of these options. Just be aware that different versions of the same nondairy milk can have very different nutritional profiles, so before buying a carton, be sure to read both the list of ingredients and the Nutrition Facts label to see if that product is right for you.

Soymilk. Available both plain and flavored, soymilk is made from soybeans that have been cooked and ground. Of all the nondairy alternatives, soymilk comes closest to cow's milk in protein content, with about six grams of protein per cup. Unfortified soymilk is also a good source of potassium, iron, and the B vitamins, but does not provide much calcium. Some brands are fortified with calcium, vitamin D, and vitamin B_{12}, which is helpful for people who may not obtain sufficient amounts of these nutrients from their diet. Soymilk provides about 100 calories per cup. It is low in saturated fat and is cholesterol- and lactose-free. If you are getting vitamins D and B_{12}

from supplements or another food source, we recommend buying organic plain unsweetened soymilk. Fortified soymilk is advisable only if you are not getting these nutrients from supplements or other foods. A whole food plant-based diet supplies more than enough calcium, so calcium-enriched products are not necessary.

Nut milk. These days, almond milk is easy to find even in supermarkets, where it is available in a variety of forms, including both unsweetened and sweetened, as well as flavored. Cashew and hazelnut milk are also available in some markets. All nut milks contain little protein, with about one gram per cup. However, almond milk often provides a good amount of calcium, as well as vitamin E. Nut milks are also a good option if you are trying to reduce calories, as unsweetened nut milk contains about 30 calories per cup. And, of course, all nut milks are cholesterol-free, lactose-free, and low in saturated fat. For a good nutritional profile, opt for enriched unsweetened nut milks.

Hemp milk. Although milk can be made from different seeds, the type of seed milk most commonly found in stores is hemp milk, which is prepared from the seeds of the hemp plant. (Note that it does not contain the THC found in the leaves of the plant.) This delightful beverage has a nutty taste and is one of the most nutritious milks on the market. It contains all nine of the essential amino acids, which make it a great source of protein. It also offers a perfect balance of omega-3 and omega-6 amino acids, and so is naturally anti-inflammatory. If you are allergic to dairy, soy, or nuts, hemp milk is a great option because it contains no known allergens.

Seasonings and Flavorings

Many people fear that when they switch to a plant-based diet, they will have to miss out on great-tasting meals. Nothing could be further from the truth. Fruits, vegetables, grains, and other plant-based foods each have their own distinctive flavors, which most people appreciate more fully when they stop overloading their dishes with salt, sugar, and oil. Moreover, there is a wide range of natural ingredients that can enhance the flavor of your meals. Some of them you are probably already using, while some may be new to you. We discuss these ingredients below.

Coconut aminos. A soy sauce alternative, coconut aminos are a fermented product made from raw coconut sap and salt. They are low-glycemic, vegan, and gluten-free, and they boast seventeen amino acids—the building blocks of protein. This product has about 65 percent less sodium than regular soy sauce. Use it as you would use soy sauce, or simply add it to foods as a tasty condiment.

Dulse. Mildly flavored, dulse is a sea vegetable that tastes like the ocean when used right out of the package. When pan-fried, though, it has smoky and savory characteristics that may remind you of bacon. A great natural source of iodine, dulse helps to maintain a healthy thyroid. Simmer it in soups or stews, toss it into salads, or cook it in a pan and use it to make a great vegan BLT sandwich. (See page 113 for the recipe.)

Herbs and spices. As you'll see when you flip through our recipes, the sky's the limit when it comes to using herbs and spices to season your dishes. Although we believe that all our dishes are well seasoned—using everything from basil and tarragon to cayenne and chipotle pepper—we urge you to be bold and experiment with your favorite herbs and spices, including fresh herbs when they're available, so that each dish suits your tastes. It's worth noting that herbs and spices are concentrated sources of health-protecting antioxidants, such as vitamins A, C, and E. So while you're adding flavor and zest to your food, you'll also be enhancing your dish with valuable nutrients. Just make sure that seasoning blends don't contain salt.

Liquid smoke. Made literally from wood smoke that is cooled to form droplets and then filtered, liquid smoke imparts a smoky flavor without the carcinogens associated with charbroiling meats. Add it to pea soup, bean dishes, and other foods that can benefit from a little smoky taste. One small bottle will last a long time.

Miso. A fermented paste usually made from cooked soybeans, sea salt, and grains, miso is full of flavor and somewhat salty. Although most people think of it as the principle ingredient in Japanese miso soup, this versatile product can be used to add great taste to a number of foods, from roasted vegetables and grain dishes to dips and salad dressings.

Several types of miso are available. *White miso,* prepared from fermented soybeans and rice, is mild, slightly sweet in taste, and less salty than the darker varieties, making it very versatile. Its mild flavor is partly due to its relatively short period of fermentation. *Yellow miso* is usually made with fermented soybeans and barley. It's a little stronger and saltier than white miso, but is milder than the red variety. *Red miso,* which is generally made with fermented soybeans and a grain such as barley, has a longer fermentation period than the other types. This is the saltiest and most pungent of the soybean-based miso varieties, and should be used with hearty fare. Prepared from chickpeas (instead of soybeans) and rice, *chickpea miso* is relatively mild in flavor and low in salt. It is a great choice for people who can't eat soybeans.

Besides adding flavor to food, miso offers numerous health benefits. It aids digestion, restores beneficial probiotics to the intestines, strengthens the immune system, and is a good source of protein, the B vitamins, and antioxidants. To preserve miso's beneficial effects, add it to food toward the end of the cooking process and avoid boiling it. Store leftover miso in an airtight container in the refrigerator, where it will keep for several months.

Nutritional yeast. A deactivated yeast that is related to brewer's yeast, this product is grown on a food source and then harvested, heated, dried, and crumbled. It is called "nutritional" because it provides significant amounts of thiamin, riboflavin, niacin, pyridoxine, folic acid, vitamin B_{12}, protein, and fiber. Available in flakes and powders, both of which are bright yellow in color, it can be added to soups, sauces, salads, popcorn, and spreads, where it lends a cheesy, nutty taste. In fact, this food is often used as a cheese substitute.

Salt. Although your dishes should ideally be free of added salt—especially if you have high blood pressure or another health issue for which salt is contraindicated—some of our recipes include small amounts of salt or sodium-containing ingredients (like coconut aminos) to help you accustom your taste buds to a whole food plant-based diet. When choosing salt, we urge you to select either sea salt or pink Himalayan sea salt, both of which—

depending on where they were sourced—contain a number of minerals, such as potassium, phosphorus, iron, iodine, manganese, and zinc. Regardless of the product you choose, the goal is to use a minimum of salt and to add flavor with herbs, spices, and other no- or low-sodium ingredients.

Toasted sesame seed oil. Made by pressing toasted sesame seeds, this oil is deep orange in color and has a pronounced nutty flavor. Toasted sesame seed oil is not used for cooking. Instead, it is used in tiny amounts to season a cooked dish or to flavor salad dressings. Store it in a cool, dry place for several months.

Vinegar

Made primarily from fruits and grains, vinegar has long been a valued ingredient not only because it preserves food, but also because it is such a wonderful flavoring agent. The following vinegars are used in the recipes in this book. Store your vinegars in the pantry, where they will keep indefinitely. Don't worry if sediment forms at the bottom of the bottle. It's harmless. But if it bothers you, strain the vinegar through a coffee filter.

Apple cider vinegar. Made from fermented apple juice, apple cider vinegar has a very strong, even harsh flavor. But when balanced properly with other ingredients, it makes a wonderful contribution to salads and many other dishes. Plus, it is thought to have many health benefits, including the ability to help control blood sugar, promote weight loss, and lower cholesterol.

Balsamic vinegar. Made from whole grapes complete with juice, skin, seeds, and stems, true balsamic vinegar is cooked down and then aged for a minimum of twelve years. With a complex rich flavor, a unique sweetness, a port-like aroma, and an almost syrupy consistency, this is like no other vinegar. If you are going to use your balsamic vinegar in cooking, buy a moderately priced bottle. If you intend to use it straight from the bottle, go for a pricier brand and make sure it comes from Modena, Italy.

Rice vinegar. Made from fermented rice or rice wine, this vinegar is traditionally used in Japanese and Chinese cooking. It is less acidic than western vinegars, and has a delicate, mild, and somewhat sweet flavor. Choose an unseasoned variety, as seasoned rice vinegar contains added sugar and salt.

Wine vinegar. The most versatile of vinegars, wine vinegar is made from red or white wine, which is why there are red wine vinegars and white wine vinegars. A staple in both Mediterranean and American cooking, wine vinegar adds a tangy robust taste to salads and other foods. It has lower acidity than cider vinegar, but is stronger in flavor than rice vinegar.

Canned Foods

Although this cookbook emphasizes whole fresh foods, we realize that certain canned products can be a big help as you strive to get healthy flavorful meals on the table. In this book, we use canned beans, canned tomato paste, canned tomatoes, and prepared vegetable broth, which often comes in cans. When purchasing these items, look for organic brands that are low in sodium or have no added salt, as this will allow you to better control the salt in your diet. (Remember that most excess dietary salt comes from prepared and processed foods.) To avoid bisphenol A (BPA), a chemical used in the lining of some cans to prevent corrosion, it makes sense to choose brands that use BPA-free cans. This chemical is capable of interfering with the body's hormones, especially estrogen, and has been linked to diseases such as cancer and diabetes. Usually, companies whose cans are BPA-free state this fact on the label.

BASIC TOOLS AND EQUIPMENT

For the most part, you'll need the same kitchen utensils and equipment to prepare the recipes in this book that you would use for any type of cooking. This is great, because you probably already have most of what you require, including good sharp knives, measuring cups, mixing bowls, and other standard kitchen tools. In a few areas, though, you may want to make a new purchase or two to ensure success. These areas include nonstick cookware; cookware used for steaming; a few small appliances; and storage containers.

Nonstick Cookware

Many of our recipes rely on nonstick cookware because it allows you to prepare your foods with no oil or with only a tiny amount of nonstick cooking spray. But as you may know, numerous brands of nonstick pots and pans are made using poly- and perfluoroalkyl substances (PFAS), which release carcinogenic chemicals into both the air and your food when heated. In addition, dangerous chemicals can get into your food if the nonstick coating flakes off during cooking.

Fortunately, several types of nontoxic nonstick cookware are now on the market. Green-Pan, for instance, uses a ceramic nonstick layer derived from sand that will not release

toxic fumes when heated. Other brands you might want to consider are Mercola, Beka Eco-Logic, BioChef, Mauviel, Ozeri Green Earth, and Ecopan. These lines of cookware use a variety of innovative materials—such as bamboo powder and plastics manufactured from algae—that make them easy to use and easy to clean while keeping both your food and your family safe.

A final word should be said about not only skillets, but cookware in general. Whenever possible, it's advisable to get heavy cookware with tight-fitting covers. You'll note that many recipes in this book use techniques that require you to cook food with the lid on the pot. (Read about the techniques on pages 24 to 25.) Also, a heavy pot makes it easier to cook vegetables, grains, and other foods without sticking. Your investment in good cookware will pay off in terms of beautifully prepared meals.

Cookware for Steaming

Steaming is a great way to prepare vegetables without the use of oil. Several types of cookware are available for this purpose. You can buy an electric steamer, which often doubles as a rice maker; or you can use a steamer rack or an inexpensive bamboo steamer, which can be positioned in a large heavy pot over simmering water.

If you choose to use an electric steamer, you will simply follow the manufacturer's directions. If using a steamer rack or bamboo steamer, you will fill a large pot with two to three cups of water and bring the water to a rolling boil. Add your vegetables—or tofu or whatever you're cooking—to the rack or bamboo steamer, cover, and steam the food over boiling water for about five minutes, or until the vegetables become tender but not overcooked.

Basic Appliances

Blenders, food processors, juicers, and pressure cookers are a big help when preparing plant-based dishes. In some instances, they can help you make quick work of an otherwise time-consuming job, like chopping vegetables or cooking dried beans. And when preparing certain dishes—like juices and smoothies—they are a true necessity. Let's discuss each of these appliances in turn.

Blenders. A blender is essential for grinding nuts, flaxseeds, and small quantities of grain. And, of course, it is needed to make smoothies, as well as some sauces, soups, salad dressings, and dips. Generally, a blender is more effective than a food processor for turning foods into silky smooth liquids.

When you're following a whole food plant-based diet, it's important to have a high-speed blender—a blender with a peak horsepower of two or higher. Scott burned out many blenders through the years until he invested in a high-speed model, and he's never looked back. The best-known brands are Vitamix and Blendtec. Either of these will allow you to mill grains, make smooth soups and smoothies, create nut butters, and do a variety of other tough jobs without the machine sputtering, smoking, or conking out. These blenders are pricey, and if you can't afford one, pick up the best blender with the highest peak horsepower you can afford, and put a high-speed brand on your birthday wish list. It will make an invaluable contribution to your whole food plant-based kitchen. Although the hand-held blender called an immersion blender it not absolutely necessary, it's nice to have for making individual smoothies and for puréeing soups directly in the pot.

Food processors. A good heavy-duty food processor will make your kitchen life much easier. You can use your food processor to chop, slice, and grate foods; to make salsa and guacamole; and to process ingredients that are too thick or tough for a regular blender. If you have a large high-speed blender and good knife skills, you probably don't need a food processor. But if you have an ordinary blender; you're interested in the machine's chopping and slicing capabilities; or you want a machine that processes bread dough, a food processor would make a good investment. Just about any good food processor can do the job. If you have a large family, though, be sure to get a 14-cup model.

Juicers. A juicer separates a fruit or vegetable's nutrient-packed juice from its fiber so that you have a healthy beverage that's full of vitamins, minerals, enzymes, and antioxidants. Although we generally recommend eating whole foods—which means including the fiber—freshly made juices are valuable because they make nutrients easy to process by the body so that you can benefit from the nutrients quickly. And, of course, they produce much more nutritious beverages than you'll ever find in a store. It is important to remember that one of the aims of juicing is to increase your consumption of greens and other vegetables, adding just enough fruit to make the beverage flavorful.

There are a lot of good heavy-duty juicers on the market, with brand names like Champion and Omega. When making a selection, think about what you will juice, and make sure that the juicer you buy can handle it. For instance, some juicers can't efficiently process greens and wheatgrass. If you want to include these foods in your beverages, check to see that the brand you're considering can do the job. Also make sure that the juicer is easy to clean. If cleanup is a hassle, you will probably use the appliance once or twice, and then put it away, never to be used again.

Pressure cookers. The recipes in this book are designed to be used with standard cookware, but in a few cases, we offer the option of preparing the dish in a pressure cooker. This piece of cookware is a great addition to a whole food plant-based kitchen, because it allows you to quickly cook dried beans, grains, and slow-cooking vegetables like collards. Basically, a pressure cooker is a large heavy pot with a lid that locks in place. By trapping steam from boiling liquid inside the pot, it creates superheated pressure that cooks the food in a fraction of the time needed to prepare food in regular cookware. (A pound of beans, for instance, can be cooked in well under an hour.) Choose either a stove-top or electric model, depending on your preferences. Many of the electric pressure cookers reduce cooking time by up to 70 percent, and their one-touch preset options are a great time saver.

Storage Containers

Food-safe containers are a necessity for storing uncooked grains, cereals, flours, beans, and lentils, as well as leftovers and any grains or other foods that you have cooked in batches to speed meal preparation. Although plastic containers are inexpensive, lightweight, and convenient, chemicals can leach from the plastics into the foods they contain, especially if you heat the foods in the containers. If you prefer plastic, we suggest you check the codes found in the tiny triangles on the bottoms of the con-

tainers, which indicate the types of plastic used. Containers marked with codes 1, 2, 4, and 5 are your safest bets. Nevertheless, we suggest that you never heat your food in a plastic container, as high temperatures can cause the chemicals to break down. Plastic containers should be used only for storing uncooked foods and for transporting food from place to place.

The safest storage options—for holding everything from dried beans to hot foods—are glass containers with tight-fitting lids. You can use the containers again and again, as they won't leach potentially harmful chemicals into your food. And if you ever decide to dispose of them through recycling, they won't pose risks to the environment, either. Of course, ceramic, stoneware, and stainless steel containers can also be useful, but they don't have the advantage of being transparent so you can quickly see what's being stored.

COOKING WITHOUT OIL

Cooking meals on a whole food plant-based diet is not at all difficult. But if you're used to sautéing in oil, you will have to acquaint yourself with the techniques used to prepare food without this high-calorie ingredient. Fortunately, there are three simple ways to do this. (For information on steaming, see page 22.)

Cooking with Water or Vegetable Broth

One way to deliciously cook your food without oil is to use a small amount—about two tablespoons—of water or vegetable broth in your nonstick skillet. Simply heat the skillet until a drop of water added to the skillet rolls around the pan like a drop of mercury. Then add the cooking liquid along with the food. Cook, stirring often to prevent sticking, for several minutes or until the food is done according to the recipe instructions or your liking. If at any point, your food begins to stick to your cookware, add a little more liquid and/or lower the heat under the skillet. The recipe for Big Country Cheesy Scramble, found on page 28, demonstrates how this technique can be used to cook a skillet full of onions, bell peppers, and other vegetables.

Using Nonstick Cooking Spray

Another way to cook foods without oil—or, rather, with only an infinitesimal amount of oil—is to spray your nonstick pan lightly with cooking spray before you add the food to the pan. (See page 17 to learn how to choose a spray.) Then cover the food and cook over low to medium heat, without stirring, until the food is done to taste.

As you'll see in recipes like Soul Food Greens, found on page 162, you can add vegetables in layers according to the recipe, replacing the cover of the skillet or pot quickly after each addition. By not stirring, you will keep the thin film of cooking spray on the bottom of the pot to prevent sticking, and by replacing the lid after the addition of each ingredient, you will allow the heat and steam to build up in the pot and cook the food. In Soul Food Greens, this method actually enables the onions on the bottom of the dish to caramelize for great flavor. If at any point your food does start to stick, simply add a few tablespoons of liquid such as water or vegetable broth, stir the ingredients, replace the lid, and continue to cook.

Dry Sautéeing

In some recipes, we dry sauté vegetables in a nonstick pan. For instance, in Red Tomato Sauce on page 82, a chopped onion is cooked in a nonstick skillet over medium-high heat—with no liquid and no cooking spray—until translucent and lightly browned. The trick to using this technique successfully is to stir frequently to prevent sticking and burning. If the food starts to stick or begins to brown too quickly, turn the heat down and add a small amount of liquid.

BATCH COOKING AND OTHER TIME-SAVING TECHNIQUES

A busy schedule can wreak havoc with your plans to make healthy plant-based meals. While there's no denying that it takes time to chop and cook fresh vegetables and to cook dried beans and whole grains, there are several steps you can take to speed meal preparation so that it's always possible to get a nourishing meal on the table.

First, make salad preparation faster by buying prewashed greens or washing, drying, and storing greens in airtight containers as soon as you get them home. As long as you get the greens completely dry and keep them in well-sealed containers, they should last for several days. Also clean and cut up favorite salad veggies such as bell peppers and cucumbers at the start of the week, and keep them in well-sealed glass containers in the fridge so that you can quickly assemble a salad at any time.

If you've already looked through the Hearty Bowls chapter, which starts on page 135, you'll know that a variety of healthful main dish bowls can be made in very little time if you have cooked grains on hand. The same is true of many of our other dishes, as well. Our advice is to batch cook some of your favorite grains over the weekend or whenever you have a few hours to spare, and store them in convenient portions—1 cup or 2 cups, for instance—in the refrigerator or freezer. Cooked grains will last at least a few days in the refrigerator and up to several months in the freezer. Beans can be cooked in advance and kept in the refrigerator in their cooking liquid for up to a week, or stored in the freezer for several months. (Be sure to drain the liquid before freezing the beans.) Another option is to cook extra grains and beans when you make a meal, and store the leftovers for future meals. Frozen beans and rice can be thawed overnight in the refrigerator or more quickly thawed in a large bowl of warm water. If you find that you simply don't have the time to batch cook, consider investing in a pressure cooker, which can prepare these foods in no time at all. (See page 24 for more information on pressure cookers.) Another option is to use a slow cooker, which can prepare the beans while you're at work or out of the house for another reason.

While you are in the kitchen waiting for the beans or grains to cook, you might want to whip up a couple of sauces or condiments. Golden Hemp Seed Sauce (page 83), Fresh Salsa (page 62), Oven-Caramelized Onions (page 86), and many other creations will allow you to flavor plain cooked beans, rice, tofu, and veggies. This means that you'll not only get your meal on the table, but you'll also make it utterly irresistible. Plus all of these sauces add nutrition to your meal.

You now know why a whole food plant-based diet can make such a positive difference to your health, and you are acquainted with the ingredients, cookware, and culinary techniques that will allow you to make delicious wholesome dishes. Rest assured that whether you are an experienced cook or you have never prepared anything more challenging than a simple sandwich, our recipes are easy to follow and our dishes are easy to love. Just as important, by offering an abundance of the nutrients your body needs to thrive, the recipes presented in the following chapters will help you and your family enjoy greater health, now and for a lifetime.

2.

Breakfast

xperts agree that the best way to start your day is with a healthy breakfast. But if you are just beginning to make the transition to a whole foods plant-based diet, you may wonder exactly what you're going to eat every morning. You may even be worried that your new lifestyle will limit your choices. Fortunately, so many delicious foods are available to you that you can have a different breakfast every day of the month!

This chapter begins by offering scrambles and skillet dishes that are anything but boring. Hash Me No Question, for example, is a savory dish of both russet and sweet potatoes, onion, shallots, bell pepper, roasted garlic, and spices. Big Country Cheesy Scramble is another satisfying choice. Who wouldn't want to get out of bed for these hot and hearty meals?

If you love pancakes and waffles, you're in for a treat, because the following pages offer a number of truly tempting recipes, from the World's Healthiest Pancakes to filled Buckwheat Crepes. You'll even find a recipe for crisp Mochi Waffles, which can be prepared in a matter of minutes by using a convenient yet wholesome product that you can find in most health food stores.

Cereals are another breakfast favorite, and this chapter gives you several tasty options. If the weather outside is frightful, pick from among a number of hot dishes, including Creamy Cheesy Grits and Cherry Vanilla Cream Porridge. If it's simply to warm to cook, try Apple Nut Muesli with Berries or Milan's Guilt-Free Granola. You can't go wrong with these fruit-sweetened treats.

Don't feel that you must be limited by traditional breakfast choices, either. In the following pages, you'll find several breakfast sandwiches, including a fabulous Maple-Smoked Tempeh BLT, that you and your family are sure to love. We've even included a delightful breakfast salad that combines sweet berries, coconut, and raisins; protein-packed seeds; and salad greens. To round out our breakfast collection, we've added sweet broiled plantains, a nutrient-rich fruit parfait, comforting stewed apples, and some heavenly muffins.

Starting your day with wholesome foods is not just healthy; it's truly delicious. And it does not have to be difficult. The following recipes will help you make the change to nourishing breakfast foods that will delight your taste buds and keep you going strong all morning long.

Big Country Cheesy Scramble

This satisfying breakfast scramble is bursting with the flavors of onion, bell pepper, garlic, and shallots. Nutritional yeast lends the dish a wonderful cheese taste.

YIELD: 4 servings

2 packages (8 ounces each) extra-firm tofu

2 tablespoons lower-sodium vegetable broth or water

1 red onion, chopped

1 green bell pepper, thinly sliced

1 red bell pepper, thinly sliced

1 large shallot, minced

4 cloves garlic, minced

2 cups lightly packed coarsely chopped spinach

1/4 cup fresh basil leaves plus 8 basil leaves for garnish

2 tablespoons nutritional yeast

2 tablespoons coconut aminos

1. Wrap each block of tofu in a clean absorbent kitchen towel. Then place a heavy object—a large skillet or a plate weighted with a can, for instance—on top of the tofu to press out any liquid. Set the tofu aside to drain for 15 to 20 minutes.

2. Heat a large nonstick skillet over medium heat. Add the vegetable broth or water, onion, bell peppers, and shallot to the skillet, and cook, stirring frequently, for 7 to 10 minutes, or until the onions are translucent and the peppers are tender.

3. Add the garlic to the vegetable mixture, and cook for about 3 minutes, or until fragrant.

4. Toss the spinach and 1/4 cup of basil into the mixture, and cook for about 3 minutes, or until the greens are wilted.

5. While the spinach and basil are cooking, unwrap the tofu and use a fork to crumble it into bite-sized pieces. Move all your veggies to one side of the skillet, and add the crumbled tofu to the other side of the skillet. Cook, stirring occasionally, for 3 to 5 minutes, or until the tofu is heated through.

6. Stir the veggies and tofu together. Add the nutritional yeast and coconut aminos, mixing well, and cook for 3 additional minutes.

7. Divide the scramble equally among 4 plates. Garnish each plate with 2 basil leaves, and serve hot.

Spuds, Veggies, and Greens

If you love a hot and savory breakfast, this is the dish for you!
An inspired combination of potatoes, veggies, and greens, it will awaken
your morning taste buds and prepare you for the day ahead.

YIELD: 4 servings

2 tablespoons lower-sodium vegetable broth or water

2 medium yellow onions, thinly sliced into rings

4 medium Yukon gold potatoes (unpeeled), cut into bite-sized pieces

1 clove garlic, minced

$1/2$ teaspoon ground black pepper

1 red bell pepper, thinly sliced

1 yellow bell pepper, thinly sliced

2 cups lightly packed chopped kale

1. Place a large nonstick skillet over high heat, and add the broth or water and the onions. Cook, stirring often, for about 5 minutes, or until the onions are transparent.

2. Stir in the potatoes, garlic, and black pepper, and cook for 3 to 4 minutes.

3. Layer the remaining vegetables over the potato mixture. Turn the heat to low, cover, and cook for 10 to 15 minutes, or until the potatoes are soft.

4. Carefully mix the potatoes and other veggies together, and serve hot.

Green with Health

Dark leafy greens have the highest nutrient density—nutrients per calorie—of any whole food. Kale, collard greens, and watercress top the list of powerhouse greens with their super-high levels of antioxidants, anti-inflammatory nutrients, and phytochemicals. Working together, these nutrients enhance the health of your eyes, heart, and brain and help protect your body from cancer.

Hash Me No Questions

Delighting the senses with a variety of colors, flavors, and satisfying textures, this hearty hash—which boasts three kinds of potatoes—is comfort food at its best.

YIELD: 4 to 6 servings

2 large russet potatoes

1 large sweet potato

3 medium purple potatoes

1/4 cup lower-sodium vegetable broth or water, divided

1 large red onion, chopped

1 large red bell pepper, chopped

1 large green bell pepper, chopped

1 large shallot

2 whole heads Roasted Garlic (see page 31)

1 tablespoon finely chopped fresh rosemary

1 teaspoon ground smoked black pepper

2 tablespoons coconut aminos

1. Preheat the oven to 425°F. Scrub and dry the potatoes, and pierce each one with a fork to prevent it from bursting during baking.

2. Place the potatoes directly on the center oven rack. Bake for 45 minutes, or until the potatoes are soft when you squeeze them. (Note that the smaller potatoes will finish cooking first.) Remove the potatoes from the oven and set aside to cool.

3. Remove the skin from the sweet potato, but leave the skin on the other potatoes. Dice the potatoes and set aside.

4. Heat a large nonstick skillet over medium heat. Add 2 tablespoons of vegetable broth or water and the onion, bell peppers, and shallot. Cook, stirring frequently, for about 12 minutes, or until the onion begins to caramelize.

5. Cut open the top of the roasted garlic heads, and squeeze the garlic into the skillet. Stir to mix, and cook for 2 to 3 minutes. Transfer the onion mixture to a bowl, and set aside.

6. Wipe out the skillet with a paper towel and heat over medium-high heat. Add the remaining 2 tablespoons of vegetable broth or water and the reserved diced potatoes. Cook, stirring occasionally, for about 10 minutes, or until they begin to brown.

7. Stir the reserved onion mixture into the potatoes, and add the rosemary and pepper. Cook for 5 minutes, stirring occasionally to prevent sticking.

8. Remove the skillet from the heat, and stir in the coconut aminos to loosen up the hash. Divide the hash equally among the serving plates and serve hot.

Morning Sun and Greens

Leafy greens are a great source of nutrients, so why not begin the day by giving your body what it needs? Sweet berries, coconut, and raisins—along with crunchy protein-packed seeds—make this dish as scrumptious as it is nutritious.

YIELD: 4 servings

4 cups mixed salad greens

2 cups fresh mixed berries of your choice, or 2 cups warmed frozen berries of your choice

1 cup unsalted raw sunflower seeds

2 cups sunflower sprouts

1 cup shredded unsweetened coconut

½ cup raisins

Ground cinnamon

1. Place 1 cup of greens on each of 4 serving plates. Top each salad with ½ cup of berries, ¼ cup of sunflower seeds, ½ cup of sunflower sprouts, ¼ cup of coconut, and 2 tablespoons of raisins.
2. Lightly sprinkle each salad with cinnamon to taste, and serve.

Roasted Garlic

When garlic is slow-roasted, it becomes sweet, mild tasting, and creamy. The caramelized cloves are amazingly versatile, too. Squeeze them on your favorite bread or crackers, or stir them into skillet dishes, casseroles, or dips. You may be surprised to learn that garlic is easy to roast without the oil that is used in most recipes, and it stores well. Roast several heads of garlic at once, place them in an airtight container, and keep them in the refrigerator for up to a week.

1 whole head garlic

1. Preheat the oven to 350°F.
2. Place the entire head of garlic (unpeeled and uncut) in the oven, directly on the center rack, positioning a baking sheet on the rack below. Roast for 20 to 25 minutes, or until the cloves are soft when squeezed. Remove the garlic from the oven, and allow the heads to cool.
3. To use, cut open the cloves with a sharp knife and squeeze out the garlic. Place any unused heads of roasted garlic in an airtight container, and store in the refrigerator for up to a week.

World's Healthiest Pancakes

Whole grains provide a wonderfully nutty taste to these pancakes while packing each forkful with nutrition. Coconut and dates add the sweetness that makes pancakes a universal favorite. Top these pancakes with fresh fruit, maple syrup, or applesauce.

YIELD: 4 servings

1 cup uncooked buckwheat groats	1/4 cup shredded unsweetened coconut
1/2 cup uncooked brown rice	2 pitted dates
1/2 cup uncooked millet	1 1/2 cups unsweetened soy, nut, or seed milk
1/2 cup chopped kale	1 teaspoon baking powder
1/4 cup freshly ground flaxseed meal	1 teaspoon vanilla extract

1. Place all of the ingredients in a blender, and process on high speed for 2 to 3 minutes, or until the mixture is smooth. If necessary, add 1 to 2 tablespoons of water to create a thick but pourable batter.

2. Lightly spray a large nonstick skillet with nonstick cooking spray, and heat to medium.

3. Pour 2 to 3 tablespoons of the batter onto the skillet, creating a 4- to 5-inch pancake. Cook until the center begins to bubble and the edges appear slightly brown. Flip and cook until the second side is brown. Transfer the pancake to a plate, and cover to keep warm while you make the rest of the pancakes.

4. Serve the pancakes hot with the toppings of your choice.

Variation

■ To make World's Healthiest Chocolate Pancakes, add 1/4 cup of unsweetened cocoa powder to the batter, and cook as directed above. Top the pancakes with sliced bananas and a light drizzle of maple syrup.

Easy Oat Pancakes

These pancakes take just a few minutes to whip up for a nutritious breakfast treat that makes getting out of bed in the morning a pleasure. Serve them with fresh seasonal fruit, some Broiled Plantains (see page 44), or some Spiced Stewed Apples (see page 51). For a delicious topping, try the Tahini Vanilla Whip (see page 68), or simply add a drizzle of maple syrup.

YIELD: 3 to 4 servings

$\frac{1}{2}$ cup uncooked old-fashioned rolled oats

3 tablespoons flaxseeds

$\frac{1}{2}$ cup garbanzo flour

$1\frac{1}{2}$ teaspoons baking powder

$\frac{1}{2}$ teaspoon baking soda

$1\frac{1}{2}$ cups unsweetened soy, nut, or seed milk

1 tablespoon apple cider vinegar

---

1. Place the oats and flaxseeds in a blender, and grind to a flour-like consistency. Transfer the flour to a medium-sized mixing bowl.

2. Add the garbanzo flour, baking powder, and baking soda to the mixing bowl, and stir to combine the ingredients.

3. Place the milk and vinegar in a small bowl, and stir together. Add the milk mixture to the dry ingredients, and stir to form a batter. Don't worry about lumps.

4. Lightly spray a large nonstick skillet with nonstick cooking spray, and heat to medium-high. Drop $\frac{1}{4}$-cup portions of the batter onto the skillet, cooking 4 pancakes at a time. Cook until the center begins to bubble and the edges begin to dry out. Flip and cook until the second side is brown. Transfer the pancakes to a plate, and cover to keep warm while you make the rest of the pancakes. (This batter will make about 14 pancakes.)

5. Serve the pancakes hot with the toppings of your choice.

Buckwheat Crepes

This vegan low-fat whole grain crepe is surprisingly thin and pliable. Serve it with a fruit filling for breakfast, a weekend brunch, or a nice dessert. With a savory filling, it can be an elegant appetizer or even a main course. You don't need a special crepe pan—just a good nonstick skillet.

YIELD: 5 servings

Crepes	Filling
1/4 cup uncooked buckwheat groats	1 recipe Tahini Vanilla Whip (see page 68) or Orange Peanut Butter Whip (see page 68)
1/4 cup garbanzo flour	
2 tablespoons flaxseeds	1 recipe Spiced Stewed Apples (see page 51)
2 cups unsweetened nut, seed, or soy milk	Fresh berries for garnish

1. Place all of the crepe ingredients in a blender, and blend until smooth.

2. Lightly spray a large nonstick skillet with nonstick cooking spray and heat it over medium-high heat.

3. Measure out around 1/4 cup batter for a small crepe or 1/2 cup for a larger crepe. Pour the batter into the skillet, and either pick up the skillet and tilt it in a circular motion to distribute the batter as thinly and evenly across the bottom of the pan to form a somewhat round crepe, or use a silicon spatula to spread the batter out as thinly and evenly as possible. This must be done quickly, because the crepe will start to cook immediately. Cook for about 3 minutes, or until lightly browned on the bottom. Turn the crepe over, and quickly cook on the other side. As the crepes are done, stack them on a plate and cover them to keep warm. Repeat until all the batter has been used. (This batter will make about 5 large or 10 small crepes.)

4. To assemble, place one crepe at a time on a plate, and spread with a tablespoon of the tahini or peanut butter whip. Using a slotted spoon, top the whipped topping with a spoonful of the stewed apples, and roll up the crepe. Arrange any extra whip or apples on top of or alongside the crepes. Garnish with fresh berries, and serve.

Variation

■ Feel free to experiment with different fillings. Try fresh or stewed seasonal fruit, unsweetened vegan yogurt, nuts, and anything else that suits your fancy.

Helpful Tip

If you have never made crepes before, start by making small crepes, because they are easier to prepare. The larger ones require a little more skill.

Mochi Waffles

Mochi is a Japanese confection made from a special variety of rice called sweet rice. Brown rice mochi is available in the freezer section of health food stores. It comes in a sheet and contains nothing but brown rice. When cut into squares and cooked in a nonstick waffle iron, it puffs up and becomes super crisp and light. Serve it with fresh fruit, and maybe Broiled Plantains (see page 44) or Spiced Stewed Apples (see page 51). Tahini Vanilla Whip or Orange Peanut Butter Whip (see page 68) would make delicious toppings.

YIELD: 6 servings

12-ounce package brown rice mochi,
cut into 6 squares

1. Spray a nonstick waffle iron lightly with nonstick cooking spray. Preheat the iron according to the manufacturer's directions.

2. When the waffle iron is hot, place the mochi in the iron and close. Cook for about 5 minutes, or until the mochi is puffed, light brown, and crisp. If the waffle iron requires turning, turn the waffle and cook on the second side until light brown and crisp.

3. Serve the waffles hot with the topping of your choice.

Helpful Tip

One 12-ounce package of mochi can be cut into six squares to make six waffles, but most waffle irons can cook only two to four of these waffles at a time. If you want to make more, you'll have to work in batches. So cook as many pieces of mochi as you like, wrap up and refrigerate any leftover pieces, and store them in the refrigerator for up to four days.

Creamy Cheesy Grits

*One of Milan's favorite dishes, these southern-style grits are both creamy
and cheesy thanks to generous amounts of cashew cream and nutritional yeast.
Enjoy this stick-to-your-ribs treat without guilt.*

YIELD: 4 servings

4 cups plus 2 tablespoons lower-sodium vegetable broth, divided

1 yellow onion, diced

1 shallot, minced

2 cloves garlic, minced

3/4 cup uncooked coarse- or medium-ground yellow cornmeal*

1/2 cup Basic Cashew Cream (see page 71)

1/4 cup nutritional yeast

1 teaspoon ground smoked black pepper

1/4 cup cilantro sprigs

---

*While you can find a product labeled "grits" in the super-market, any coarse or medium grind of cornmeal will work well. If you want to avoid GMO corn, buy an organic product.

1. Heat a medium-sized nonstick saucepan over medium-high heat. Add 2 tablespoons of the vegetable broth, the onions, and the shallot, and sauté, stirring frequently, for 5 to 7 minutes, or until the onions are translucent.

2. Add the garlic to the saucepan and cook for about 3 minutes, or until fragrant.

3. Pour 3 cups of the remaining vegetable broth into the saucepan, and bring to a boil over high heat. Slowly pour the grits into the boiling mixture while whisking to remove any lumps.

4. Return the grits to a boil; then decrease the heat to a simmer. Cook, whisking occasionally to prevent sticking, for about 5 minutes, or until most of the liquid has been absorbed and the grits begin to thicken. Add the remaining cup of broth, and simmer over low heat until thickened, whisking occasionally.

5. Stir the Basic Cashew Cream, nutritional yeast, and smoked black pepper into the grits, and simmer over low heat, stirring occasionally, for 20 to 30 minutes, or until the grits are soft and tender.

6. Divide the grits equally among 4 bowls and garnish with the cilantro. Serve immediately.

Variation

■ For added flavor, texture, and taste, crumble up some maple-smoked tempeh bacon (see page 48), and stir it into the grits or sprinkle it over the top.

Oh, Happy Day Oats and Berries

*Old-fashioned rolled oats make this breakfast quick and easy to prepare—
a great choice on a busy morning—while warm berries make
it a sweet treat that the whole family will enjoy.*

YIELD: 4 servings

4 cups water

2 cups uncooked old-fashioned rolled oats

1 teaspoon Date Paste (see page 45)
or pure monk fruit powder (optional)

1 cup frozen or fresh berries of
your choice

1 cup whole or chopped unsalted
raw walnuts

1. Place the water in a medium-sized saucepan, and bring to a boil over high heat. Stir in the oats, adding the Date Paste or monk fruit powder if desired. Reduce the heat to low and cook at a simmer, stirring occasionally, for 5 to 10 minutes, or until the oatmeal has reached the desired consistency.

2. While the oatmeal is cooking, place the berries in a small saucepan, and cook over low heat for 2 to 3 minutes, or just until warm.

3. Divide the oatmeal among 4 bowls. Top each serving with about ¼ cup each of warm berries and nuts, and serve immediately.

Getting to the Heart of the Matter

Heart disease is America's leading cause of death, affecting nearly one out of every two people during their lifetime. But this all-too-common disorder can be virtually banished through a simple change of lifestyle. Remove processed food and animal products from your life, and shift to a plant-based diet. The result will be better heart health and enhanced overall wellness.

Peachy Cream Oats

*Cashew cream is a delicious (and convincing) alternative to dairy cream,
and when paired with peaches, you have a flavor combination that's hard to beat.
The steel-cut oats will fill you up and power you throughout the morning.*

YIELD: 4 servings

4 cups water	1 recipe Basic Cashew Cream (see page 71)
1 cup uncooked steel-cut oats	1 cup sliced fresh peaches, or 1 cup frozen sliced peaches, warmed

---

1. Place the water in a medium-sized saucepan, and bring to a boil over high heat. Stir in the oats, reduce the heat to low, and cook at a simmer, stirring occasionally, for 20 to 30 minutes, or until the oatmeal has reached the desired consistency. Remove from the heat, cover, and allow to stand for 2 to 3 minutes.

2. Divide the oatmeal among 4 bowls. Top each serving with $1/4$ cup of Basic Cashew Cream and $1/4$ cup of peaches, and serve immediately.

Simple Teff Porridge

Teff is such a delicious grain with its dark brown color, fine texture, and faint molasses-like flavor. It is available in most health food stores and truly worth getting to know. The dates add sweetness to this dish, but if you like it even sweeter, add a pinch of monk fruit powder.

YIELD: 2 to 3 servings

$1/2$ cup uncooked teff, rinsed and drained	4 pitted dates, chopped
$1 1/2$ cups water	$1/2$ teaspoon vanilla extract

---

1. Place the teff, water, and dates in a medium-sized saucepan, and stir to combine. Bring the mixture to a boil over high heat. Reduce the heat to low, cover, and cook at a simmer, stirring occasionally, for 15 to 20 minutes, or until the water has been absorbed and the teff is cooked.

2. Stir the vanilla into the porridge, and divide among 2 to 3 bowls. Serve immediately as is or topped with vegan milk and/or fresh fruit.

Cherry Vanilla Cream Porridge

Millet is a mild-flavored, nourishing, quick-cooking grain that is also gluten-free. This vanilla-and-cherry cream of millet can brighten up any cold grey morning.

YIELD: 2 to 3 servings

½ cup uncooked millet

3 cups water

2 cups unsweetened frozen cherries

1 teaspoon vanilla extract

1–2 tablespoons shredded unsweetened coconut (optional)

---

1. Place the millet in a blender, and grind it to a cornmeal-like texture. Transfer the ground millet to a medium-sized saucepan, add the water, and stir to combine.

2. While stirring constantly, bring the mixture to a boil over medium-high heat. Reduce the heat to low, cover, and cook for 3 minutes, or until thick and creamy.

3. Stir the cherries and vanilla into the porridge, cover, and turn off the heat. Allow the saucepan to sit for about 5 minutes, or until the cherries have thawed.

4. Divide the porridge among 2 to 3 bowls. Top with shredded coconut, if desired, and/or with fresh fruit or vegan milk or yogurt. Serve immediately.

Sugar—Sweet to the Tongue, Bitter to the Body

The average person consumes one hundred and fifty pounds of refined and artificial sweeteners a year, including twenty-two teaspoons of sugar daily. This shouldn't be too surprising, since studies have shown that sugar and sweets are more addictive than heroin! The problem is that sugar triggers an acute inflammatory response that contributes to heart disease, diabetes, cancer, and many other disorders. Sugar also alters our gut bacteria, which is responsible for a good part of our immune system. And, of course, sugar is high in calories and low in nutrients. By following a whole food plant-based diet, you will gradually lose your taste for refined sugar and begin to appreciate the natural sweetness of healthy foods.

Overnight Berry Muesli

Often called a "superfood" because it's so packed with nutrients—including antioxidants—dried Himalayan goji berries are also pretty and very tasty. Make this muesli before you go to bed, and it will be ready when you wake up in the morning.

YIELD: 1 generous or 2 small servings

⅓ cup uncooked old-fashioned rolled oats

¼ cup dried goji berries

2 tablespoons raisins

2 tablespoons shredded unsweetened coconut

1 tablespoon freshly ground flaxseed meal

1 cup hot water

1 cup frozen blueberries

1. Place the oats, goji berries, raisins, coconut, and flaxseed meal in a medium-sized bowl. Add the hot water and stir. Stir in the frozen blueberries, cover, and refrigerate overnight.

2. The next day, serve the muesli as is or topped with unsweetened soy, nut, or seed milk and/or vegan yogurt.

Orange Chia Muesli

Here is an easy, versatile, and yummy way to get your day started. If you're serving several people, double or triple the recipe—it will still work beautifully. Since no cooking is needed, this is a great choice on a warm day.

YIELD: 1 generous or 2 small servings

⅓ cup uncooked old-fashioned rolled oats

2 tablespoons raisins

2 tablespoons chia seeds

1-inch-square piece orange peel (optional)

⅓ cup orange juice (juice from 1 orange, freshly squeezed)

1 cup unsweetened soy, nut, or seed milk

1 banana, peeled and sliced

1 orange, peeled, sliced, and sectioned

1–2 tablespoons shredded unsweetened coconut

1. Place the oats, raisins, chia seeds, and orange peel, if using, in a blender. Grind to a coarse meal, and transfer to a medium-sized bowl.

2. Add the orange juice and milk to the oat mixture, stirring to combine. Allow to sit for at least 5 minutes.

3. Top the muesli with the banana and orange, sprinkle with a bit of shredded coconut, and serve.

Variations

■ Depending on what you have on hand, feel free to use a different type of fruit juice and/or dried fruit. You can also replace the juice with nut, seed, or soymilk. And you can vary the fresh fruit according to the season.

Apple Nut Muesli with Berries

You can't beat this breakfast in warm weather. Like Orange Chia Muesli (see page 40), it is prepared without the use of a hot stove, and the lemony flavor makes it refreshing while the apples add their own unique flavor and sweetness. By using different types of berries, you can keep this cereal fresh and new every day.

YIELD: 2 servings

1/2 cup uncooked old-fashioned rolled oats	1-inch-square piece lemon peel
2 tablespoons raisins	3/4 cup unsweetened soy, nut, or seed milk
2 tablespoons chopped unsalted raw walnuts	2 small apples, grated (peel if not organic)
	Fresh seasonal berries for garnish

1. Place the oats, raisins, walnuts, and lemon peel in a blender. Grind to a coarse meal, and transfer to a medium-sized bowl.

2. Add the milk and apples to the oat mixture, stirring to combine. Allow to sit for at least 5 minutes.

3. Divide the muesli between 2 bowls. Top with the berries and, if desired, with extra vegan milk or yogurt before serving.

Festive Winter Porridge

Cranberries are so high in antioxidants that it's a shame to save them for holiday dinners and load them down with sugar. Raisins and apples provide sweetness, but if you want your oatmeal a little sweeter, add a pinch of pure monk fruit powder. Turmeric has great anti-inflammatory powers, but if you don't like the flavor, just omit it. This dish packs a high-nutrient punch even without the turmeric.

YIELD: 2 to 3 servings

2½ cups water	1 cup cranberries, fresh or frozen
2 small apples, diced (peel if not organic)	3 tablespoons raisins
¾ cup uncooked old-fashioned rolled oats	6 cloves
	½–1 teaspoon ground turmeric (optional)

1. Place the water, apples, oats, cranberries, raisins, cloves, and turmeric, if using, in a medium-sized saucepan, and stir to combine.

2. Bring the mixture to a boil over high heat. Immediately reduce the heat to low, cover, and cook at a simmer for 15 to 20 minutes, or until most of the water has been absorbed and the apples are tender.

3. Remove and discard the cloves, and divide the porridge among 2 to 3 bowls. Serve immediately as is or topped with fresh berries and/or vegan milk or yogurt.

Variation

■ To cook Festive Winter Porridge more quickly, simply place the pot over higher heat, and the dish will be done in 5 to 10 minutes. Unlike the slower-cooking method, though, this one needs a little more attention, so watch the porridge closely and stir often.

Milan's Guilt-Free Granola

If you're looking for a delicious granola that's great for breakfast and snacks—and doesn't have the oil and refined sugar found in so many commercial brands—look no further. This cereal is loved by kids and adults alike and will fill your home with the irresistible aromas of cinnamon, maple syrup, and roasting nuts.

YIELD: 4 to 6 servings

3 cups uncooked old-fashioned rolled oats

$1/2$ cup chopped unsalted raw walnuts

$1/2$ cup chopped unsalted raw pecans

$1/2$ cup chopped dates

2 tablespoons ground cinnamon

$1/2$ teaspoon ground nutmeg

$3/4$ cup water

$1/2$ cup maple syrup

1 teaspoon vanilla extract

1. Preheat the oven to 350°F. Line a large rimmed baking pan with parchment paper, and set aside.

2. Place the oats, walnuts, pecans, dates, cinnamon, and nutmeg in a large bowl, and stir to mix. Set aside.

3. Place the water, maple syrup, and vanilla in a small saucepan, stir to mix well, and cook over medium-low heat, stirring often, for 2 to 3 minutes, or until well combined and hot.

4. Pour the wet ingredients over the dry ingredients and stir well, making sure that everything is thoroughly combined.

5. Spread the granola mixture evenly over the prepared pan, and bake, stirring occasionally, for 35 minutes or until golden brown and crisp. Remove the pan from the oven, and allow the granola to cool to room temperature.

6. Serve immediately with your favorite unsweetened nut or seed milk, or store in an airtight container for up to 2 weeks.

Breakfast Banana Wrap

*Make this delicious simple-to-prepare sandwich with whole wheat pita bread
for a breakfast that you can enjoy immediately or take with you if you must.*

YIELD: 2 servings

2 sweet medium-sized apples,
grated (peel if not organic)

1 tablespoon lemon juice

2 whole wheat pitas

1/4 cup nut butter of your choice

2 small bananas, sliced lengthwise
and then halved crosswise

2 tablespoons raisins or chopped dates

1. Place the grated apple and lemon juice in a small bowl, and stir to mix. Set aside. (The lemon juice will help prevent the apple from browning.)

2. Heat the pitas in a dry skillet for a minute or so on each side. Spread half of the nut butter on one side of each warm pita, and top with half of the grated apples, banana slices, and raisins or chopped dates.

3. Roll up the pitas and enjoy immediately. To eat later, "wrap the wraps" in waxed paper, twist the ends of the paper to hold the sandwich together, and pack in your lunch box to eat within an hour or two.

Broiled Plantains

*Plantains are large cooking bananas. When they are underripe, they are usually
cooked and served as a starchy vegetable, but when they are so black that they look
ready for the compost heap, they are super sweet and delicious and make a great
addition to a breakfast of pancakes, whole grain toast, or waffles.*

YIELD: 4 servings

2 ripe plantains

1. Preheat the oven broiler. Spray a cookie sheet with nonstick cooking spray.

2. Peel the ripe plantains and cut them in half lengthwise. Then cut each piece crosswise so that you get 4 pieces from each plantain.

3. Arrange the plantain quarters on the prepared sheet, and smash them with a spatula to provide more browning surface. Spray the tops lightly with nonstick cooking spray.

4. Place the plantains under the preheated broiler and broil for 3 to 4 minutes, or until the tops are brown and caramelized. Turn the plantains over, and broil until the second side is brown. Serve immediately.

Variations

■ If you are making just one plantain, you can broil it in a toaster oven. Prepare the plantain as directed in Step 2 of the recipe, and place the pieces directly on the wire rack. Cook until brown and caramelized, turning once.

■ To pan-fry plantains, prepare them for cooking as directed in Step 2 of the recipe. Then spray a nonstick skillet with nonstick cooking spray, and arrange the plantain pieces in the pan. Cook over medium-high heat for 3 to 4 minutes, or until the bottom is brown. Turn and cook on the second side.

■ For a warm and delicious breakfast sandwich that's a nice change from bananas and peanut butter, spread whole grain toast with almond butter or another nut butter. Then add slices of pan-fried or broiled plantain.

Date Paste

Simple to prepare, date paste is a wonderful sweetener—creamy, delicious, and high in nutrients—that is also extremely versatile. It is a great topping on fruit parfaits (see the recipe on page 47) and is equally good in smoothies and baked goods. Once made, this all-natural sweetener can be kept in the refrigerator for up to a week or stored in the freezer for up to three months.

YIELD: 1¹/₂ cups

1 cup pitted dates, preferably Medjool   1 cup water, divided

1. Place the dates in a small bowl, and add the water to cover. Soak overnight or for at least 8 hours.

2. Drain the water from the dates, reserving the water.

3. Place the dates in a blender or food processor along with a few tablespoons of the reserved soaking water, and blend or process until the mixture is smooth and creamy. If necessary, add a little more of the reserved water.

4. Use immediately, or store in the refrigerator for up to a week or the freezer for up to three months. Note that the paste may darken in the refrigerator, but this will not affect its flavor.

Warm Apple Breakfast Crisp

The smell of baked apples and cinnamon is better than any alarm clock to open sleepy eyes. This hearty breakfast—perfect for a cold morning—can be prepared the night before through Step 4. The next day, just pop the pan in the oven for a half hour and enjoy!

YIELD: 4 servings

4 apples of your choice, cored and thinly sliced (peel if not organic)*

1/4 cup Date Paste (see page 45)

1 teaspoon ground cinnamon

---

*Choose the apples according to your taste preferences. Granny Smith will give you a tart taste while Pink Lady creates a sweeter crisp.

Crumble Topping

1 cup uncooked old-fashioned rolled oats

1/2 cup unsalted raw walnuts

1/2 cup unsalted raw pecans

1/2 cup pitted dates

2 tablespoons water

1 teaspoon vanilla extract

1. Preheat the oven to 350°F.

2. To make the crumble, place all of the crumble ingredients in a food processor, and blend until the mixture has a crumbly appearance and can be compressed in your hand. Set aside.

3. To make the apple filling, place the sliced apples, Date Paste, and cinnamon in a medium-sized bowl. Stir with a wooden spoon or spatula until well mixed.

4. Arrange the apple mixture evenly across the bottom of an ungreased 8 inch-square oven-safe dish. Evenly sprinkle the crumble over the apples.

5. Bake for 25 to 30 minutes, or until the apples are bubbly. Remove from the oven and allow to cool for 10 minutes before dividing among 4 bowls. Serve as is, or top with almond milk or Basic Cashew Cream (see page 71) and a light sprinkling of ground cinnamon.

Fruit Parfait

This presentation is so beautiful that your family may ask you why you're serving dessert for breakfast! But don't be fooled by its pretty looks and luscious taste; this parfait is full of the nutrients you need to start your day.

YIELD: 4 servings

¹/₂ cup uncooked buckwheat groats	2 teaspoons ground cinnamon
2 tablespoons old-fashioned rolled oats	2 teaspoons vanilla extract
Water for soaking grains	¹/₂ cup sliced fresh strawberries
1¹/₂ cups unsweetened soy, nut, or seed milk	¹/₂ cup fresh blueberries
2 ripe bananas, mashed	2 tablespoons Date Paste (see page 45)
¹/₄ cup chia seeds	

1. The night before you plan to serve the parfaits, place the buckwheat groats and rolled oats in a small bowl, and add water to cover. Stir lightly, cover, and refrigerate overnight.

2. Also the night before, place the milk, mashed bananas, chia seeds, cinnamon, and vanilla in a medium-sized bowl. Blend well using either a hand or electric blender until no clumps of chia remain. Cover and refrigerate overnight.

3. In the morning, place the buckwheat mixture in a strainer, and rinse with cold water until no slimy residue remains. Add the rinsed buckwheat mixture to the chia mixture, and stir well.

4. When you are ready to make your parfaits, mix the strawberries and blueberries in a small bowl, reserving a few berries for a garnish. Place 1 tablespoon of berries in each of 4 glass bowls, dessert glasses, or mason jars. Top with 2 tablespoons of the buckwheat mixture, followed by a tablespoon of the berries. Continue to alternate layers of berries and buckwheat until the glasses are full.

5. Drizzle some Date Paste over the top of each parfait. Top with 2 to 3 of the reserved berries, and serve.

Maple-Smoked Tempeh BLT

If you thought eating vegan meant giving up bacon, think again!
Piled high with smoky tempeh bacon, crisp lettuce, and fresh tomatoes,
this BLT will have you doing your happy dance.

YIELD: 4 servings

4 whole grain onion rolls, or 4 rolls of your choice	1 tablespoon maple syrup
4 slices beefsteak tomato	1 tablespoon vegan Worcestershire sauce
4 leaves romaine lettuce	1 tablespoon balsamic vinegar
Maple-Smoked Tempeh Bacon	1 tablespoon smoked paprika
2 tablespoons coconut aminos	1 teaspoon ground smoked black pepper, or 1 teaspoon ground black pepper plus 1 teaspoon liquid smoke
2 tablespoons water	8 ounces tempeh

1. To make the bacon, in a small mixing bowl, combine the coconut aminos, water, maple syrup, Worcestershire sauce, balsamic vinegar, smoked paprika, and smoked black pepper (or regular pepper plus liquid smoke), making sure that ingredients are thoroughly mixed. Set aside.

2. Slice the tempeh as thin as you can without breaking it apart (about $1/8$ inch thick). The thinner you slice it, the crisper it will be. Make short slices rather than trying to make longer ones. Dip each piece of tempeh into the reserved maple syrup mixture, making sure that each piece is well coated on both sides.

3. Arrange the dipped tempeh slices in a single layer in a large baking dish. Pour the remaining marinade over the tempeh, and allow the slices to marinate for 30 minutes. While the tempeh is marinating, preheat the oven to 450°F.

4. Place a metal rack on top of a large baking sheet, and arrange the tempeh in a single layer on the rack. Bake for 20 minutes or until the tempeh is golden brown. Because the rack allows air to circulate completely around the tempeh, there is no need to flip the slices. Remove the pan from the oven, and set the tempeh aside to cool just until warm.

5. Slice the rolls in half lengthwise and arrange them directly on the oven rack, sliced sides down. Toast for 3 to 5 minutes, or until warm and crusty. Be sure to watch them closely to prevent burning.

6. For each BLT, arrange some of the tempeh bacon slices on the bottom of a toasted roll. Top with a slice of tomato, a leaf of lettuce, and the top of the roll. Serve warm.

Variation

■ For added flavor and creaminess, layer some sliced avocado over the lettuce, or spread the rolls with a generous amount of Guacamole (see page 63) before adding the tempeh, tomato, and lettuce.

Blueberry Muffins

These fat- and sugar-free delights are almost as much blueberry as they are muffin!

YIELD: 12 muffins

1½ cups whole grain spelt flour	1¼ cups fresh blueberries
½ cup garbanzo flour	1½ cups unsweetened soy, nut, or seed milk
1½ teaspoons baking powder	½ cup mashed firm silken tofu
½ teaspoon baking soda	1 tablespoon apple cider vinegar
½ teaspoon pure monk fruit powder	1 teaspoon vanilla extract

1. Preheat the oven to 350°F. Lightly spray a standard 12-muffin tin with nonstick cooking spray, and coat the cups generously with flour.

2. Place the spelt flour, garbanzo flour, baking powder, baking soda, and monk fruit powder in a large mixing bowl, and stir well to combine. Add the blueberries, and mix again to distribute them evenly throughout the flour. Set aside.

3. Place the milk, tofu, vinegar, and vanilla extract in a blender or food processor, and blend until smooth.

4. Pour the blended milk mixture into the flour mixture, and stir just enough to combine the ingredients into a batter. Do not overmix.

5. Spoon equal amounts of batter into the prepared muffin cups. (We use a ¼-cup measuring cup with a handle to ladle out the batter.) Bake for 15 to 18 minutes, or until the muffins are firm to the touch.

6. To release the muffins from the tin, run a knife around the edge of each muffin and invert the tin. Serve warm or at room temperature.

Carrot Ginger Muffins

A generous dose of freshly grated ginger gives these muffins a subtle touch of heat to warm you on a cold morning. If some of the muffins aren't eaten on the day they are baked, slice them in half and freeze them in a plastic bag. Then pop the frozen halves in the toaster to heat and serve. If you don't have a sweet tooth, leave out the monk fruit powder.

YIELD: 12 muffins

1½ cups whole grain spelt flour	1 cup grated carrots
½ cup garbanzo flour	½ cup raisins
2 teaspoons ground cinnamon	3 tablespoons freshly grated ginger root
2 teaspoons baking powder	1⅓ cups unsweetened soy, nut, or seed milk
1 teaspoon baking soda	
½ teaspoon pure monk fruit powder, or to taste	2 tablespoons apple cider vinegar
	1 teaspoon vanilla extract

1. Preheat the oven to 350°F. Lightly spray a standard 12-cup muffin tin with nonstick cooking spray, and coat the cups generously with flour.

2. Place the spelt flour, garbanzo flour, cinnamon, baking powder, baking soda, and monk fruit powder in a large mixing bowl, and stir well to combine.

3. Stir the carrots, raisins, and grated ginger into the flour mixture, making sure that all the raisins are separate rather than being clumped together.

4. Place the milk, vinegar, and vanilla extract in a smaller mixing bowl, and stir to combine. Add the milk mixture to the flour mixture, and stir just enough to combine the ingredients into a thick batter. Do not overmix.

5. Spoon equal amounts of batter into the prepared muffin cups. (We use a ¼-cup measuring cup with a handle to ladle out the batter.) Bake for about 15 minutes, or until the muffins are firm to the touch and a toothpick inserted in the center of a muffin comes out clean.

6. To release the muffins from the tin, run a knife around the edge of each muffin and invert the tin. Serve warm or at room temperature.

Helpful Tip

Fresh ginger has fine hair-like fibers, which, needless to say, do not look good sticking out of baked muffins. So after grating the ginger, chop it with a knife to make sure that these fibers are not visible.

Spiced Stewed Apples

*This is a soothing and warming dish that is delicious alone
and also goes wonderfully with whole grain toast, waffles, or pancakes.*

YIELD: 2 servings

2 large sweet apples, diced (peel if not organic)	1 cinnamon stick
$1/4$ cup water	1 tablespoon freshly grated ginger root
8 cloves	$1/8$ teaspoon pure monk fruit powder, or to taste (optional)

1. Place the apples, water, cloves, cinnamon, and ginger in a medium-sized saucepan, and stir to combine.

2. Bring the mixture to a boil over medium heat. Reduce the heat to low, cover, and cook at a simmer, stirring occasionally, for 5 to 10 minutes, or until the apples are soft.

3. Remove and discard the cloves and cinnamon stick. Taste, and stir in the monk fruit powder, if desired. Divide between 2 bowls and serve immediately.

Open-Faced Breakfast Sandwiches

*These sandwiches are hearty, sweet, and filling. When served with fresh berries, they
make a delightfully easy breakfast. Sacha inchi seeds are available in health food stores
and are worth seeking out. They are high in protein, fiber, and omega-3 fatty acids.*

YIELD: 2 servings

1 recipe Spiced Stewed Apples (see above)	2 slices whole grain bread, toasted
$1/4$ cup Tahini Vanilla Whip (see page 68) or Orange Peanut Butter Whip (see page 68)	2 tablespoons sacha inchi seeds, coarsely ground in blender or chopped (optional)

1. While the apples are cooking, whip up the tahini or peanut butter whip, and toast the bread.

2. To assemble, generously spread each piece of toast with the whipped spread, pile high with warm stewed apples, and sprinkle with sacha inchi seeds. Serve immediately.

NOT FITTING IN

In June of 2013, my wife and I decided to take our son Nigel to Universal Studios Orlando to celebrate his upcoming seventh birthday. Neither my wife nor my son had ever been to Florida. We planned on being in Florida on my son's actual birthday in mid-June. It was going to be awesome.

The only request my son made during our entire trip was for me to ride the Harry Potter ride with him. We had spent several weeks researching the rides prior to our vacation and Nigel had deemed the Harry Potter ride the most epic of all. He wanted to experience this epic ride with his dad. I was over four hundred and twenty pounds at the time, so in the back of my mind I worried about whether or not I would fit in one of the ride's seats. Nevertheless, I promised my son that wild horses could not stop me from getting on the Harry Potter ride with him. My health was about to make a liar of me.

On the day of our big Universal Studios Orlando visit, we arrived an hour or so before the park was scheduled to open and managed to be at the front of the line. When the gates swung open we made a beeline for the Harry Potter ride. There was a sample of the seating on display as we approached the platform. As we made our way past the display, one of the park attendants signaled to me and asked me to step out of line. He suggested I try the seating before getting on the ride.

My son didn't know what was going on. As I went to sit down, it was obvious this wasn't going to end well. The attendant began trying to close the harness, but soon had to ask another attendant for help. I sat there for what felt like forever as these two grown men practically fractured my ribs trying to secure the harness. I realized I was not going to be able to go on this ride with my son.

After a few minutes of intense effort, the attendants stepped back and told me I would not be able to take part in the attraction. My son still didn't understand what was happening. He simply heard the attendant tell me I had to leave. Nigel immediately began to cry as my wife tried to take him on the ride instead. I stood there and watched as he called out to me. I could hear him trying to explain to the man running the ride that it was his birthday, and that I had promised to go on the Harry Potter ride with him. As I stood there watching my wife practically drag my son across the platform, he screamed, "But it's my birthday! Please let my dad ride with me!"

I was devastated. Tears began to flow freely down my face, and I made myself a promise. This was going to be the last time I ever let my son down.

Excerpt from *The Change* By Milan Ross and Scott Stoll. Reprinted with permission of Square One Publishers. Copyright © 2016 by Milan Ross and Scott Stoll.

3.

Juices and Smoothies

Juices and smoothies are among the most easy-to-prepare and delicious of all foods. These treats are versatile, too. They work well for breakfast, snacks, and dessert, and they are great for an on-the-go lifestyle. In just a few minutes, you can whip up a delicious beverage, pour it into an insulated cup, and drink it as you make your way to work, play, or school. If your mornings are especially hectic, you can assemble all your smoothie ingredients in the blender container the night before, and store it in the fridge. In the morning, just attach the container to the blender, and you'll be enjoying a homemade smoothie in a matter of seconds.

Juices and smoothies are loaded with nutrition in the form of fruits; vegetables; antioxidant-rich herbs and spices; nondairy milk; and seeds such as flax or chia. It's easy to "sneak in" high-nutrient veggies such as kale, because your favorite fruits, as well as sweet veggies such as carrots and beets, make the mixture as luscious as it is healthful. Your family will never know that Green Julius packs a powerful nutrient punch because orange juice, pure vanilla extract, and a judicious amount of natural sweetener combine to make a creamy delight. Be aware, too, that it's not what you eat but what you absorb that makes you healthy. Smoothies and juices increase the absorption of key nutrients by breaking down the cell walls of plants.

Although you can find many premade juices and smoothies on the shelves of your local stores, the fruit and veggie beverages that you make at home offer more nutrients than any packaged product, because nutrients tend to degrade as a product sits. That's why it's so important to prepare these treats fresh and consume them as soon as possible.

In the pages that follow, you'll find some of our favorite juice and smoothie combinations, all of which provide both great taste and excellent nutrition. Although we hope that you enjoy each and every one, we also want you to use these ideas as springboards to your own creations. The next time you visit your local grocery store, explore the produce section with juices and smoothies in mind. Remember that frozen fruit can also be a good choice, especially when making cold and frosty smoothies. Your creations are limited only by your imagination.

JUICES

Purple People Eater

Beets and kale give this beverage its vivid purple color, which makes it a winner with kids of all ages. But the Purple People Eater is much more than a visual stunner. Subtly sweet and very delicious, it packs a serious nutrient punch.

YIELD: 4 servings

8 medium carrots (peeled)	4 ounces kale (about 2 cups chopped)
3 red delicious apples or other sweet apples, peeled and cored	1 stalk celery
	$1/2$ medium beet, peeled

1. Cut the fruit and vegetables as necessary to fit your juicer's feed tube.

2. Juice all the ingredients and stir well.

3. Divide the juice among glasses and drink as soon as possible.

Summer Breeze

Did you know that the unique taste of watermelon blends beautifully with many herbs and spices? Just one sip of this refreshing summertime drink will make a believer out of you.

YIELD: 4 servings

6 ounces watermelon (about $1^1/2$ cups cubed)	8 large basil leaves
	1-inch piece ginger root, peeled

1. Juice all the ingredients and stir well.

2. Divide the juice among glasses and drink as soon as possible.

Happy Day

A great way to start your day, this juice blends the sweetness of carrots, apples, and oranges with the warm and spicy flavors of ginger and turmeric.

YIELD: 4 servings

8 medium carrots, peeled

2 large Granny Smith apples or other tart apples, peeled and cored

1 blood orange, peeled and sectioned

1-inch piece ginger root, peeled

1-inch piece turmeric root, peeled

1. Cut the fruit and vegetables as necessary to fit your juicer's feed tube.
2. Juice all the ingredients and stir well.
3. Divide the juice among glasses and drink as soon as possible.

Kale-Aid

A healthy twist on lemonade, Kale-Aid will quench your thirst with plenty of delicious flavor, but no added sugar.

YIELD: 4 servings

5 small gala apples or other apples, peeled and cored

3 medium carrots, peeled

4 ounces kale (about 2 cups chopped)

1 lemon, peeled and sectioned

1. Cut the fruit and vegetables as necessary to fit your juicer's feed tube.
2. Juice all the ingredients and stir well.
3. Divide the juice among glasses and drink as soon as possible.

Eye Opener

*Both tart and sweet, this beverage offers the health benefits of turmeric,
a natural anti-inflammatory that also promotes good digestion.*

YIELD: 4 servings

2 large Granny Smith apples or other tart apples, peeled and cored

1 medium grapefruit, peeled and sectioned

1-inch piece turmeric root, peeled

1. Cut the fruit as necessary to fit your juicer's feed tube.
2. Juice all the ingredients and stir well.
3. Divide the juice among glasses and drink as soon as possible.

The Super Hero

*Boasting two superfoods—kale and spinach—this is truly the super hero of juices.
Carrots and apples add further nutrients along with plenty of taste appeal.*

YIELD: 4 servings

12 medium carrots, peeled

2 large honeycrisp apples or other apples, peeled and cored

4 ounces kale (about 2 cups chopped)

4 ounces spinach (about 2 cups chopped)

1 cucumber, peeled

1 stalk celery

1. Cut the fruit and vegetables as necessary to fit your juicer's feed tube.
2. Juice all the ingredients and stir well.
3. Divide the juice among glasses and drink as soon as possible.

SMOOTHIES

Every Day

*A tasty beverage that everyone loves, Every Day is simple to prepare
when time is at a premium.*

YIELD: 2 to 3 servings

2 cups frozen berries of your choice

1 cup frozen mango chunks,
or 1 frozen peeled banana

1 cup water or unsweetened almond milk

$1/4$ cup freshly ground flaxseed meal

2–3 leaves kale

1. Place all the ingredients in a blender, and blend at low speed for 20 seconds. Then purée at high speed until very smooth.
2. Divide the smoothie among glasses and drink as soon as possible.

Caribbean Dream

*One sip of this smoothie will transport you to an idyllic beach surrounded by
aquamarine waters and the sound of steel drums. The healthiest piña colada
you will ever drink, Caribbean Dream is also one of the tastiest.*

YIELD: 2 to 3 servings

2 cups chopped collard greens

2 cups frozen pineapple chunks

1 cup frozen mango chunks

1 cup coconut cream

1 cup water

1. Place all the ingredients in a blender, and blend at low speed for 20 seconds. Then purée at high speed until very smooth.
2. Divide the smoothie among glasses and drink as soon as possible.

Green Julius

In 1929, Julius Freed invented the Orange Julius—a creamy orange juice drink—and started a juice and smoothie revolution. So, we asked, why not add kale and make the Green Julius a beverage for the twenty-first century? Enjoy this frothy, creamy delight at breakfast, as an afternoon snack, or maybe both!

YIELD: 2 to 3 servings

2 cups fresh-squeezed orange juice	8 dried stevia leaves, or
2 cups ice	8 drops whole leaf liquid stevia
2–3 leaves kale	1 teaspoon vanilla extract

1. Place all the ingredients in a blender, and blend at low speed for 20 seconds. Then purée at high speed until very smooth.

2. Divide the smoothie among glasses and drink as soon as possible.

Spice Cake and Greens

Eating healthier doesn't mean giving up your favorite flavors—including the mouth-watering taste of spice cake. Cinnamon, nutmeg, and ginger combine to make this smoothie uniquely delicious.

YIELD: 2 to 3 servings

4 cups spinach leaves	2 teaspoons ground cinnamon
2 cups frozen pineapple chunks	$\frac{1}{2}$ teaspoon ground nutmeg
1 cup frozen mango chunks	$\frac{1}{4}$ teaspoon ground ginger
1 cup unsweetened almond milk	

1. Place all the ingredients in a blender, and blend at low speed for 20 seconds. Then purée at high speed until very smooth.

2. Divide the smoothie among glasses and drink as soon as possible.

Guilt-Free Chocolate Smoothie

A favorite of both children and adults, this smoothie's rich chocolate flavor disguises its secret ingredient: kale. We often enjoy Guilt-Free Chocolate Smoothie at breakfast, but it also makes a cool, refreshing drink after playing or working on a hot summer's day.

YIELD: 2 to 3 servings

3 cups ice	6 pitted dates and 12 dried stevia leaves or 12 drops whole leaf liquid stevia
1 cup unsweetened almond milk or other nut or seed milk	
	2–3 leaves kale
1/3 cup unsweetened cocoa powder	2 teaspoons vanilla extract

1. Place all the ingredients in a blender, and blend at low speed for 20 seconds. Then purée at high speed until very smooth.

2. Divide the smoothie among glasses and drink as soon as possible.

Pumpkin Pie

You don't have to wait for the holidays to enjoy the sweet and spicy creaminess of a pumpkin pie. As a bonus, our smoothie is packed with antioxidants, vitamins, and minerals that will boost the health of your skin, eyes, and immune system.

YIELD: 2 to 3 servings

1 cup almond milk or water	3–4 pitted dates
1 cup ice	8 drops whole leaf liquid stevia, or 8 leaves dried stevia
1 cup spinach leaves	
1 frozen peeled banana	2 leaves kale
1/2 cup canned pumpkin purée	2 teaspoons ground pumpkin pie spice

1. Place all the ingredients in a blender, and blend at low speed for 20 seconds. Then purée at high speed until very smooth.

2. Divide the smoothie among glasses and drink as soon as possible.

Blues for the Blues

The combination of greens and berries is known to improve mood and increase alertness. Let Blues for the Blues lift your spirits and power you through to lunch without the mid-morning crash that so often comes after a coffee or espresso.

YIELD: 2 to 3 servings

1 cup water or unsweetened almond milk	$1/2$ apple or pear, whole or sliced
1 cup frozen blueberries	2–3 leaves kale
$1/2$ cup frozen blackberries	5 drops whole leaf liquid stevia, or 6 dried stevia leaves
$1/2$ cup frozen strawberries	$1/8$ cup freshly ground flaxseed meal

1. Place all the ingredients in a blender, and blend at low speed for 20 seconds. Then purée at high speed until very smooth.

2. Divide the smoothie among glasses and drink as soon as possible.

Creamy Light Green Smoothie

Mildly flavored fennel and cucumber work well in many smoothies, and give this one a refreshing flavor. The bananas provide sweetness and, along with the cashews, make this smoothie irresistibly creamy.

YIELD: 2 to 3 servings

1 cup unsweetened soy, nut, or seed milk or water	$1/3$ cup unsalted raw cashews
1 frozen peeled banana	Juice from $1/2$ lemon
1 cup sliced cucumber ($1/2$ medium)	1-inch-square piece lemon peel
1 cup sliced fennel bulb ($1/3$ large)	$1/2$ teaspoon vanilla extract
	1–2 dates (optional)

1. Place all ingredients in a blender, and blend at low speed for 20 seconds. Then purée at high speed until very smooth.

2. Divide the smoothie among glasses and drink as soon as possible.

4.

Dips, Spreads, and Appetizers

Dips and spreads are among the most versatile of foods. Besides scooping them up with crackers, cut-up vegetables, and spears or slices of fruit, you can use them in a variety of dishes, both sweet and savory. Salsa, for instance, makes a flavorful condiment that will enliven a plain dish of rice, a bowl of beans, or your favorite veggie burger. White Bean and Roasted Garlic Purée can be used in a wrap or mounded on a bed of salad greens for a fast and filling lunch. And our sweeter offerings, like Basic Cashew Cream, can double as luscious frostings for cookies and cakes. This chapter offers a bounty of versatile dips, as well as savory snacks such as Curry Baked Kale Chips and Garlic Nut Thins.

Once you whip together a dip or spread, you can use it to make an almost limitless array of appealing appetizers. The recipes in this chapter represent just a few ways you can pair your creamy concoctions with fruits and veggies to make delicious finger foods. Create your own gourmet bites by preparing produce to serve as scoops and "crackers"— think turnip slices, cherry tomato halves,

endive leaves, and apple slices—and add the toppings of your choice. Then make your appetizers as beautiful as they are wholesome by garnishing them with chopped or halved nuts, minced parsley, toasted seeds, thinly sliced strawberries, or whatever suits your fancy. The possibilities are endless, and the delights you produce will be out of the ordinary enough to be conversation breakers as well as seriously tasty treats.

If you're used to thinking of appetizers as being guilty pleasures, this chapter will be something of a revelation, because only wholesome ingredients have been used in these recipes. You'll soon learn that dips and spreads can be made creamy through the use of nut butters, tahini sauce, silken tofu, beans and peas, avocados, and a variety of other healthy vegan foods. And there's no need to worry about your creations being bland. Fresh herbs like cilantro and basil, jalapeño peppers, garlic, fresh lemon and lime juice, and a host of other ingredients make our dips and spreads as scrumptious as they are nutritious. No matter which recipes you choose, you're sure to please friends and family alike.

Fresh Salsa

*Enjoy this salsa as a healthy dip for whole grain chips, or use it to spice up
a plain dish of beans and rice or your favorite veggie burger.*

YIELD: About 1³/₄ cups

1 medium tomato, finely chopped	¹/₂ to 1 jalapeño pepper, seeded and minced
¹/₂ cup finely chopped bell pepper (any color)	¹/₄ cup chopped fresh cilantro
	1 tablespoon chopped fresh basil
¹/₄ cup minced sweet onion	2 tablespoons lime juice

1. Place all of the ingredients in a bowl, and mix well. If you prefer a smoother salsa, place the ingredients in a food processor, and process until you reach the desired consistency.

2. Serve immediately, or transfer to a covered container and store in the refrigerator for up to 4 days.

Cilantro Pesto

*Even people who claim not to like cilantro have been seen enjoying this! Rather than tossing
it with pasta, try it as a dip with crackers or crudités, or use it to liven up a sandwich.*

YIELD: About 1 cup

4 cups coarsely chopped fresh cilantro (3–4 bunches)	1 clove garlic, pressed
	2 tablespoons water, or as needed
¹/₂ cup pine nuts (pignoli)	¹/₄ cup dulse flakes

1. Place the cilantro, pine nuts, and garlic in a food processor or high-powered blender. Blend until the cilantro and nuts are well chopped and the mixture is well blended, adding water as needed to help it along.

2. Transfer the mixture to a bowl, add the dulse flakes, and mix well.

3. Use immediately, or transfer to a covered container and store in the refrigerator for up to 4 days.

Guacamole

Guacamole is such a simple dish that its success depends on the quality of the ingredients. If you use perfectly ripe avocados and tomatoes, it's hard to go wrong. Enjoy your freshly made guacamole as a dip with raw veggies; use it as a spread for whole grain bread; and spoon creamy dollops on soups, bean dishes, grains, and salads.

YIELD: About $2^1/_2$ cups

2–3 small avocados, or 1 large

2–3 tablespoons lemon or lime juice

1–2 cloves garlic, pressed

1 small tomato, finely chopped

$^1/_3$ cup finely chopped bell pepper (any color) or poblano chile pepper

2 tablespoons finely minced sweet onion

$^1/_2$ teaspoon ground cumin

Pinch of cayenne or chipotle pepper, to taste

Fresh cilantro leaves for garnish

---

1. Cut the avocados in half lengthwise and remove the pits. Scoop out the flesh into a medium-sized mixing bowl. Add the lemon or lime juice and the garlic, and mash with a potato masher.

2. Add the tomato, bell or poblano pepper, onion, cumin, and cayenne or chipotle pepper to the bowl, and mix until well blended.

3. Transfer the mixture to a serving bowl, and garnish with cilantro. Serve immediately (it's best served fresh), or transfer to a covered container and store in the refrigerator for a day or two.

The Health Benefits of Garlic

Garlic is a culinary treasure and nutritional powerhouse that adds flavor as it enhances your health. Studies have found that it can reduce blood pressure by opening up blood vessels, lower cholesterol and triglycerides, inhibit blood clots, decrease inflammation, help prevent cancer, and fight bacterial and viral infections. Maximize your garlic's health benefits by chopping or crushing the cloves and allowing them to sit for ten minutes before cooking. This enables enzymes to convert the phytochemical allin into allicin, the major biologically active component of garlic.

Warm Spinach Artichoke Dip

When you decided to switch to a whole food plant-based diet, you may have thought that you'd have to give up all your favorite appetizers. Think again! This warm dip is delicious with raw vegetables or your favorite crackers, so be sure to make enough because it will go quickly.

YIELD: 1³/₄ cups

14-ounce can water-packed artichoke hearts, drained

2 cups fresh spinach (lightly packed)

1 small onion

5 cloves Roasted Garlic (see page 31)

1 tablespoon fresh lemon juice

¹/₂ teaspoon coconut aminos

¹/₂ teaspoon ground black pepper

---

1. Preheat the oven to 350°F.
2. Place all of the ingredients in a food processor, and pulse until the mixture has the consistency of salsa.
3. Transfer the artichoke mixture to a small casserole, and place in the preheated oven for 10 minutes, or until warm. Serve with fresh-cut vegetables such as cucumber, carrots, zucchini, peppers, and radishes, or with whole grain crackers.

Artichoke Dip

This couldn't be easier to prepare! Try it as a dip for raw veggies, a flavorful spread for sandwich wraps, or a creamy salad dressing. It's also a delicious ingredient in Twice-Baked Artichoke-Stuffed Potatoes (see page 122).

YIELD: 2 cups

14-ounce can water-packed artichoke hearts, drained

12.3-ounce package firm silken tofu

1 teaspoon dried tarragon

1 clove garlic

¹/₈ teaspoon ground white pepper

1 tablespoon minced fresh parsley

1. Reserve 2 of the artichoke hearts, and place the remainder in a blender or food processor.

2. Add the tofu, tarragon, garlic, and pepper to the blender or processor, and blend until smooth and creamy. Transfer the mixture to a medium-sized mixing bowl.

3. Chop the 2 reserved artichoke hearts, and add them to the artichoke mixture. Add the parsley, and mix well. Serve immediately, or transfer to a covered container and store in the refrigerator for 3 to 4 days.

Green Hummus

Here is a yummy change from the usual chickpea or black bean hummus.
It can be made with either edamame or split peas for different but equally good results.
The mint gives this hummus an unexpected and refreshing taste. Serve with
a crudité platter or use it to stuff a pita pocket or top a salad.

YIELD: About 2 cups

2 cups cooked edamame or split peas	1/4 teaspoon sea salt
1/3 cup tahini sauce	2 tablespoons chopped fresh mint, plus extra for garnish
2 tablespoons lemon juice	Paprika for garnish
1–2 cloves garlic	

1. Place all of the ingredients except for the extra mint and the paprika in a food processor or blender, and blend until smooth. If the mixture is too thick, add water, one tablespoon at a time, to achieve the desired consistency.

2. Transfer the mixture to a serving bowl, and garnish with the extra mint and a sprinkle of paprika. Serve immediately, or transfer to a covered container and store in the refrigerator for up to 4 days.

Variation

■ To make *Traditional Hummus*, follow the above recipe substituting cooked, rinsed, and drained chickpeas (canned are fine) for the edamame or split peas. Omit the mint, and add another tablespoon of lemon juice, if desired.

White Bean and Roasted Garlic Purée

*Try this creamy purée on whole grain bread or toast, in a wrap,
or simply mounded on a bed of salad greens.*

YIELD: About 2 cups

2 cups cooked or canned Great Northern
or other white beans, rinsed and drained

1–2 tablespoons Roasted Garlic,
to taste (see page 31)

1 tablespoon white balsamic
or white wine vinegar

1 tablespoon minced fresh sage,
or ½ teaspoon dried sage

¼ teaspoon sea salt

2 tablespoons water, or as needed

1. Place all of the ingredients except for the water in a food processor or blender, and blend until smooth, adding water as needed to get the desired consistency.

2. Transfer the mixture to a bowl and serve immediately, or transfer to a covered container and store in the refrigerator for up to 4 days.

Baba with a Twist

Miso contributes to the marvelous flavor of this eggplant dish, allowing it to be lower in sodium than usual and providing the beneficial probiotic properties for which this traditional Japanese food is known. Spread it on whole grain bread and pair it with a salad.

YIELD: About 2 cups

1 medium eggplant (about 1 pound)

3 tablespoons minced fresh parsley

2–3 tablespoons lemon juice, or to taste

2 tablespoons tahini sauce

2 teaspoons chickpea miso

½ teaspoon liquid smoke (optional)

1 clove garlic, pressed

Paprika or smoked paprika for garnish

1. Preheat the oven to 400°F.

2. Rinse the eggplant and pierce it all over with the tines of a fork. Place it on a baking sheet and bake for about 50 minutes, or until the eggplant is soft and looks shriveled, turning the eggplant over 2 to 3 times during baking so it cooks evenly. Allow to cool until comfortable to handle.

3. Cut the eggplant in half, and use a spoon to scrape the insides out onto a cutting board. Coarsely chop the flesh. You can process it in a blender or food processor instead of chopping it, but the chopped eggplant gives the spread a pleasing texture.

4. Transfer the chopped eggplant to a large mixing bowl, and stir in all of the remaining ingredients except for the paprika. Mix well, sprinkle with paprika, and serve immediately, or transfer to a covered container and store in the refrigerator for up to 4 days.

Hempannaise

Whenever you want an oil-free, low-sodium plant-based alternative to mayonnaise, try Hempannaise. Although it doesn't taste like mayo, it has a tangy creaminess that makes it a great sandwich spread as well as the perfect mayo substitute when preparing potato salad.

YIELD: About 1¹/₄ cups

¹/₂ cup raw hemp seeds	1 tablespoon Dijon-style mustard
¹/₂ cup diced avocado	1 clove garlic
¹/₃ cup water	1 teaspoon chickpea miso
2 tablespoons lemon juice, or to taste	

1. Place all of the ingredients in a blender, and blend until smooth and creamy.

2. Use immediately, or store in an airtight container in the refrigerator for up to 4 days.

Variation

■ To make *Chipotle Sauce*, omit the mustard from the Hempannaise and add ¹/₄ teaspoon ground chipotle pepper and 1 teaspoon smoked paprika.

Tahini Vanilla Whip

This easy-to-prepare spread is great on bread and muffins, and can make fresh fruit, pancakes, mochi waffles, or porridge taste like dessert!

YIELD: 1 cup

½ cup tahini sauce	1 teaspoon vanilla extract
½ cup unsweetened soy, nut, or seed milk	⅛ teaspoon pure monk fruit powder, or several drops whole leaf liquid stevia, to taste

1. Place the tahini in a small bowl, and slowly stir in the milk, whipping it with a fork until it becomes light and fluffy.

2. Stir the vanilla and monk fruit powder into the tahini mixture. Serve immediately, or transfer to a covered container and store in the refrigerator for up to 4 days.

Orange Peanut Butter Whip

Whip this spread up in two minutes to serve on whole grain toast or muffins for a delicious breakfast treat. It also makes a wonderful icing for cakes or cookies.

YIELD: About ¾ cup

½ cup unsweetened, unsalted crunchy peanut butter	⅛ teaspoon pure monk fruit powder, or several drops whole leaf liquid stevia, to taste
1 tablespoon minced orange peel or zest, or less to taste	⅓ cup orange juice, preferably fresh squeezed
½ teaspoon vanilla extract	

1. Place the peanut butter, orange peel, vanilla extract, and monk fruit powder in a small bowl, and stir to mix well.

2. Slowly stir the orange juice into the peanut butter mixture until it has a spreadable whipped consistency. Use immediately, or transfer to a covered container and store in the refrigerator for up to 4 days.

Variations

■ To make a dressing for fruit salad, thin the mixture with additional orange juice.

■ For a different flavor, replace the orange juice and orange peel with $1/3$ cup apple juice and $1/2$ teaspoon ground cinnamon.

Savory Peanut Whip

If this seems like an unusual use of peanut butter, think of spicy peanut sauce. It takes almost no time to prepare this savory whip, which is delicious on toast with lettuce or arugula, and also makes a great topping for veggie appetizers. Although Savory Peanut Whip is really good when made with red miso, any type of miso will work.

YIELD: About 1 cup	
$1/2$ cup unsweetened, unsalted crunchy peanut butter	1 teaspoon red miso
$1/4$ cup water	1 clove garlic, pressed
$1^1/2$ tablespoons lime juice	$1/3$ cup minced celery
1 teaspoon grated ginger root	1 scallion, chopped

1. Place the peanut butter in a medium-sized bowl, and slowly stir in the water and lime juice, mixing with a fork.

2. Add the ginger, miso, and garlic, mixing well. Then add the celery and scallion, and mix well. Use immediately, or transfer to a covered container and store in the refrigerator for up to 4 days.

Cashew Sandwich Spread

If you juice, there is always the question of what to do with the leftover pulp. Here is a simple spread made with leftover vegetable pulp that is delicious as a sandwich spread, a savory topping for crackers, or a veggie roll filling. If you don't juice, simply substitute grated carrots and minced cucumber and celery for the pulp.

YIELD: About 2 cups

1 cup unsalted raw cashews	1/4 cup coarsely chopped sweet onion or scallions
1/3 cup carrot pulp	
1/3 cup cucumber pulp	2 tablespoons lime juice
1/3 cup celery pulp	1/2 teaspoon fennel seed
	1/4 teaspoon sea salt, or to taste

1. Place the cashews in a medium-sized bowl and add enough water to cover the nuts by 1 inch. Allow them to soak at room temperature for at least 2 hours or up to 8 hours. Drain and rinse the cashews.

2. Place the soaked cashews and all of the remaining ingredients in a food processor or high-powered blender, and blend until the cashews are coarsely ground, using the plunger or scraping the sides of the machine as needed. If using a regular (not high-powered) blender, do this in two or more batches.

3. Transfer the mixture to a bowl and serve immediately, or transfer to a covered container and store in the refrigerator for up to 3 days.

Helpful Tip

This recipe is pretty flexible, so you can use the suggested types of pulp or opt for all carrot and cucumber. Cabbage and bell pepper pulp would work well, too. If you use celery, make sure to pick out the strings. As long as you use around 1 cup of pulp—or, if you prefer, 1 cup of minced vegetables—it will be fine.

Basic Cashew Cream

This recipe transforms buttery cashews into a rich cream that makes a fabulous dip for fresh fruit; is delicious on cereal, fruit, and desserts; and is a wonderful nondairy substitute for cheese, cream, and sour cream. You can even use it to frost cakes. Scott's children absolutely love it and affectionately call it "dipping sauce." The cream keeps for several days, so prepare extra and enjoy it throughout the week.

YIELD: 1¹/₂ cups

1 cup water

1 cup unsalted raw cashews

2 tablespoons Date Paste (see page 45)

1. Place the water, cashews, and Date Paste in a blender, and process on high speed for 2 minutes or until creamy.

2. Use immediately, or transfer to a covered container and store in the refrigerator for up to 7 days.

Variations

■ To make a lower-glycemic version of Basic Cashew Cream, omit the Date Paste and add ¹/₄ teaspoon of pure monk fruit powder.

■ To make *Basic Cashew Cream with Vanilla,* follow the main recipe but add 1 teaspoon of vanilla extract to the blender.

■ To make *Vanilla Monk Fruit Cashew Cream,* follow the main recipe but add 1 teaspoon of vanilla extract and replace the Date Paste with ¹/₄ teaspoon of pure monk fruit powder. This is a good option for people with high blood sugar or diabetes, as monk fruit powder has no effect on blood glucose levels

Curry Baked Kale Chips

Homemade kale chips are crisper and fresher than any you can buy, and offer a good way to turn kale haters into kale lovers. Change the seasoning to suit your tastes—see the Variations at the end of the recipe—and serve these savory chips as a healthy appetizer or snack, or as an accompaniment to a meal of bean soup and salad.

YIELD: 4 servings

12 ounces kale	1 tablespoon coconut aminos
1/3 cup nutritional yeast	1 tablespoon curry powder, or more to taste
1–2 tablespoons lemon juice	Pinch of cayenne pepper (optional)

1. Preheat the oven to 350°F.

2. Wash the kale, strip it from its thick stems (discard the stems), and lightly dry it in a salad spinner. It should retain a bit of moisture but not be dripping wet.

3. Place the prepared kale in a large bowl. Add the nutritional yeast, lemon juice, coconut aminos, curry powder, and, if desired, the cayenne. Mix well, using your hands to coat the leaves as evenly as possible.

4. Spray two 13 by 18-inch baking sheets lightly with nonstick cooking spray. Arrange the kale in an even layer over the baking sheets, keeping the larger pieces near the edges of the pans.

5. Bake for about 8 minutes. Then remove the baking sheets from the oven and carefully turn the leaves over, again arranging them in a single layer and placing the larger pieces towards the edges of the pans.

6. Return the sheets to the oven and bake for another 7 or 8 minutes, or until the leaves are crisp and brittle. Turn the oven off. If any leaves are not done, return them to the oven and allow them to stay there until crisp, checking every 5 minutes. Even though the oven is off, the remaining heat will continue to cook and crisp the kale. Cool before serving, or transfer to a covered container and store for 3 or 4 days.

Variations

■ To make *Spicy Southwestern-Style Kale Chips,* substitute 2 teaspoons of smoked paprika, 1 teaspoon of dried basil, 1 teaspoon of ground cumin, and 1/4 teaspoon or more of ground chipotle for the curry powder.

■ To make *Italian-Style Kale Chips,* substitute 2 teaspoons of Italian seasoning, 3 to 6 cloves of pressed garlic, and freshly ground black pepper to taste for the curry and cayenne. Replace the lemon juice with balsamic vinegar.

Garlic Nut Thins

These crisp savory crackers are good with spreads, soups, or salads.

YIELD: 24 crackers

¹/₂ cup flaxseeds	¹/₂ cup water
¹/₂ cup unsalted raw walnuts	1 tablespoon coconut aminos
¹/₂ cup garbanzo flour	1 tablespoon pressed garlic
Pinch of cayenne pepper (optional)	

1. Preheat the oven to 300°F. Lightly spray a cookie sheet with nonstick cooking spray and sprinkle it generously with flour. Set aside.

2. Place the flaxseeds in a blender and grind them to a powder. Transfer the ground seeds to a small mixing bowl. Place the walnuts in the blender and grind them to a powder. Add the ground nuts to the mixing bowl. Add the garbanzo flour and the cayenne, if using, to the bowl, and stir to mix.

3. Place the water, coconut aminos, and garlic in a small bowl, and stir to mix. Add the liquid mixture to the dry mixture, and stir to make a thick dough.

4. Drop the dough by the teaspoon onto the prepared cookie sheet to make 24 neat mounds. Using a fork dipped in water, flatten each cracker by pressing with the tines of the fork and then sliding the fork off, rather than lifting it from the dough. Do this 3 to 4 times for each cracker to make the dough as thin as possible.

5. Bake for 12 minutes. Carefully turn each cracker over, and bake for 10 to 12 additional minutes, or until the crackers are browned and fairly crisp. Turn the oven off, and allow the crackers to cool in the oven for an hour or two. The crackers should be crisp when completely cool. If they are not, turn the oven to 300°F and bake for a few minutes longer. Cool completely.

6. Serve the crackers immediately, or place in an airtight container and store in the refrigerator for up to a week.

Topped Turnip Slices

Pass these pretty slices around at your next party, and your guests will be amazed to learn that they have been eating turnips! Slightly spicy, these appetizers are both inexpensive and easy to make. For an especially attractive plate, combine watermelon radishes and white turnips.

YIELD: 30 appetizers

4 medium-sized white turnips, watermelon radishes, or both	1 recipe Yeasty Smoked Pecan Topping (see page 84)
1 recipe Artichoke Dip (see page 64)	1/4 cup minced fresh parsley

1. Scrub the turnips or radishes, and trim off the roots and tops. Using a sharp knife, slice them into rounds, making the slices as thin as possible while keeping them even and whole. Each turnip will make about 8 slices, allowing for a few imperfect cuts that you may want to discard or use for something else.

2. Place a dollop of artichoke dip on each slice, sprinkle it with the nut topping, and add a pinch of minced parsley. Serve immediately, or cover and chill for a couple of hours. If they are made too far in advance and not refrigerated, the Topped Turnip Slices will lose their crispness.

Variations

Instead of using the toppings recommended in the main recipe, try the following:

- Cilantro Pesto (see page 62) topped with a cherry tomato half.

- Cashew Sandwich Spread (see page 70) sprinkled with minced parsley and red bell pepper.

- Hempannaise (see page 67) sprinkled with Yeasty Smoked Pecan Topping (see page 84) or one of its variations.

Endive Boats with Savory Peanut Dip

Belgian endives separated into individual leaves are perfect containers for dips and toppings. The filled leaves look elegant when lined up on a tray and have a mild crisp taste.

YIELD: About 30 appetizers

3 Belgian endives	1/4 cup chopped unsalted dry roasted peanuts
1 recipe Savory Peanut Whip (see page 69)	1/4 cup chopped fresh cilantro or scallions

---

1. Cut about 1/4 inch off the bottom stem end of each endive to allow the leaves to separate. Keep cutting off the stem end as needed to separate the leaves as you go. Leaves that are too large or small to make a nice appetizer can be saved and chopped for a salad. Each head should provide about 10 useable leaves.

2. Fill each leaf with a dollop of peanut whip, sprinkle with chopped peanuts, and top with cilantro or scallions. These endive boats can be made a few hours in advance, covered, and stored in the refrigerator.

Variations

Instead of using the fillings recommended in the main recipe, try the following:

■ Guacamole (see page 63) topped with Fresh Salsa (see page 62) and sprinkled with fresh sweet corn, cut off the cob and used either raw or quickly steamed.

■ Green Hummus (see page 65) topped with minced raw red bell pepper or sliced roasted red bell pepper and minced parsley.

■ Hempannaise (see page 67) topped with French Herbed Walnut Topping (see page 85) and minced fresh parsley.

Apple Slice Sweet Bites

Thin slices of fresh fruit topped with either Orange Peanut Butter Whip or Tahini Vanilla Whip make super-yummy treats that are appreciated by both kids and adults. Don't skip the garnish, which adds eye appeal and flavor.

YIELD: About 30 appetizers

3 apples

Juice of 1 lemon

1 recipe Tahini Vanilla Whip (see page 68) or Orange Peanut Butter Whip (see page 68)

Garnishes of your choice, such as thin slices of strawberry or orange, halved blueberries, chopped or halved nuts, etc.

1. Holding the apple with the stem side up, use a sharp knife to make thin vertical slices, stopping at the core. Discard the outside slice from each side. Cut any fruit that remains attached to the core into vertical slices, again discarding the outside cuts.

2. Brush both sides of each slice with lemon juice. Place a dollop of the chosen whip on each slice, and top with the garnish of your choice. These appetizers can be made a few hours in advance, covered, and stored in the refrigerator.

The Life-Changing Power of Positive Words

As you transition to a healthier way of eating, it's important to change the way you think about your ability to succeed. If your self-talk includes phrases such as "I can't," "I always fail," and "It's too difficult," you will sabotage your opportunity for success. Replace your internal monologue with hope-filled words: "I can change," "I enjoy change," "I will succeed," and "I can overcome my challenge." When you start putting a positive spin on your old script, the power of words will increase both your motivation and your success.

5.

Sauces, Condiments, and Toppings

If you have always thought of sauces as cream-, butter-, and cheese-laden indulgences that add flavor at the price of sound nutrition, think again. The sauces, condiments, and toppings in this chapter certainly add great taste, but do so without compromising your health or expanding your waistline. What's more, they're a snap to make even if you're new to whole food plant-based cooking.

The chapter begins with a range of delicious sauces and gravies, including flavorful Easy BBQ Sauce, rich-tasting Porcini Sauce, velvety Walnut Gravy, and more. Try them over a serving of beans, a veggie burger, a dish of grains of pasta, or a bowl of steamed veggies. In fact, just about any meal can benefit from a tasty sauce, and we offer a delicious option for every occasion.

While creamy sauces can contribute a good deal to plant-based cuisine, sometimes a soup, salad, or skillet dish needs a little crunch. If so, try Yeasty Smoked Pecan Topping, which combines toasted nuts with irresistible flavors, including sage and garlic. If you prefer Indian Cuisine, you'll want to make some Taste of India Topping. Or add a classic European touch with French Herbed Walnut Topping.

A spoonful of chutney or relish can quickly turn a ho-hum bowl of grains or veggies into a memorable meal. This chapter offers Creamy Green Chutney, a healthy version of an Indian favorite; and Sweet Pepper and Corn Relish, which packs a punch of piquant flavor along with a burst of vibrant color. Or prepare Oven-Caramelized Onions, a condiment that can add richness to almost any savory dish.

If you're worried that making sauces and condiments will prove too time-consuming while you're putting together healthy meals, you'll be glad to learn that most of our creations can be made up to a week in advance. So whenever you have a little extra time, you can whip up a few sauces or toppings, and then enjoy them in your menus for the coming week.

Pairing the right sauce, condiment, or topping with the right dish is part of the fun of cooking, and is also a great way to change up dishes so that they never become boring. So get ready to elevate your foods to new heights—without a lot of fuss or a bit of guilt.

Easy BBQ Sauce

A tablespoon of this sauce stirred into a serving of beans or spread over a veggie burger, tofu, or tempeh will provide a boost of flavor without all the sodium and sugar found in most commercial sauces. Make it as mild or spicy as you like.

YIELD: About 1¼ cups

6-ounce can tomato paste	1 teaspoon dried basil
¼ cup water	2 teaspoons liquid smoke
2–3 soft pitted Medjool dates	2 cloves garlic, or more to taste
2 tablespoons coconut aminos	½ teaspoon ground chipotle pepper, or more to taste
2 tablespoons balsamic vinegar	

1. Place all of the ingredients in a blender, and blend until smooth.

2. Serve immediately, or store in an airtight container in the refrigerator for up to a week.

Tahini Yeast Sauce

This sauce couldn't be easier to make, because all you do is mix the ingredients together. It is creamy, savory, and tangy with a nice garlicky edge. Although it is made with "health food" ingredients, it is usually well liked by everyone. Use it with vegetable and grain dishes, or try it in the Quinoa, Kale, and Carrot Bowl on page 147.

YIELD: 1¼ cups

½ cup tahini sauce	½ cup nutritional yeast
1 clove garlic, pressed	¾ cup water or liquid left over from cooking vegetables, as needed
2 teaspoons white or yellow miso	

1. Place the tahini, garlic, and miso in a small mixing bowl, and stir until the miso is well blended with the other ingredients. Add the yeast, and mix well.

2. Slowly stir in the water to the desired consistency. Serve immediately, warm or at room temperature, or store in an airtight container in the refrigerator for up to 4 days. If you choose to heat the sauce, warm it gently without boiling to preserve the probiotic properties of the miso.

Walnut Gravy

Made entirely without oil, this velvety gravy adds delicious richness to grain, tempeh, tofu, seitan, and vegetable dishes. If it thickens up too much upon sitting, just whisk in a little water when it is reheated.

YIELD: About 2 cups

$^1/_4$ cup whole grain spelt flour or garbanzo flour

1 cup unsalted raw walnut halves

2 cups water or unsalted vegetable broth

2 tablespoons coconut aminos

$^1/_4$ teaspoon ground white pepper, or to taste

1. Preheat the oven to 350°F.

2. Sprinkle the flour in an even layer about $^1/_8$-inch thick on a baking sheet, and spread the walnuts over and around the flour. Bake for about 10 minutes, or until the flour and nuts begin to brown, being careful not to burn them.

3. Place the browned flour and nuts in a blender with the water or vegetable broth, and blend until smooth.

4. Transfer the mixture to a medium-sized saucepan, and stir in the coconut aminos. While stirring with a whisk, bring the mixture to a simmer. Cook at a simmer for a minute or so, or until the gravy has thickened to your liking. Add pepper to taste and serve immediately, or store in an airtight container in the refrigerator for up to 4 days.

Porcini Sauce

There is nothing in the vegetable kingdom that provides such a rich meaty flavor as porcini mushrooms, and dried mushrooms are even more flavorful than fresh. Actually, it's not the mushrooms but the soaking water that has the most flavor, which makes dried porcinis perfect for a sauce. This ingredient is not inexpensive, so you may want to save it for a special meal. Porcini Sauce is wonderful over grain dishes, pasta, tempeh, tofu, vegetables, and more.

YIELD: About 2 cups

2–3 ounces dried porcini mushrooms	1 tablespoon miso, preferably red miso, but any type will work
2$^{1}/_{2}$ cups water	1 tablespoon minced fresh sage
2 tablespoons arrowroot powder	$^{1}/_{4}$ teaspoon ground white pepper

1. Place the mushrooms in a medium-sized heatproof bowl. Add the water, and stir. Allow to soak for at least 30 minutes or until the mushrooms are rehydrated.

2. Swish the mushrooms around in the soaking water and squeeze them a bit to dislodge any lingering dirt or sand. Remove the mushrooms from the water, reserving the water.

3. Place a dish towel, cotton napkin, cheesecloth, or paper coffee filter in a strainer, and position the strainer over a bowl. Pour the soaking water through the cloth and into the bowl.

4. Transfer most of the liquid to a medium-sized saucepan, reserving about $^{1}/_{4}$ cup.

5. Place the rehydrated mushrooms in a medium-sized bowl. Add water to cover, and swish around to dislodge any grit that may remain in the mushrooms. Remove the mushrooms from the water, discarding the water.

6. Place the rinsed mushrooms in the saucepan with the soaking water, and bring to a boil over medium-high heat. Reduce the heat to low and simmer for about 3 minutes to cook the mushrooms.

7. Add the arrowroot powder to the $^{1}/_{4}$ cup of reserved soaking water, and mix well to dissolve the powder. Stirring constantly, pour the arrowroot mixture into the pan with the simmering mushrooms. The sauce should immediately thicken. Return the sauce to a simmer.

8. Remove the pan from the heat, and stir in the miso, sage, and white pepper. Serve immediately, or store in an airtight container in the refrigerator for up to 4 days. When reheating, warm the sauce gently without boiling to preserve the probiotic properties of the miso. Add more water if the sauce becomes too thick.

Hemp Seed Sauce

Hemp seeds are a good way to add protein to your diet, and in this recipe, they make a creamy sauce that can be spooned over grain or vegetable dishes.

YIELD: About 1$\frac{1}{2}$ cups

1$\frac{1}{2}$ cups water or unseasoned vegetable broth

1 cup raw hemp seeds

2 teaspoons chickpea miso

Ground white pepper to taste

1. Place the water or broth and the hemp seeds in a blender, and blend until very smooth and creamy.

2. Pour the blended mixture into a saucepan and, stirring constantly with a wire whisk, cook over medium-high heat until the mixture comes to a boil and thickens.

3. Remove the saucepan from the heat, and whisk in the miso and white pepper. To preserve the health benefits of the miso, do not boil the sauce after the miso has been added. Serve immediately, or store in an airtight container in the refrigerator for up to 4 days. When reheating, warm the sauce gently without boiling to preserve the probiotic properties of the miso. Add more water if the sauce becomes too thick.

Caramel Sauce

Autumn and the changing color of the leaves reawaken fond memories of crisp apples dipped in caramel. This delicious date-sweetened sauce will be loved by all and can be paired with apple slices for a quick dessert.

YIELD: 1$\frac{1}{4}$ cups

1 cup pitted Medjool dates, room temperature

$\frac{3}{4}$ cup coconut butter

1. Place the dates and coconut butter in a blender, and process on high speed until creamy.

2. Serve immediately, or store in an airtight container in the refrigerator for up to 7 days.

Coconut Cream Cilantro Sauce

*This sauce is delicious served over beans, steamed vegetables, salads,
black bean-and-vegetable burritos, and a host of other dishes. Your
family and friends will ask you to make it again and again.*

YIELD: 2 cups

13.5-ounce can coconut milk

4-ounce can mild green chilies, drained

$\frac{1}{2}$ cup fresh cilantro
(loosely packed)

1. Place all of the ingredients in a blender or food processor, and process until the mixture is well blended and creamy, with only very small pieces of cilantro visible.

2. Serve immediately at room temperature, or store in an airtight container in the refrigerator for up to 7 days.

Red Tomato Sauce

*This is a classic Italian red sauce—smooth and rich. The secret ingredient is San
Marzano tomatoes, which are sweeter and meatier than other tomatoes. Serve the sauce
over whole grain pasta, zucchini noodles, or your favorite grain. Double or triple the
recipe, and freeze some for those busy days when time is short.*

YIELD: 2 cups

28-ounces can whole San Marzano
tomatoes, undrained

1 medium onion, diced

2 cloves garlic, minced

2 fresh basil leaves, minced

1 bay leaf

1 tablespoon Date Paste (See page 45)

$\frac{1}{8}$ teaspoon ground nutmeg

1. Place the tomatoes and their juice in a blender or food processor, and process until completely smooth. Set aside.

2. Preheat a large nonstick saucepan over medium-high heat. Add the diced onion, and dry sauté until the onions are translucent and slightly brown. Add the garlic and continue to cook, stirring continuously, for 2 minutes.

3. Add the puréed tomatoes, basil, bay leaf, Date Paste, and nutmeg to the onion mixture, and stir to combine. Lower the heat to a simmer and cook, stirring often, for 20 minutes.

4. Remove and discard the bay leaf before serving the sauce hot. Store any leftover sauce in an airtight container in the refrigerator for up to 5 days.

Golden Hemp Seed Sauce

Use this golden sauce in place of cheese sauce on vegetables, whole grain pasta, or grain dishes, knowing that you are getting protein, omega-3s, B vitamins, and more—all in a tasty sauce.

YIELD: About 2 cups

1¹⁄₂ cups water or unseasoned vegetable broth	¹⁄₂ red, orange, or yellow bell pepper, coarsely diced
1 cup hemp seeds	¹⁄₃ cup chopped onion
¹⁄₂ cup nutritional yeast	1 tablespoon chickpea miso
	Ground white pepper to taste

1. Place the water or broth in a blender with the hemp seeds, yeast, bell pepper, and onion. Blend until very smooth and creamy.

2. Pour the blended mixture into a small saucepan and, stirring constantly with a wire whisk, cook over medium-high heat until the mixture comes to a boil and thickens.

3. Remove the saucepan from the heat, and whisk in the miso and white pepper. To preserve the health benefits of the miso, do not boil the sauce after the miso has been added. Serve immediately, or store in an airtight container in the refrigerator for up to 4 days. When reheating, warm the sauce gently without boiling to preserve the probiotic properties of the miso. Add more water if the sauce becomes too thick.

Yeasty Smoked Pecan Topping

It's simple to make a crisp yeasty nut topping that can add flavor and texture to salads, soups, vegetables, and grain dishes. The main recipe features smoky pecans, while the Variations guide you in making Taste of India Topping or French Herbed Walnut Topping simply by changing the ingredients. The cooking directions are the same for all three treats, but each variation provides an entirely different flavor, so you might want to make all three at once and give your family several delicious choices.

YIELD: About 1¼ cups

1 cup unsalted raw pecan halves	1 heaping teaspoon dried sage
1 tablespoon cider vinegar	3–4 cloves garlic, pressed
1 tablespoon coconut aminos	¼ cup nutritional yeast
1 tablespoon smoked paprika	

1. Preheat the oven to 350°F.

2. Place the nuts in a medium-sized bowl. Add the cider vinegar, and mix well. Then add all of the remaining ingredients, finishing with the yeast, and mix until the nuts are evenly coated with the mixture.

3. Arrange the coated nuts in a single layer on a baking sheet, and bake on the middle rack of the oven for 14 to 15 minutes, or until the nuts are dry and toasted. If you are not sure if they are done, turn the oven off and allow the mixture to cool outside the oven for about 5 minutes. If the nuts appear wet, return them to the oven (which will still be hot, so don't turn it back on), and bake for a few more minutes, checking frequently to avoid burning.

4. Allow the nuts to cool to room temperature. Then coarsely grind them in a blender or food processor. Use immediately, or store in an airtight container in the refrigerator for up to one month.

Variations

■ To make *Taste of India Topping,* replace the ingredients in the main recipe with 1 cup cashews, 1 tablespoon coconut aminos, 1 tablespoon lime juice, 1 tablespoon curry powder (hot or mild), and ¼ cup nutritional yeast. Mix as directed in Step 2 of the recipe, tossing the nuts first in the liquids and then in the remaining ingredients. Bake and process as directed in Steps 3 and 4.

■ To make *French Herbed Walnut Topping,* replace the ingredients in the main recipe with 1 cup walnut halves, 1 tablespoon coconut aminos, 1 tablespoon wine vinegar, 1 tablespoon Herbes de Provence herb blend, and $1/4$ cup nutritional yeast. Mix as directed in Step 2 of the recipe, tossing the nuts first in the liquids and then in the remaining ingredients. Bake and process as directed in Steps 3 and 4.

Helpful Tip

Fill a Mason jar with one of these toppings and tie with a ribbon to make a hostess gift that that is both healthy and delicious. As a nice touch, attach the recipe to the jar so that the recipient can make the topping again and again.

Spinach Pesto Sauce

One bite of this sauce on your favorite pasta or steamed vegetables will remind you of a summer garden fragrant with herbs. Best of all, this healthy pesto—packed with fresh spinach and basil, but no oil or cheese—can be enjoyed without guilt.

YIELD: $1^3/4$ cups

4 sun-dried tomatoes (no oil)	1 large tomato, cut into 4 pieces
2 cups fresh spinach (lightly packed)	3 cloves garlic, minced
1 cup fresh basil (tightly packed)	$1/4$ cup water
$1/2$ cup pine nuts (pignoli)	

1. Place the sun-dried tomatoes in a small heatproof bowl, and add boiling water to cover. Allow to soak for 1 hour. Then drain the tomatoes, discarding the water.

2. Place the drained tomatoes and all of the remaining ingredients in a blender or food processor, and process on high speed until well blended and creamy.

3. Serve at room temperature over pasta or cooked vegetables, or transfer the mixture to a saucepan and cook over low heat for about 10 minutes, or until warm, before serving. Store any leftover sauce in an airtight container in the refrigerator for up to 7 days.

Omega Cereal Topping

This easy-to-make topping is full of omega 3s. It takes just minutes to prepare and tastes great over porridge, fruit, or even Nice Cream (see Variation on page 178).

YIELD: 2¹/₂ cups

1 cup flaxseeds	1 tablespoon ground cinnamon
1 cup chia seeds	¹/₈–¹/₄ teaspoon pure monk fruit powder
¹/₂ cup unsalted raw walnuts	

---

1. Place the flaxseeds and chia seeds in a blender, and grind to a powder. Add the remaining ingredients to the blender, and process until the walnuts are coarsely ground.

2. Use immediately, or transfer to a jar and store in the refrigerator for up to 3 weeks.

Helpful Tip

If you're using a Vitamix or other high-powered blender, you will be able to make this topping in one batch. If you're using a smaller or less powerful blender, you may have to grind the flax and chia seeds in two batches and grind the walnuts separately. Transfer the ground ingredients to a jar, add the cinnamon and monk fruit powder, and shake the jar to mix.

Oven-Caramelized Onions

Caramelized onions can be used to add flavor and richness to almost any savory dish. When you make them in the oven, they need less stirring and attention than they do when prepared on the stovetop. A well-seasoned cast-iron skillet is perfect for this recipe. If you don't have one, select a heavy pot with an oven-proof lid. If you use sweet onions, you may be amazed by how much sweeter they become when caramelized.

YIELD: About 1¹/₂ cups

6 cups sliced onions (about 2 large)

1. Preheat the oven to 375°F.

2. Lightly spray a well-seasoned cast-iron skillet or another heavy pot with lid with nonstick cooking spray, and place the onions in the skillet. Cover and place in the oven.

3. Bake covered for about 30 minutes. The onions will be sizzling hot. Stir and quickly return to the oven with the lid slightly ajar. Bake for another 20 minutes.

4. Turn the heat up to 425°F. Remove the lid, setting it aside, and stir the onions. Bake uncovered for 15 additional minutes, or until the onions have reduced to about 1½ cups. They will not be as brown as they would if they were cooked in oil, but if desired, you can turn on the broiler for a couple of minutes to brown them a bit more, being careful not to burn them.

5. Use immediately. They will probably not be around too long, but if you have leftovers, you can store them in a covered container in the refrigerator for up to 4 days.

Creamy Green Chutney

Here is a low-salt, medium spicy version of the cilantro mint chutney that is often served in Indian restaurants. But this condiment is delicious on so many foods! Use it to spice up bean, rice, and vegetable dishes, as well as curries.

YIELD: About ¾ cup

1 cup fresh cilantro (lightly packed)	½-inch piece ginger root, peeled and sliced
1 cup fresh mint (lightly packed)	
1 scallion, coarsely chopped	2 tablespoons lime juice
⅓ cup unsalted raw cashews	1 teaspoon chickpea miso
¼ cup water, or more as needed	⅛ teaspoon cayenne pepper, or to taste

1. Place all of the ingredients in a blender, and blend until smooth and creamy. Add slightly more water if you would like a thinner consistency.

2. Serve immediately, or store in an airtight container in the refrigerator for up to 1 week.

Variation

■ Instead of using cayenne pepper, use a chopped jalapeño pepper (1 whole or 1 half pepper), or the fresh chile pepper of your choice.

Sweet Pepper and Corn Relish

Spoon this relish over burgers, rice, scrambled tofu, or beans for zingy sweet-sour flavor and a burst of color. It is prettiest when made with three different colors of bell peppers, but is just as good when prepared with only orange, yellow, or red peppers.

YIELD: About 2 cups

1/2 cup finely diced orange bell pepper	2 tablespoons apple cider vinegar
1/2 cup finely diced yellow bell pepper	1 tablespoon Dijon-style mustard
1/2 cup finely diced red bell pepper	1 teaspoon chickpea miso
1/2 cup sweet frozen corn (no need to defrost)	1 teaspoon dried basil
3 tablespoons minced onion	1/4 teaspoon ground allspice
	1/8 teaspoon ground turmeric

1. Place the bell peppers, corn, and onion in a medium-sized bowl, and stir to mix.

2. Place the vinegar and all of the remaining ingredients in a cup or small bowl, and stir to mix.

3. Add the vinegar mixture to the bell pepper mixture, and stir until the vegetable mixture is evenly coated. Set aside for 30 minutes, allowing the flavors to blend, and stir before serving. Place any leftovers in an airtight container and store in the refrigerator for up to one week.

Spicing Your Way to Health

You may think of spices simply as flavorings, but these ingredients are actually nutritional power-houses. After all, spices come from plants, which are packed with phytonutrients, including antioxidants, anti-inflammatories, and more. That dash of cardamom boosts your body's natural killer cells, which play a major role in fighting tumors and viruses. Cinnamon reduces inflammation and improves blood sugar control. Nutmeg has strong antibacterial properties and also aids digestion. And turmeric, which includes an active ingredient called curcumin, has been shown to alleviate inflammatory disorders and help prevent or treat several types of cancer.

6.

Salads and Dressings

Looking for a delicious dish that's easy to prepare, packed with nutrition, and can serve as an appetizer, a main dish, or a side? You need look no further, because salads are among the most healthful and versatile dishes you'll ever find. And whether you want a simple mixture of greens and veggies or a salad that is a meal in itself, you will not be disappointed by the selections that follow.

The chapter begins with several outstanding dressings that can provide interest to any salad using only wholesome ingredients and, remarkably, no oil. And from Toasted Pumpkin Seed Dressing to Creamy Pine Nut Dressing, every one's a winner.

Green salads and veggie salads are so healthful, appetizing, and easy to prepare that we've included a wide selection. Don't expect to be bored, though, because our recipes feature yummy additions such as caramelized almonds; fresh berries; sweet shredded coconut; crunchy sunflower, pumpkin, and poppy seeds; and chewy raisins. And each of these creations is paired with a dressing that perfectly complements the flavors of the ingredients.

These days, produce aisles and farmers markets offer such a wide assortment of fruits and veggies that there's no excuse to serve the same old salad at every meal. This chapter offers a number of not-so-usual recipes, such as Celery Root-Cucumber Salad; Grapefruit, Jicama, and Fennel Salad; and Sci-Fi Salad, which features kohlrabi. You'll also find some new takes on familiar recipes, such as Southwestern Black Bean Salad, Potato Dill Salad, and Unbeetable Berry Slaw.

As you scan the many offerings in this chapter, don't forget that even a simple mixture of fresh greens can be turned into a satisfying main dish by topping it with a protein-packed Black Bean Burger (see page 123) or Lentil Burger (page 110), or by adding a mound of creamy Green Hummus (page 65), Guacamole (page 63), or White Bean and Roasted Garlic Purée (page 66). Also keep in mind that any fruit or vegetable—whether it is an old favorite or a new discovery—can make a nutritious, flavorful addition to just about any salad. So don't hesitate to exercise your creativity and add the goodness of salads to your meals.

SALAD DRESSINGS

Pear-Licious Dressing

This sweet and creamy dressing celebrates the abundance of a fall harvest and seasonal fruits like Barlett pears. It's great on green salads of any kind, and is especially good on spinach and kale salads.

YIELD: 1¹/₄ cups

1 ripe Bartlett pear, cored and cut into chunks

¹/₄ cup apple juice

¹/₃ cup unsalted raw cashews

1 tablespoon balsamic vinegar

1. Place all of the ingredients in a blender or food processor, and process on high speed until the mixture is smooth and creamy.

2. Serve immediately over salad greens, or store in an airtight container in the refrigerator for up to 7 days.

Berry Dressing

This colorful, sweet dressing makes a great dip for raw vegetables and adds a brilliant dash of color to a green salad. Garnish with some whole berries and you'll have an eye-catching dish that won't last long.

YIELD: 1 cup

6 strawberries

¹/₄ cup raspberries

¹/₄ cup blueberries

1 tablespoon lemon juice

1 teaspoon lemon zest

2 fresh basil leaves

1. Place all of the ingredients in a blender, and purée until the dressing is smooth and creamy.

2. Serve immediately over salad greens, or store in an airtight container in the refrigerator for up to 7 days.

Toasted Pumpkin Seed Dressing

This savory salad dressing blends the subtle sweetness of apples with the bold flavor of toasted pumpkin seeds. Scott's children love it drizzled over a bowl of tossed greens.

YIELD: 1$^1/_2$ cups

$^1/_3$ cup unsalted raw pumpkin seeds

1 cup water

$^1/_2$ cup balsamic vinegar

1 apple slice

1 teaspoon garlic powder

---

1. Preheat the oven to 325°F. Spread the pumpkin seeds in a single layer over a large baking sheet, and bake in the preheated oven for about 4 minutes, or until the seeds begin to brown slightly. (Watch carefully to avoid burning.) Remove the pan from the oven and allow the seeds to cool to room temperature.

2. Place the toasted pumpkin seeds, water, and vinegar in a blender, and process on high speed until the mixture is smooth and creamy. Add the apple slice and garlic, and blend again until smooth and creamy.

3. Serve immediately over salad greens, or store in an airtight container in the refrigerator for up to 14 days.

Gaining Freedom From Processed Foods

Many experts consider processed foods to be the number-one addiction in the United States. The excessive amounts of sugar, fat, and salt in these foods stimulate the release of the neurotransmitter dopamine, which provides you with a sense of pleasure and reward. Over time, as you continue eating processed fare, you have to eat larger amounts to bring about the same rewarding effects. In fact, food products are crafted to create quick, intense emotional hits that leave you wanting more. But when you remove processed foods from your diet and start eating meals of fresh vegetables, fruits, and other plant foods, in just one week, the reward center of your brain begins to normalize. In two weeks, your taste buds begin to change, and you find the flavor of vegetables and fruits more enjoyable. In three months, your reward circuitry returns to normal, and you gain freedom from processed foods.

Tomato Dressing

This totally fat-free dressing livens up salad greens while providing
a healthy dose of B vitamins.

YIELD: 1 cup

1 medium tomato, coarsely chopped (about 1 cup)

2 tablespoons lemon juice

1 tablespoon coconut aminos

1–2 cloves garlic

1 teaspoon dried basil

1/4 cup nutritional yeast, or more as needed

1. Place the tomato, lemon juice, coconut aminos, garlic, and basil in a blender, and purée until the dressing is smooth.

2. Add the nutritional yeast to the blender, and purée again. If the dressing is too thin, add a little more yeast.

3. Serve immediately over salad greens, or store in an airtight container in the refrigerator for up to 4 days.

Ranch Dressing

This creamy multipurpose dressing can be used on salads, sandwiches,
or raw vegetables. We worked to make this one great, so enjoy!

YIELD: 1 1/2 cups

1 cup Basic Cashew Cream (see page 71)

1 tablespoon plus 1 teaspoon white vinegar

1 tablespoon dried or chopped fresh chives

1 teaspoon coconut aminos

1 teaspoon dried parsley

1/2 teaspoon dried dill

1/2 teaspoon garlic powder

1/2 teaspoon onion powder

1/8 teaspoon ground black pepper

1. Place all of the ingredients in a medium-size bowl, and whisk until well-blended.

2. Serve immediately on your favorite salad, use as a veggie dipping sauce, or store in an airtight container in the refrigerator for up to 7 days.

Creamy Pine Nut Dressing

This dressing is so delicious that you won't believe it is actually good for you! Try it on a green salad or on steamed vegetables such as broccoli, cauliflower, or asparagus. It also makes a great dipping sauce for crudités.

YIELD: About 1 cup

$\frac{1}{2}$ cup pine nuts (pignoli)	1 tablespoon Dijon-style mustard
$\frac{1}{2}$ cup water	1 clove garlic
2 tablespoons lemon juice	1 teaspoon chickpea miso

1. Place all of the ingredients in a blender, and purée until the dressing is very smooth and creamy.

2. Serve immediately over salad greens or veggies, or store in an airtight container in the refrigerator for up to 7 days.

Understanding Calorie Density

Calorie density is a measure of how many calories are found in a given weight of food, usually a pound. Some foods—vegetables, fruits, grains, and legumes, for instance—are low in calorie density. Foods like bread, muffins, chocolates, and oils, on the other hand, are high in calorie density. Not surprisingly, research has found that it's best to build your diet on foods that have relatively few calories per pound. In fact, the calorie-per-pound ratio in plant foods is perfect for maintaining a healthy weight without counting calories. Also, plant foods tend to be highest in nutrient density, meaning that they provide more nutrients per calorie than you're likely to find in calorie-dense choices. So when you fill up on plant-based foods, you're getting the nutrients you need without the excess calories you're trying to avoid.

SALADS

Mixed Greens with Caramelized Almonds and Raspberries

The delicate flavor of the Pear-Licious Dressing combines with greens to create this mildly sweet salad. Sunflower seeds and caramelized almonds add a burst of flavor and crunch to each bite. If you like bitter-sweet combinations, be sure to include some arugula or radicchio in your salad mixture.

YIELD: 4 servings

4 cups lightly packed leafy greens

1/2 cup raspberries

1/4 cup unsalted raw sunflower seeds

1/4 cup Pear-Licious Dressing, or to taste (see page 90)

1 Bartlett pear, cored and thinly sliced

Caramelized Almonds

1/4 cup unsalted raw almonds

1 tablespoon pure monk fruit powder

1. To make the caramelized almonds, heat a small dry skillet on low heat for 3 to 5 minutes. When the pan is warm, add the almonds and monk fruit powder, and stir frequently for 5 to 10 minutes, or until the almonds are light brown in color. Remove the almonds from the skillet and set aside to cool.

2. To assemble the salad, place the leafy greens in a large bowl and top with the raspberries, sunflower seeds, and reserved almonds. Lightly drizzle the pear dressing over the top of the salad as evenly as possible. Garnish the top with thin slices of pear, and serve immediately.

Fresh Ginger and Bok Choy Salad

Fresh ginger adds zest and vibrancy to a green salad inspired by Asian cuisine. This is a wonderful dish to bring to social events or serve to special guests.

YIELD: 4 to 6 servings

2 baby bok choy, chopped (about 4 cups)

2 tablespoons raisins

1 tablespoon shredded unsweetened coconut

1 tablespoon sesame seeds

Ginger Dressing

1 tablespoon minced fresh garlic

1½ teaspoons grated fresh ginger root

2 large pitted dates, chopped

Juice of 1 lemon

2 teaspoons coconut aminos

---

1. To make the dressing, place all of the dressing ingredients in a blender, and process on high speed until the mixture is smooth and creamy. Set aside.

2. To assemble the salad, place the bok choy in a salad bowl, add the prepared dressing, and toss until the greens are well coated. Sprinkle the raisins, coconut, and sesame seeds over the top, and serve immediately.

Why Is It So Important to Eat a Variety of Whole Plant Foods?

It is the combination of minerals, vitamins, fiber, and phytochemicals (active chemicals found in plants) that exerts positive effects on the body. In other words, the whole is greater than the sum of its parts, and no one nutrient can do the job of keeping you healthy. That's why it's vital to eat as many fruits, veggies, and grains as possible in whole form, so that you get all the nutrients each plant has to offer, and to include many different plant foods in your menus. Each meal should be like a nutritional symphony whose components work together to nourish, energize, protect, and heal your body.

Summer Italian Vegetable Feast

Scott's wife, Kristen, grew up in a traditional Italian family that had a passion for great-tasting food. This salad is a healthy version of an old family favorite that harkens back to the days when family and food were celebrated around the dinner table.

YIELD: 4 to 6 servings

2 medium tomatoes, halved and thinly sliced

1 medium red onion, thinly sliced

1 cucumber, thinly sliced

1½ cups thinly sliced button mushrooms

1 cup string beans, lightly steamed

1 red bell pepper, sliced

15 fresh basil leaves, chopped

Balsamic Dressing

3 tablespoons balsamic vinegar

2 tablespoons sesame seeds

1 teaspoon dried thyme

1. To make the dressing, place the dressing ingredients in a small bowl, and whisk until well mixed. Set aside.

2. To assemble the salad, place all of the ingredients in a large bowl, and toss to mix. Pour the dressing evenly over the vegetables, and toss until well coated. Serve immediately.

Four Ways That Plants Satisfy Your Hunger

You know that a whole food plant-based diet provides an abundance of nutrients, but are you aware that it also satisfies your hunger in unique ways? Here's how:

■ A plant-based diet calms the cravings that result from a standard western diet's overload of sugar, fat, and salt. Removing processed food and adding more plants heals your brain's reward system and restores normal satisfaction and pleasure to your meals.

■ High-volume dishes like a large salad or a bowl of steamed vegetables fill your stomach and activate stretch receptors in the stomach wall, telling your brain to turn off hunger signals.

■ Plant foods rich in micronutrients like phytochemicals and minerals shut down hunger signals and reduce levels of hormones like insulin and leptin, helping to regulate food intake.

■ The fiber found in plant foods like chickpeas feeds the bacteria in your gut, collectively known as the microbiome. After feasting on fiber, beneficial strains of gut bacteria secrete by-products that signal fullness and meal satisfaction to the brain.

Tropical Quinoa Salad

Scott's children love mangos and just about anything that contains mangos,
including this delicious tropical salad. Quinoa, a complete protein,
lends a delightfully chewy texture to the dish.

YIELD: 4 to 6 servings

1 cup uncooked quinoa

2 cups water

1/2 red onion, diced

1/2 cup chopped Portobello mushrooms

1 clove garlic, minced

1 1/2 cups shredded kale

4 ripe mangos, peeled and chopped,
or 2 cups frozen mango, warmed

1/2 cup raisins

1/4 cup finely chopped fresh cilantro

Tahini Dressing

1/2 cup water

2 tablespoons tahini sauce

1 clove garlic, minced

1/8 teaspoon pink Himalayan sea salt

1. Rinse the quinoa and place it in a 2-quart pot with the water. Bring to a boil over high heat. Reduce the heat to low, cover, and cook at a simmer for 15 to 20 minutes, or until the quinoa is tender and the water has been absorbed. Allow to cool to room temperature. (The quinoa may be prepared the day before and stored in the refrigerator until you're ready to prepare the salad. Allow it to reach room temperature before using.)

2. To make the dressing, place all of the dressing ingredients in a small bowl and whisk until well mixed. Set aside.

3. Heat a medium-size nonstick skillet over medium-high heat. Add the onions and dry-sauté, stirring continuously, until they become translucent and slightly brown.

4. Turn the heat under the skillet down to medium-low, and add the mushrooms and garlic. Cook, stirring frequently, for 3 minutes. Add the kale and cook, stirring occasionally, for another 3 minutes. Remove the vegetables from the heat and allow them to cool to room temperature.

5. To assemble the salad, place the quinoa in a large salad bowl. Add the mushroom mixture, mangos, raisins, and cilantro, and stir gently until the ingredients are well blended. Drizzle the Tahini Dressing evenly over the salad, and serve immediately.

Sweet Pineapple Salad

Simple, sweet, and satisfying is how we describe this salad to friends and family.
The pineapple juice you collect while cutting the fruit is the dressing, and it combines
perfectly with the other ingredients to create a delicious whole food salad.

YIELD: 4 to 6 servings

2 cups bite-size pieces fresh pineapple (reserve any pineapple juice that forms as you cut the fruit)

4 cups tightly packed whole leaf spinach

1/2 cup raisins

1/4 cup shredded unsweetened coconut

2 tablespoons poppy seeds

1 tablespoon unsalted raw sunflower seeds

1 tablespoon unsalted raw pumpkin seeds

1. Place all of the ingredients except for the reserved pineapple juice in a large bowl, and toss to mix.

2. Add the reserved juice, and toss again. Serve immediately or chill until ready to serve.

Unbeetable Berry Slaw

The vivid colors of this salad hint at the delightful mixture of sweet and bold flavors.
A perfect addition to the holiday table, this fruit-and-vegetable slaw is
equally at home on an everyday lunch or dinner table.

YIELD: 4 to 6 servings

1 1/2 cups shredded purple cabbage

1 cup shredded beets

1 cup shredded carrots

3/4 cup blueberries

3/4 cup raspberries

1/4 cup chopped unsalted raw walnuts

Juice of 2 oranges

1. Place all of the ingredients except for the orange juice in a large bowl, and toss to mix.

2. Pour the orange juice over the slaw, and toss again until well mixed. Serve immediately or chill until ready to serve.

Southwestern Black Bean Sala

This salad is a huge hit at every party, witnessed by the empty bowl at the end of the event and numerous requests for the recipe. Colorful and delicious, it is also so nutritious that it can serve as an entire meal.

YIELD: 4 to 6 servings

1 cup cooked or canned black beans, rinsed and drained

1 cup corn kernels, fresh or frozen (thawed)

1 cup peas, fresh or frozen (thawed)

1 cup chopped orange or red bell pepper

1 cup sliced plum tomatoes

1 avocado, diced

$\frac{1}{2}$ red onion, finely chopped

$\frac{1}{2}$ cup chopped fresh cilantro

Lime-Chili Dressing

Juice of 2 limes

2 cloves garlic, minced

$\frac{1}{2}$ teaspoon pink Himalayan sea salt

$\frac{1}{4}$ teaspoon chili powder

1. To make the dressing, place all of the dressing ingredients in a small bowl, and whisk until well mixed. Set aside.

2. To assemble the salad, place all of the salad ingredients in a large bowl, and stir to mix well. Add the dressing, and mix until the ingredients are well coated. Serve immediately or chill until ready to serve.

The Immune-Boosting Benefit of Beans

People who follow a plant-based diet know that beans are delicious, filling, and an inexpensive source of plant protein. What they might not know is that beans also boost the immune system. These super-versatile foods come packaged with their own antioxidants—substances that defend the body's cells from damage. They are also high in fiber, which feeds the good gut bacteria that protect the body from disease-causing microbes.

Every-Day Salad

Every successful dietary change is supported by a core group of easy-to-make recipes that become a staple in your home. This salad can be prepared quickly and—as long as you don't add the dressing until serving time—will keep well in the refrigerator for up to two days.

YIELD: 4 to 6 servings

4 cups chopped Romaine lettuce	$1/2$ cup halved grape tomatoes
2 carrots, chopped	$1/2$ cup bean or broccoli sprouts
1 red bell pepper, thinly sliced	$1/4$ cup Ranch Dressing, or to taste (see page 92)
1 medium cucumber, thinly sliced	

1. Place all of the ingredients except for the Ranch Dressing in a large bowl, and toss to mix.

2. Pour the Ranch Dressing over the salad, and toss again until the ingredients are well coated. Serve immediately.

Yummy Green Salad

Swiss chard is packed with nutrition and has a milder, gentler taste than kale. This salad is a family affair, as the Swiss chard, spinach, and beets are all related. The blend of sweet and savory flavors is not to be missed.

YIELD: 4 to 6 servings

	Dressing
2 cups lightly packed chopped Swiss chard	10 pitted dates, chopped
2 cups lightly packed whole leaf spinach	2 cups chopped fresh parsley
1 cup shredded raw beets	2 tablespoons water
$1/4$ cup unsalted raw sunflower seeds	2 tablespoons nutritional yeast
$1/4$ cup raisins	1 tablespoon tahini sauce
	1–2 cloves garlic

1. To make the dressing, combine all of the dressing ingredients in a blender, and process on high speed until the mixture is smooth and creamy, adding more water if a thinner consistency is desired. Set aside.

2. To assemble the salad, place the Swiss chard, spinach, and beets in a large bowl, and toss gently to mix. Sprinkle the sunflower seeds and raisins over the top, and drizzle evenly with the dressing. Serve immediately.

Red, White, and Blue —and Greens!

Celebrate any time of the year with this distinctive salad that tastes as good as it looks. The flavorful berry dressing blends with colorful ingredients to create a dish that is both sweet and tangy with a satisfying crunch.

YIELD: 4 to 6 servings

4 cups lightly packed mixed spring greens	**Honey-Cinnamon Pecans**
1/4 cup Berry Dressing, or to taste (see page 90)	2 teaspoons honey
1/2 cup chopped raw cauliflower	1/4 teaspoon ground cinnamon
1/2 cup sliced strawberries	1/4 cup chopped pecans
1/4 cup blueberries	

1. Preheat the oven to 350°F. Coat a small baking sheet with nonstick cooking spray.

2. To make the pecans, place the honey and cinnamon in a small saucepan, and stir over low heat until the honey thins. Add the pecans and stir until the nuts are well coated. Transfer the nuts to the prepared baking sheet, arranging them in a single layer, and bake for 10 minutes, or until golden brown. (Watch carefully to avoid burning.) Remove the pecans from the oven and allow to cool.

3. To assemble the salad, place the greens in a large bowl, and add the dressing. Toss to coat the greens. Add the cauliflower, strawberries, blueberries, and reserved pecans, and toss lightly before serving.

Celery Root-Cucumber Salad

Did you ever wonder what to do with celery root? Also known as celeriac, this is not the prettiest vegetable at the market, but it has a clean celery flavor and a carrot-like texture. In France, it is often grated and served raw in a salads or crudité platters. This easy-to-make, fresh-tasting salad is a nice change from the usual.

YIELD: 4 servings

1 cup grated peeled celery root (about 1 small)

1 cup grated cucumber (about 1 medium)

1 cup diced avocado (about 1 small)

1/4 cup chopped scallions

2 tablespoons dulse flakes

2 tablespoons lemon juice

1. Place all of the ingredients in a salad bowl, and toss to combine.
2. Serve immediately, or refrigerate for up to 2 days before serving.

Helpful Tip

If you have leftover celery root, grate it for use in another salad, or dice it and add to a soup or stew.

Grapefruit, Jicama, and Fennel Salad

This salad is so flavorful and refreshing that it does not need oil or salt to be appealing. Use a good hand grater, a mandolin, or a food processor to make the shaved fennel and grated jicama. Serving this salad on a bed of mature arugula leaves gives it a spicy edge and makes it pretty. Baby arugula is nice, too, but not as spicy.

YIELD: 4 to 5 servings

1 grapefruit, sliced, sectioned, and seeded (about 1 1/2 cups)

1 cup shaved fennel bulb

1 cup grated jicama

1/2 cup unsalted raw pecan halves

1/4 cup chopped scallions, both green and white parts

2 tablespoons balsamic vinegar

2 cups arugula

Fennel tops for garnish

1. Combine the grapefruit, fennel, jicama, pecans, scallions, and vinegar. Mix well, and set aside.

2. Divide the arugula among 4 or 5 salad plates, spreading the arugula into a bed on each plate. Top with the vegetable mixture, garnish with the fennel tops, and serve immediately. If you would like to make this salad in advance, leave out the arugula—which would be wilted by the vinegar—and add it just before serving. Without the arugula, the salad will keep in a covered container in the refrigerator for 2 to 3 days.

Curly Endive Salad with Avocado and Tomato

Curly endive, also called frisée, is a somewhat coarse and bitter green. But when it's finely chopped, as it is in this dish, it makes a wonderful salad—which is great, because this low-calorie, high-fiber vegetable is so good for you! When you chop the endive, imagine that you are chopping parsley, and it will be perfect.

YIELD: 3 to 6 servings

3 cups finely chopped curly endive	2 tablespoons key lime juice or regular lime or lemon juice
2 cups diced avocado (about 2 small)	
1 cup halved or quartered cherry or grape tomatoes	1 teaspoon ground cumin
	1 teaspoon dried basil
2 tablespoons minced sweet onion	1 clove garlic, pressed
	1–2 tablespoons coconut aminos

1. Place all of the ingredients in a salad bowl, and toss to combine.

2. Serve immediately or, if you would like to make this salad in advance, leave out the coconut aminos, and add them just before serving. Without the aminos, the salad will keep in a covered container in the refrigerator for at least 2 days.

Sci-Fi Salad

A kohlrabi looks like a vegetable from outer space, with its leaves growing from long stems and a large bulb on the bottom. But don't let its unusual appearance put you off. The leaves can be cooked like collard greens, and the bulb is mild and delicious diced or grated in salads. Kids seem to like kohlrabi raw, but it can also be cooked in a soup or stew.

YIELD: 6 servings

1 medium kohlrabi bulb, peeled and diced (2 cups)

1 medium apple, diced (peel if not organic)

1 medium orange, sliced, sectioned, and seeded

1/2 cup unsalted raw walnut halves

3–4 tablespoons lemon juice, or to taste

2 tablespoons minced fresh parsley

1 tablespoon grated orange zest

1 teaspoon dried tarragon

Ground black pepper, to taste

1. Place all of the ingredients in a medium-sized bowl, and toss to combine.

2. Cover and chill for at least 30 minutes or up to 2 days. Mix once more before serving.

Potato Dill Salad

Fresh dill weed and cucumber make this hearty salad taste light and fresh. It's a good dish for a picnic.

YIELD: 4 to 6 servings

1 1/2 pounds red potatoes (peel if not organic), cut into 1/2-inch to 3/4-inch dice (4 1/2 cups diced)

1 cup frozen peas

1 cup finely diced red or yellow bell pepper (about 1 medium)

1 cup diced cucumber (about 1 medium)

1/3 cup chopped scallions

1/3 cup chopped fresh dill

2 tablespoons capers, drained

1 recipe Hempannaise (see page 67)

1. Place the potatoes in a large pot, and add about 2 inches of cold water. (It's not necessary to entirely cover the potatoes with water.) Cover the pot and bring to a boil over high heat. Then lower the heat to a simmer and cook for 15 minutes, or just until tender when pierced with a fork. Drain well, reserving the cooking water for another purpose, such as a soup or sauce.

2. Transfer the potatoes to a large bowl. Add the peas to the potatoes while they are still hot. Toss to mix; then allow to cool for at least 5 minutes.

3. Add all of the remaining ingredients to the potato mixture, and toss to mix well. Serve immediately on a bed of salad greens, or chill for up to 3 days before serving.

Chopped Herb Garden Salad

The crisp sweetness of Belgian endive contrasts with the bitterness of radicchio and an unexpected mixture of flavorful herbs, making this salad wonderfully fresh and appealing, not to mention pretty. Use this dish to dress up a special meal or, if you have your own herb garden, enjoy it at any meal!

YIELD: 4 servings

2 cups chopped Belgian endive (about 3 medium)	1/4 cup lightly packed chopped fresh dill
2 cups chopped radicchio (about 1/2 medium)	1/4 cup chopped scallions
1/4 cup lightly packed fresh basil leaves, halved or quartered if large	6–8 nasturtium flowers, separated into petals (optional)
1/4 cup lightly packed fresh mint leaves, halved or quartered if large	1/2 cup chopped unsalted raw walnuts
	2 tablespoons balsamic vinegar
	1 tablespoon coconut aminos

1. Place the endive, radicchio, basil, mint, dill, and scallions in a salad bowl, and toss lightly to mix.

2. Scatter the flower petals and walnuts over the top of the salad. Drizzle with the vinegar and coconut aminos, toss again, and serve. If you would like to make this salad in advance, leave out the vinegar and aminos, and add them just before serving. Without these ingredients, the salad will keep covered in the refrigerator for 2 to 3 days.

FROM PRESCRIPTIONS TO RECIPES

I knew I could not recommend a diet book as the solution for my patients, so I turned my attention back to academic research as I searched for an answer. Over the course of two years, I reviewed thousands of studies and found one common thread. The body of research consistently showed that the higher the intake of plant-based food, such as vegetables, fruits, beans, etc., the healthier the body, and the more disease-resistant the body remains over time. . . . I began to use my prescription pad at my medical practice to write recipes for smoothies, lunches, and dinners. I started to see amazing results in some of my patients, including the reversal of high blood pressure and type 2 diabetes, as well as the discontinuation of many medications. For the first time, many of my patients reported the resolution of pain and significant long-term weight loss without feelings of deprivation or sacrifice. One patient even lost over one hundred pounds without exercising and reported that she no longer felt hungry all the time. She had literally eaten her way to a healthy weight. . . .

The one-week program we run is a unique opportunity for people to step back from their busy schedules, bad habits, tempting food environments, and the stressors and pressures of life and recapture perspective, vision, inspiration, and motivation. Ultimately, it teaches attendees how good it feels to take care of their bodies through dietary and lifestyle changes. It is a comprehensive health education program that embraces the most up-to-date science of nutrition, achievable kinds of exercise (or, as we like to say, movement), and culinary education, encouragement, and coaching.

Food is the centerpiece of the retreat, so we work closely with the chef and kitchen staff of the hotel at which the retreat is held. Under our guidance, they prepare delicious, healthy meals for the program's participants every day. Each dish is meant to please the palate and fulfill the needs of the body. It is always a fun and uniquely transformational week, as evidenced by the incredible stories of people who altered the trajectory of their lives by attending the program.

So many of those who have taken part in this seven-day retreat have attained healthy lives and found freedom. They have found freedom from fatigue, pain, sleep disruption, constipation, memory impairment, and decreased mobility. They have found freedom from the emotional pain associated with disease, including depression, anxiety, irritability, fear, and hopelessness. They have found freedom from the relationship problems associated with dealing with disease. They have found freedom from the occupational disruption caused by disease. They have found freedom from the spiritual distraction of disease. Every year, we at the immersion program hear from people whose lives have been beautifully transformed.

Excerpt from *The Change* By Milan Ross and Scott Stoll. Reprinted with permission of Square One Publishers. Copyright © 2016 by Milan Ross and Scott Stoll.

7.

Sandwiches, Wraps, and Burgers

If you're like most people, you love sandwiches. But if you've just begun to follow a whole food plant-based diet, you may worry that your sandwich days are over. Fortunately, this couldn't be further from the truth. There are literally *dozens* of healthful sandwich options, ranging from hearty burgers that would satisfy the most devoted meat lover to sandwiches that are suitable for an elegant ladies luncheon. This chapter presents some of our favorites.

For burger lovers everywhere, our sandwich collection features a wide assortment of these treats. For those who like the rich flavor of a grilled beef burger, Full-Flavor Smokehouse Burgers are a great choice. Barbecue sauce, meaty tasting mushrooms, and a few minutes on the grill make these burgers wonderfully smoky and satisfying. Or try spicy Chili Burgers, smoky Lentil Burgers, or fruit-sweetened Aloha Burgers. Add the toppings of your choice, and enjoy.

Soy products like tempeh and tofu and naturals for vegan sandwiches, and in the following pages, you'll find a number of recipes that use these versatile high-protein ingredients in creative ways. Try Dulse, Lettuce, Tomato, and Tempeh Sandwiches, which are reminiscent of a BLT; flavorful Open-Faced BBQ Tofu Sandwiches; or Ladies Luncheon Sandwiches, a healthy version of that fifties favorite Chicken à la King. If you love hummus, you'll want to make a batch of Tried and True Hummus Veggie Sandwiches, which pair wholesome homemade hummus with creamy avocado and other veggies. Or indulge your love of sweet and spicy barbecue sauce by preparing Barbecue-Style Cauliflower in a Pita Pocket.

Like all the recipes in this book, those that follow are sure to inspire you to concoct dishes of your own. When searching the fridge for sandwich ideas, keep in mind that just about any veggie or bean mixture can be tucked into a pita pocket or rolled into a wrap. And don't forget about luscious spreads like Green Hummus (see page 65), Guacamole (page 63), and Cashew Sandwich Spread (page 70), any of which can be used to make a quick and flavorful sandwich. Isn't it good to know that your sandwich days are really just beginning?

Chili Burgers

Red beans and chili spices create a delicious combination. Place these burgers on whole grain buns or English muffins, and add tomato, avocado, and lettuce for a sandwich that everyone will love. For an added burst of flavor and color, try a tablespoon or two of Sweet Pepper and Corn Relish (see page 88) or Easy BBQ Sauce (see page 78).

YIELD: 5 burgers

4 whole grain hamburger buns or English muffins, split and toasted

5 thin slices tomato

2 avocados, peeled and sliced

Lettuce

Burger Mixture

3 cups cooked or canned red kidney beans, rinsed and drained

8 sundried tomato halves (no oil)

$1/2$ cup lightly toasted unsalted pumpkin seeds

$1/4$ cup roasted flaxseed

$1/4$ cup minced celery

$1/4$ cup minced onion

$1 1/2$ tablespoons chopped fresh cilantro

1 tablespoon balsamic vinegar

2 teaspoons ground cumin

1 teaspoon dried basil

1 teaspoon smoked paprika

$1/4$ teaspoon ground chipotle pepper, or more to taste

1. To prepare the burger mixture, place the beans in a large mixing bowl, and mash with a potato masher just until they hold together. The mixture doesn't have to be smooth.

2. Place the dried tomato halves and pumpkin seeds in a blender and coarsely grind. Transfer the ground mixture to the bowl with the beans.

3. Place the flaxseeds in the blender, and grind to a powder. Add the ground flaxseed to the mixing bowl along with all of the remaining burger ingredients, and stir to combine.

4. Scoop up $1/2$ to $3/4$ cup of the mixture, and shape it into a burger that is about 4 inches in diameter and $1/2$ inch thick. Repeat with the remaining mixture to make 5 burgers.

5. Spray a large nonstick skillet with nonstick cooking spray. Arrange the burgers in the skillet and cook over medium heat for about 4 minutes, or until the bottom of each burger is brown. Turn the burgers over, and cook until the second side is brown.

6. For each burger, place a cooked patty on the bottom of a bun or English muffin, and add a slice of tomato, a couple of slices of avocado, and a leaf of lettuce. Place the top of the bun or muffin on the sandwich, and serve immediately.

Helpful Tip

■ If desired, form the burgers up to a day in advance and refrigerate them, separated by pieces of waxed paper, until you're ready to cook and serve them.

Variation

■ If you prefer to skip the bun, serve the burgers over quinoa or rice and accompany with a vegetable, or use the burgers to top a green salad.

Open-Faced BBQ Tofu Sandwiches

*Whenever you make Easy BBQ Sauce and Oven-Caramelized Onions,
use the leftovers to prepare this delicious sandwich.*

YIELD: 4 sandwiches	
Four $1/4$- to $1/2$-inch-thick bread-sized slices extra-firm tofu	$2/3$ cup Oven-Caramelized Onions (see page 86)
2 heaping tablespoons Easy BBQ Sauce (see page 78)	4 slices whole grain bread, toasted
	4 large lettuce leaves

1. Lightly spray a large nonstick skillet with nonstick cooking spray. Arrange the tofu slices in the skillet and cook over medium heat for 3 to 5 minutes on each side, or until the tofu is golden brown.

2. While the tofu is browning on the second side, spread the Easy BBQ Sauce over the tops of the tofu slices. Heat up the caramelized onions in the same skillet by placing them next to the sauce-topped tofu as it browns.

3. Arrange the 4 slices of toasted bread on a flat surface. Top the bread with first the lettuce, then the tofu, and then the onions. Serve immediately.

Lentil Burgers

These smoky tasting burgers can be enjoyed at any time of the year because they're prepared in the oven. If your house is hectic during the week, make these tasty burgers in advance, freeze them, and reheat for a quick meal when time is limited.

YIELD: 6 to 8 burgers

3–4 whole grain pita pockets cut in half, or 6–8 whole grain hamburger buns

6–8 tomato slices

6–8 leaves of lettuce

$1/4$ red onion, thinly sliced

Ketchup to taste (optional)

Mustard to taste (optional)

Burger Mixture

3 cups uncooked green lentils, picked over and rinsed

1 capful apple cider vinegar

6 cups water

$1/4$ cup freshly ground flaxseed meal

$3/4$ cup water

6 sun-dried tomatoes (no oil)

1 cup millet flour

$1/2$ cup garbanzo flour

1 cup finely chopped green cabbage

3 cloves garlic, minced

2 tablespoons onion powder

1 teaspoon smoked paprika

1 teaspoon celery seeds

1. To prepare the burger mixture, place the lentils in a large pot, cover with cold water, and add a capful of apple cider vinegar. Cover and allow to soak in the refrigerator overnight. (Note that you can skip overnight soaking when making lentils, but this step can help avoid digestive issues such as gas.)

2. The next day, transfer the soaked lentils to a colander and rinse with cold water.

3. Place the lentils in a large saucepan and add the 6 cups of water. Bring to a rapid boil. Then reduce the heat to maintain a gentle simmer, cover, and cook for 20 to 30 minutes, or until the lentils are tender but not mushy, adding water if needed to cover the lentils.

4. While the lentils are cooking, combine the ground flaxseed and $3/4$ cup water in a small mixing bowl, and stir together with a wire whip or fork until the mixture is thick and gelatinous, like a beaten egg. Set aside.

5. Place the sun-dried tomatoes in a small heatproof bowl, and add just enough boiling water to cover. Allow to soak for 15 minutes. Then transfer the tomatoes and soaking water to a blender or food processor, and blend until smooth. Add more water, if needed, to create a thick tomato sauce-like consistency.

6. Preheat the oven to 350°F. Spray a large baking sheet with nonstick cooking spray, and set aside.

7. Drain the cooked lentils and place in a large mixing bowl. Add the flaxseed mixture, sun-dried tomato purée, and all of the remaining burger mixture ingredients (millet flour through celery seeds). Wearing food-safe gloves to prevent the mixture from sticking to your hands, mix until well blended.

8. Scoop up ³/₄ cup of the lentil mixture, roll it into a ball, and place it on the prepared baking sheet. Press with your hand to form a flat patty. Repeat with the remaining mixture until you have formed 6 to 8 patties.

9. Bake in the preheated oven for 15 minutes. Flip the burgers, and allow to cook for an additional 10 to 15 minutes, or until the patties are light brown on both sides and firm to the touch. Remove the pan from the oven and allow the patties to sit for 10 minutes.

10. For each burger, place a cooked patty in a pita half or on the bottom of a burger bun. Add a slice of tomato, a leaf of lettuce, some onion, and, if desired, ketchup or mustard to taste. If using a bun, place the bun top on the sandwich and serve.

Variation

■ For a lighter meal, place a lentil patty over your favorite green salad, top with your favorite oil-free dressing, and serve.

Why Don't We Cook Our Food in Oil?

Did you know that 1 tablespoon of oil contains 120 calories, and the average person today consumes 5 to 6 tablespoons of oil per day? That means that most people take in about 30 percent of their calories as oil, a refined food that contains very few micronutrients and does little to improve health. Our advice is to ditch the oil and spend that 30 percent of your calories on foods that will improve your well-being, including vegetables, fruits, grains, legumes, nuts, and seeds. (See page 24 to learn how to cook food without oil.)

Aloha Burgers

As you bite into this delicious burger, you will feel transported to an island with swaying palm trees and luscious fruit. The mango salsa adds a burst of tropical flavor to top off the subtler coconut and pineapple in the burger. This burger is perfect for a warm summer meal with friends and family.

YIELD: 6 burgers

6 whole grain hamburger buns

1/2 cup bean sprouts

Mango Salsa

1 cup cubed mango, fresh or frozen (thawed)

1/2 cup finely chopped fresh cilantro

1/4 cup minced onion

4 cherry tomatoes

1 1/2 teaspoons minced garlic

1 1/2 teaspoons lime juice

1 teaspoon minced ginger root

1/4 teaspoon chili powder

Burger Mixture

1 medium sweet potato, baked

1 1/2 cups uncooked old-fashioned rolled oats

1 cup unsalted raw walnuts

1/2 cup shredded unsweetened coconut

2 carrots, orange or purple, each cut into 2 to 3 pieces

1 medium yellow onion, diced

2 large cloves garlic, minced

2 tablespoons unsalted raw sunflower seeds

2 tablespoons chopped dried pineapple

1/4 teaspoon sea salt

1. Preheat the oven to 350°F. Spray a large baking sheet with nonstick cooking spray, and set aside.

2. To prepare the burger mixture, peel the potato, and place the flesh in a food processor. Add all of the remaining burger ingredients (oats through salt), and pulse until the mixture is finely chopped and has the consistency of a coarse cookie dough.

3. Scoop up 1/2 cup of the sweet potato mixture, roll it into a ball, and place it on the prepared baking sheet. Press it with your hand to form a flat patty. Repeat with the remaining mixture until you have formed 6 patties.

4. Bake in the preheated oven for 15 minutes. Flip the burgers, and allow to cook for an additional 10 to 15 minutes, or until the patties are light brown on both sides and firm to the touch.

5. While the patties are baking, place all of the salsa ingredients in a food processor, and pulse until the ingredients are coarsely chopped. Transfer the salsa to a bowl.

6. For each burger, place a cooked patty on the bottom of a bun, and add 1 to 2 tablespoons of the Mango Salsa and a tablespoon of sprouts. Place the bun top on the sandwich and serve.

Variation

■ For a lighter dish, place an Aloha patty over your favorite green salad. Top with the Mango Salsa and serve.

Dulse, Lettuce, Tomato, and Tempeh Sandwiches

We sometimes call this a DLT and T because it is similar in taste to a BLT, but much more flavorful. The smoky, salty quality of dulse lends the sandwich an amazingly bacon-like flavor, and the tempeh makes it hearty and satisfying. Of course, a lot depends on having really good quality whole grain bread and ripe tomatoes, preferably from your garden or a farmers market. For this recipe, use whole-leaf dulse, not dulse flakes.

YIELD: 4 sandwiches

8 ounces tempeh, cut into 4 thin (about 1/2 inch thick) bread-size pieces

Smoked paprika, as needed

2 cups leafy pieces dulse, placed loosely in cup, not packed

8 slices whole grain bread, toasted

Dijon-style mustard to taste

1 large or 2 small ripe avocados, thinly sliced

4 large leaves lettuce

1 large or 2 small tomatoes, thinly sliced

1. Lightly spray a large nonstick skillet with nonstick cooking spray, and heat over medium heat. Add the tempeh and cook for 4 to 5 minutes on each side, or until the tempeh is golden brown. Sprinkle each piece of tempeh generously with smoked paprika on both sides. Transfer to a plate, cover to keep warm, and set aside.

2. Lightly spray the same skillet with nonstick spray, and cook the dulse over medium-high heat, turning as needed, for about 4 minutes, or until the seaweed is crisp.

3. Arrange the 4 pieces of toasted bread on a flat surface, and spread with mustard to taste. Top with first the cooked tempeh, and then the crisped dulse and sliced avocado. Finish it off with lettuce and tomato. Top the sandwiches with the remaining 4 slices of toast, cut each in half, and serve immediately.

Ladies Luncheon Sandwiches

This open-faced sandwich—which features peas, carrots, celery, and tempeh in a cream sauce—is reminiscent of that fifties ladies luncheon favorite Chicken à la King. But, of course, this version is far healthier, and we think it's more delicious, too. Add a simple green salad to complete the meal.

YIELD: 4 generous sandwiches

1 pound tempeh, thinly sliced	1 cup frozen peas
1 cup finely chopped onion	1/2 cup raw unsalted cashews
1 cup finely chopped celery	1 teaspoon chickpea miso
1 teaspoon dried savory	1/4 teaspoon ground nutmeg
1 1/2 cups water	1/4 teaspoon ground white pepper
1 cup diced carrots	4 whole grain English muffins, split and toasted
1 cup sliced mushrooms	Chopped fresh parsley or chives for garnish

1. Spray a large nonstick skillet with nonstick cooking spray, and sauté the tempeh over medium heat, stirring often, until it is golden brown. Set aside.

2. Place the onion, celery, savory, and water in a medium-sized saucepan, and bring to a boil over high heat. Cover, reduce the heat to medium-low, and cook at a simmer for 3 to 4 minutes, or until the onions and celery start to get tender.

3. Add the carrots to the saucepan, cover the pot, and continue to cook at a simmer for another 4 to 5 minutes, or until the carrots are almost tender. Add the mushrooms, and simmer for another minute or 2. Then add the peas, bring the water back to a boil, and remove the pot from the heat.

4. Drain the leftover cooking water from the pot into a blender. Add the cashews, and blend until very creamy.

5. Add the cashew cream to the saucepan with the vegetables, and return the mixture to a simmer. It should thicken immediately. If the mixture becomes too thick, add a little water until you have the desired consistency.

6. Add the miso to the sauce, and stir well to dissolve. Add the nutmeg, white pepper, and reserved tempeh, and mix again.

7. Place 2 toasted English muffin halves on each serving plate. Spoon the tempeh mixture over the muffins, garnish with the parsley or chives, and serve immediately.

Variation

■ If you'd like to serve six smaller portions rather than the four generous portions provided in the recipe above, replace the English muffins with six slices of toasted whole grain bread.

Bright and Beautiful Collard Wraps

This truly delicious raw sandwich replaces standard bread wrappers with nutrient-packed collard greens. Bursting with sweet, bitter, spicy, and tangy flavors, it is a mouthful of bliss.

YIELD: 4 wraps

4 large collard green leaves

1 capful apple cider vinegar

Chickpea-Pineapple Spread

1/2 cup cooked or canned chickpeas, rinsed and drained

1/2 cup cubes fresh pineapple

1/2 beet, cut into 4 pieces

1/2 onion, chopped

2 carrots, each cut into 6 pieces

1/4 cup chopped fresh cilantro

1 clove garlic, minced

1/2 teaspoon minced ginger root

Juice of 1 lemon

Toppings

1/2 cup sprouts of your choice

1/2 cup thinly sliced cucumber

1/4 cup toasted unsalted pumpkin seeds

2 teaspoons shredded unsweetened coconut

1. To prepare the collard leaves, place them in a shallow bowl and cover with warm water and 1 capful of vinegar. Soak for 10 minutes. Then rinse and dry.

2. Cut off the stem at the base of each collard leaf. Beginning in the middle of the leaf and working towards the base, use a sharp knife to shave the thickened part of the stem away from the leaf until the stem is even with the leaf. Set aside.

3. Place all of the chickpea spread ingredients in a food processor, and process until well blended but still slightly chunky.

4. For each wrap, place a collard green on a flat surface. Place 3 to 4 tablespoons of the chickpea mixture in the center of the collard green, and top with a quarter of the sprouts, cucumber, pumpkin seeds, and coconut. Fold the sides of the leaf in toward the middle. Then roll the wrap from the bottom up until the filling is enclosed. Serve.

Flax Flatbread with Curried Chickpea Spread

*This Indian-inspired sandwich uses mango and curry to create a delightful balance
of sweet and spicy flavors. Pair the spread with home-baked flatbread,
and you'll have a lunch that's special enough for guests.*

YIELD: 6 to 8 sandwiches

Flatbread

1 1/2 cups spelt flour

1/2 cup millet flour

2 tablespoons freshly ground flaxseed meal

1/4 teaspoon pink Himalayan sea salt

3/4 cup water

Curried Chickpea Spread

2 tablespoons vegetable broth or water

1 onion, diced

1 clove garlic, minced

1 tablespoon curry powder

2 cups cooked or canned chickpeas,
rinsed and drained

1 cup mango chunks

1/2 red bell pepper

2 teaspoons dried parsley, or
2 tablespoons chopped fresh parsley

1 teaspoon ground black pepper

1 teaspoon crushed ginger root (optional)

1. To make the flatbread, place the two flours, flaxseed meal, and salt in a medium-sized mixing bowl, and stir to combine. Slowly stir in the water until the mixture is well blended.

2. Sprinkle 1 to 2 tablespoons of flour over a wooden bread board. Turn the dough onto the board, and knead for 1 to 2 minutes, or until the dough becomes stiff and firm. Form the dough into a ball, lightly sprinkle with flour, and turn the dough until it is well covered with the flour. Place the dough in a bowl, cover with a clean kitchen towel, and allow to sit for 10 minutes.

3. Place a large nonstick skillet or griddle over medium to medium-high heat, and preheat.

4. While the pan is preheating, pull off a palm-sized piece of dough, and roll it into a ball with your hands. Sprinkle 1/4 cup of flour on a bread board, place the ball of dough on the board, and carefully roll it into a thin, round flatbread that's 6 to 8 inches in diameter.

5. Place the dough in the preheated pan and cook for 30 seconds, or until light brown spots begin to appear on the bottom. Turn the dough over and cook for 30 additional seconds. Transfer the cooked flatbread from the pan to a plate, and cover with a clean kitchen towel or a sheet of aluminum foil to keep warm. Repeat with the remaining dough to make 6 to 8 flatbreads.

6. To make the chickpea spread, heat a medium-sized nonstick skillet over medium heat. Add the vegetable broth or water, onion, garlic, and curry powder, and cook, stirring frequently, for 3 to 5 minutes, or until the onion mixture is golden brown.

7. Place the cooked onion mixture and the remaining chickpea spread ingredients in a food processor, and process until the mixture is slightly chunky.

8. Arrange the warm rounds of flatbread on a flat surface, and spread each with 3 to 4 tablespoons of the curried chickpea spread. If desired, top with avocado, sprouts, or sliced tomato, and serve immediately.

Tried and True Hummus Veggie Sandwich

This is a great tasting sandwich that is easy to prepare, travels well, and is popular with both kids and adults. It's perfect to take with you whether you're hiking in the woods or traveling by plane, and it's always satisfying. Be sure to make extras, because these go fast!

YIELD: 4 sandwiches

8 slices whole grain bread	**Hummus**
1/2 avocado, thinly sliced	15-ounce can lower-sodium chickpeas, rinsed and drained
1 cup broccoli sprouts	
1/2 cucumber, thinly sliced	1/4 cup roasted red peppers, drained
1/2 medium tomato, thinly sliced	2 tablespoons tahini
4 large lettuce leaves	Juice of 1 lemon
	2 teaspoons garlic powder
	1 teaspoon unsweetened almond milk
	1/8 teaspoon pink Himalayan sea salt

1. To make the hummus, place all of the hummus ingredients in a food processor, and blend until creamy. Add a small amount of water if needed to create the desired consistency.

2. Arrange 4 slices of bread on a flat surface and spread each slice with about 2 tablespoons of hummus. (If traveling, place the lettuce directly on the bread and spread the hummus on top to prevent the bread from getting soggy.) Top with a fourth of the avocado, broccoli sprouts, cucumber, tomato, and lettuce. Top each sandwich with another slice of bread, cut in half, and serve.

Full-Flavor Smokehouse Burgers

Smoked pepper, BBQ sauce, and a few minutes on the grill impart a wonderful smokiness to these burgers, while mushrooms lend a satisfying meaty flavor. And because these burgers contain grated beets, they even look *like beef burgers.*

YIELD: 8 burgers

8 whole grain hamburger buns, split and toasted

8 thin slices tomato

8 thin slices red onion

Burger Mixture

1 cup unsalted raw walnuts

$1/2$ cup uncooked quick-cooking oats

1 medium white onion, finely chopped

4 cloves Roasted Garlic (see page 31)

1 Portobello mushroom, stemmed and finely chopped

1 teaspoon chopped fresh thyme

$1/2$ medium beet, grated

15-ounce can lower-sodium kidney beans, rinsed and drained

$1/4$ teaspoon smoked salt

$1/2$ cup cooked brown rice

3 tablespoons Easy BBQ Sauce (see page 78) or commercial smoky BBQ sauce

$1/4$ teaspoon smoked pepper

$1/8$ teaspoon oregano

$1/8$ teaspoon garlic powder

1. To prepare the burger mixture, place the walnuts in a dry skillet, and cook over medium heat, stirring frequently, until the nuts are fragrant and golden. Transfer to a food processor.

2. Place the oats in the skillet, and toast over medium heat for 3 to 5 minutes. Add to the food processor, and pulse the mixture until you have a fine meal. Set aside.

3. Lightly spray a large skillet with nonstick cooking spray, and heat to medium heat. Add the onion and sauté, stirring frequently, until translucent. Add the roasted garlic, mushrooms, and thyme, and cook until the mushrooms are soft. Remove from the heat, and stir in the grated beet until it releases its color. Set aside.

4. Place the kidney beans and smoked salt in a large mixing bowl, and mash until only a few beans remain whole. Add the cooked brown rice, reserved walnut mixture, reserved mushroom mixture, BBQ sauce, and spices, and mix thoroughly until you've formed a moldable dough.

5. Preheat an outdoor grill or grill pan to medium.

6. Divide the burger mixture into 8 equal portions, and mold into patties. Arrange the patties on the outdoor grill or grill pan, and cook for 3 to 4 minutes on each side, searing grill marks into each side.

7. For each burger, place a cooked patty on the bottom of a bun, and add a slice of tomato and a slice of onion. Place the top of the bun on the sandwich, and serve immediately.

Barbecue-Style Cauliflower in a Pita Pocket

If you like sweet and spicy barbecue sauce, you'll love this saucy pita pocket of cooked veggies. As a bonus, this warm and satisfying sandwich comes packed with nutrients that will strengthen your immune system.

YIELD: 6 sandwiches

1 recipe Easy BBQ Sauce (see page 78)	$1/2$ teaspoon celery seeds
$1/4$ cup water	$11/2$ cups chopped unsalted raw walnuts
1 head cauliflower, cut into florets with the stem chopped	6 whole grain pita pockets
$11/2$ cup chopped onion	$11/2$ cups loosely packed sunflower sprouts, or 12 lettuce leaves
1 teaspoon dried dill	$3/4$ cup quartered cherry tomatoes

1. Place the Easy BBQ Sauce in a bowl, and stir in the $1/4$ cup water to thin it down. Set aside.

2. Steam the cauliflower for about 8 minutes, or until just tender.

3. While the cauliflower is steaming, spray a large nonstick skillet with nonstick spray. Add the onions, dill, and celery seeds. Cover and cook over medium heat for 5 minutes, or until the onions are almost done. Add the walnuts, and sauté uncovered for 2 to 3 minutes more.

4. Transfer the steamed cauliflower to a cutting board, and coarsely chop, or place in a food processor and pulse until it becomes a coarse mixture with granola-size pieces.

5. Transfer the cauliflower and the BBQ sauce to the skillet with the onions. Mix well, cover, and simmer over low to keep warm while you heat the pita pockets.

6. To heat the pitas, place one piece at a time in a dry skillet over medium-high heat. Cook, pressing firmly down on the bread with a spatula from time to time for a minute or two. Turn the pita over and cook for a minute on the other side, or until heated through, but not toasted. Cover to keep warm while you heat the rest of the bread.

7. Cut each pocket in half and stuff with about 1 cup of the cauliflower mixture. Add the sprouts or lettuce and the cherry tomatoes. Serve immediately.

MAKING THE CHANGE

I couldn't believe that in just a few short days, food had managed to do what my medication could not. My blood pressure was now in the normal range. After spending more than a decade and a half struggling to get my blood pressure under control, I wasn't showing signs of hypertension anymore. How could this be? . . . It was as if a light had been turned on inside me. Knowing healthy food had already begun to change me for the better really blew my mind. I had never thought of food as a vital part of my overall health. Yes, I was aware that humans need to eat to survive, but I'd never looked at food as medicine. Why doesn't everyone know about this, I thought. Why aren't doctors telling their patients about this?

In all the years my doctor had been treating my various conditions, she had never once mentioned a plant-based diet as a treatment option. She had told me I needed to lose weight, but she had never explained that eating a diet of mostly plants could help my body repair itself. I felt like an enormous secret was being kept from the people who really needed to know it. I paid close attention as Dr. Stoll laid out a very easy-to-follow list of practical steps to avoid the pitfalls of hunger. I would never think of cravings in the same way again. . . .

This program wasn't like any diet I had ever tried. I now know the reason for that: Immersion isn't a diet at all; it's a lifestyle change. . . . The idea of preventing and reversing disease with food opened my eyes to all the possibilities a plant-based diet presented. Dr. Stoll discussed how food could be used to stop the progression of many types of disease, including heart disease and type 2 diabetes, and sometimes even reverse them. I couldn't believe what I was hearing. I began to understand that I didn't have to have high blood pressure simply because my dad, mother, and grandparents had suffered from hypertension. My heritage was not my destiny.

Throughout Dr. Stoll's speech, I found myself continually wondering if I had heard the doctor correctly. I even debated whether or not what he was saying was true. Could it really be possible? Could I actually rid myself of all the health problems I had acquired? As I sat there contemplating everything Dr. Stoll was saying, the one fact I couldn't escape was that my blood pressure had changed so quickly on the plant-based diet I had been following. This was a result even my medication struggled to accomplish. My belief in immersion and my resolve were growing stronger and stronger.

Excerpt from *The Change* By Milan Ross and Scott Stoll. Reprinted with permission of Square One Publishers. Copyright © 2016 by Milan Ross and Scott Stoll..

8.

Main Dishes

The main dish is the centerpiece of the meal and generally provides far more protein than any of the accompanying dishes. That's why non-vegans generally associate main courses with meat, poultry, and fish. But as you know, there are many delicious ways in which you can get the protein you need without eating animal products of any kind. Lentils and other legumes, soy foods like tofu and tempeh, nuts and nut butters, and grains (especially quinoa) are all good protein sources. Nearly all vegetables contain some protein, and many vegetables, such as broccoli and kale, offer more protein per calorie than steak. So as long as your main dishes are based on these foods, you'll be getting all the protein your body requires along with lots of other important nutrients that are *not* found in meat.

This chapter includes a wide range of main dishes to suit a variety of tastes. Our Black Bean Burgers combine high-protein black beans with flavorful veggies, herbs, and spices to make a dish that is sure to satisfy. Sage Rice and Lentils uses lentils, two different kinds of rice, veggies, cranberries, and herbs and spices to make a

hearty dish that's easy to put together even on a weekday. Twice-Baked Artichoke-Stuffed Potatoes are comfort food at its best. Who wouldn't love baked potatoes blended with our creamy Artichoke Dip and popped into the oven until lightly browned? Or try one of our other delicious entrées, such as Silky Indian-Style Eggplant, Shepherd's Pie, Southwest-Style Black Beans and Vegetables, Tempeh in Peanut Sauce, and Veggie Corn Cakes.

Despite the fact that this chapter focuses on entrées, you can find main dish recipes in several other chapters of this book, as well. Both our collection of Sandwiches, Wraps, and Burgers (turn to page 107) and our section on Soups and Stews (see page 149) offer recipes that work beautifully as main dishes when accompanied by a simple salad, steamed veggies, or grains. And our Hearty Bowls (see page 135) combine veggies, grains, legumes, soy products, nuts, and more to make comforting one-dish meals that are perfect for both lunch and dinner. With so many great options, you're sure to find dishes that you and your family will enjoy again and again.

Twice-Baked Artichoke-Stuffed Potatoes

These creamy stuffed potatoes have a nice crisp skin.
Paired with a big green salad, they make a satisfying meal.

YIELD: 4 to 8 servings

4 russet potatoes (about 1 pound each)	1/4 cup chopped unsalted raw walnuts
1 recipe Artichoke Dip (see page 64)	Paprika for garnish

---

1. Preheat the oven to 375°F.

2. Scrub the potatoes and cut out any eyes or other bad spots. If no bad spots have been cut away, pierce the sides with a fork. (This will allow steam to escape during cooking, preventing the potatoes from exploding in the oven.)

3. Spray the potatoes lightly with nonstick cooking spray, and arrange them on a baking sheet. Bake for about 45 minutes, or until soft when squeezed, turning once for even browning.

4. When the potatoes are done, cut each one in half lengthwise. Using a spoon, scoop most of the flesh out into a mixing bowl, leaving a 1/4- to 1/8-inch-thick shell so that the halves will hold their shape.

5. Add the Artichoke Dip to the scooped-out potatoes, and mash together. Divide the mixture evenly among the potato skins, filling the skins and mounding the mixture as high as necessary to use up all of the mixture.

6. Top each potato half with about 1½ teaspoons chopped nuts, and sprinkle with paprika. Return the potatoes to the oven for about 15 minutes, or until the tops are lightly browned. Serve hot.

The Key to Diabetes Prevention and Treatment

Type 2 diabetes has been growing at near-epidemic rates across the globe. Over time, elevated blood sugar levels can lead to nerve damage, vision problems such as glaucoma and blindness, kidney failure, and heart disease. The good news is that type 2 diabetes is large preventable and reversible with a whole food plant-based diet. In one study, 74 percent of people with type 2 diabetes were able to discontinue all of their medications after following a plant-based diet for just four weeks. During that period, 44 percent of those on insulin were able to discontinue use of the drug. In other words, the key to diabetes prevention and treatment can be found at your local grocery store.

Black Bean Burgers

Slightly spicy and quick to make with either home-cooked or canned beans,
these burgers are delicious topped with salsa and accompanied by a salad.

YIELD: 5 burgers

$2^1/_2$ cups cooked or canned black beans, rinsed and drained

$1^1/_4$ cups fine whole grain bread crumbs, from toasted bread (see Helpful Tip, below)

$^1/_4$ cup minced celery

$^1/_4$ cup minced onion

$^1/_4$ cup minced red bell pepper

$^1/_4$ cup sun-dried tomatoes (no oil) cut into small pieces

2 teaspoons coconut aminos

1 teaspoon ground cumin

1 teaspoon dried basil

$^1/_4$ teaspoon ground chipotle pepper, or to taste

1 clove garlic, pressed

1. Place the black beans in a large mixing bowl, and use a potato masher to mash the beans until they're chunky and hold together. Add all of the remaining ingredients and mix well, using your hands as needed.

2. Divide the mixture into 5 equal portions (about $^1/_3$ cup each), and shape each portion into a burger that is about $3^1/_2$ inches in diameter and $^3/_4$ inch thick.

3. Spray a large nonstick skillet with nonstick cooking spray. Arrange the patties in the skillet and cook over medium heat for 4 to 5 minutes, or until the bottom is brown. Turn the patties over, and brown on the second side. Serve immediately.

Helpful Tip

To make the bread crumbs for this recipe, toast 3 slices of whole grain bread. Allow the bread to cool to room temperature, tear the slices into pieces, and grind the toast into crumbs using either a blender or a food processor. (If the appliance is small, this may have to be done in two batches.) Be sure to measure out exactly $1^1/_4$ cups of bread crumbs, and reserve any extra crumbs for another use.

Sage Rice and Lentils

*This hearty dish is perfect for a weekday fall or winter meal, because you throw
all the ingredients in the pot and let them cook. Cranberries are full of antioxidants
and make a tangy, nutritious, and colorful ingredient, but the dish will be
tasty even when these berries are out of season.*

YIELD: 6 to 8 servings

1 cup uncooked lentils, picked over and rinsed	1 1/2 teaspoons ground sage
1 cup uncooked brown rice, rinsed and drained	1 teaspoon dried thyme
1/2 cup uncooked wild rice, rinsed and drained	4 bay leaves
2 cups thickly sliced carrots (about 4 medium carrots sliced 1/2 inch thick)	1/2 teaspoon ground cinnamon
	5 cups water
1 1/2 cups thickly sliced celery (about 3 medium stalks)	1 cup fresh or frozen cranberries (optional)
1/3 cup dehydrated shallots or onions, or 2/3 cup fresh chopped shallots or onions	Unsalted raw walnut or pecan pieces for garnish

1. Place the lentils and all of the remaining ingredients except for the cranberries and nuts in a large, heavy pot. Stir to mix, and bring to a boil over high heat. Cover, reduce the heat to low, and cook at a simmer, without stirring, for 35 minutes.

2. Quickly remove the cover and, if desired, add the cranberries without stirring. Immediately cover the pot and cook for another 10 minutes, or until all the liquid has been absorbed.

3. Garnish with a sprinkling of walnut or pecan pieces, and serve hot with a salad or steamed green vegetable and perhaps some Walnut Gravy (see page 79). If you have leftovers, toss in some nuts and use the mixture to stuff squash or peppers.

Variations

■ For Southwestern Rice and Lentils, omit the cranberries, herbs, and cinnamon, and replace with 1 1/2 teaspoons dried basil, 1 teaspoon ground cumin, and 1/4 to 1/2 teaspoon ground chipotle pepper. Serve with slices of avocado.

■ For an Indian-style meal, omit the cranberries, herbs, and cinnamon, and replace with 1 teaspoon ground turmeric, 1 tablespoon finely grated ginger root, 1 teaspoon ground cumin, a pinch of cayenne pepper, and 1/2 teaspoon fennel seed. Serve with a vegan raita.

Dandelion Greens with White Beans

In Italy, small country restaurants often serve big bowls of cooked dandelion greens.
Folk medicine says that they are good for the liver. Buy the greens at a farmers market
that offers a larger leaf cultivated version that is less bitter than the wild varieties.
(See the Helpful Tip, below.) Enjoy this dish over whole grain pasta
or Baked Italian Rice with Garlic and Herbs (see page 160).

YIELD: 3 to 4 servings

1 pound cultivated dandelion greens, washed and coarsely chopped (about 6 cups)

$^1/_2$ cup chopped onion

3–4 cloves garlic, minced

1–2 tablespoons balsamic vinegar

1 tablespoon water

1 tablespoon coconut aminos

15-ounce can white cannellini beans, rinsed and drained

1 tablespoon capers, drained

1 teaspoon dried tarragon

1. Steam the dandelion greens for about 10 minutes, or until tender. Set the greens aside, and reserve any leftover water to use as stock in soup or stews.

2. Place the onion, garlic, vinegar, water, and coconut aminos in a large nonstick skillet. Cover and cook over medium heat, stirring occasionally, for 3 to 5 minutes, or until the onion is tender.

3. Add the reserved steamed greens, beans, capers, and tarragon to the skillet mixture, and stir to combine. Cook, stirring occasionally, for 2 to 3 minutes, or just long enough to heat the beans and blend the flavors. Serve hot.

Helpful Tip

Although you may be tempted to harvest dandelion greens from your yard or the side of the road, for the most part, this should be avoided. Harvest the dandelions from your property only if you're sure that no weed killers or other pesticides have been used there. Wild growth at the side of a road or a median may also carry toxins from pesticide sprays, and tends to accumulate pollution from passing cars and trucks. So unless you know that the foraged dandelions are free of toxic chemicals, your best bet is to choose organically cultivated greens.

Silky Indian-Style Eggplant

This recipe usually includes sour cream, but silken tofu is a scrumptious substitute in this Indian-style dish. Serve it over brown rice along with a green salad for a wonderfully easy meal.

YIELD: 3 to 4 servings

1 large eggplant (about 1½ pounds)	1 teaspoon ground cumin
1 cup chopped onion	12.3-ounce package silken tofu
4 cloves garlic, minced	1 tablespoon chickpea miso
3 tablespoons water	2 tablespoons minced fresh cilantro, plus extra cilantro for garnish
1 tablespoon curry powder	

---

1. Preheat the oven to 400°F.

2. Rinse the eggplant and pierce it all over with the tines of a fork. Place it on a baking sheet and bake for about 50 minutes, or until the eggplant is soft and looks shriveled, turning the eggplant over 2 to 3 times during baking so it cooks evenly. Allow to cool until comfortable to handle.

3. Spray a large nonstick skillet lightly with olive oil, and add the onion, garlic, and water. Cover and cook over medium heat, stirring occasionally, for 5 minutes, or until the onion is tender. Add the curry powder and cumin, and cook and stir for a minute or 2 more.

4. Cut the eggplant in half, and use a spoon to scrape the insides out onto a cutting board. Coarsely chop the flesh.

5. Transfer the chopped eggplant to the skillet, and stir to combine with the onion mixture. Cook over medium heat for a couple of minutes, stirring occasionally, to blend the flavors.

6. Place the tofu and miso in a blender, and blend until smooth. Add the blended tofu mixture to the skillet. Stir over medium heat for only a minute—just long enough for the mixture to get thoroughly heated but not cook. Stir in the 2 tablespoons of cilantro, mix well, and remove from the heat. Garnish with extra cilantro, and serve immediately.

Variation

■ Substitute parsley for the cilantro, or add a pinch of cayenne pepper to spice the dish up.

Quinoa with Broccoli, Walnuts, and Tomatoes

This is an easy and flavorful one-pot meal with simple ingredients.

YIELD: 4 to 6 servings

1 cup uncooked quinoa

2 cups water

8 sun-dried tomato halves (no oil), cut into small pieces

1 teaspoon dried basil

1 pound broccoli, stems peeled and chopped, and tops in bite-sized florets

Ground black pepper, to taste

Tomato-Walnut Topping

1 cup quartered cherry or grape tomatoes

$3/4$ cup chopped unsalted raw walnuts

$1/2$ cup chopped scallions

1–2 tablespoons balsamic vinegar

1–2 cloves garlic, pressed (optional)

---

1. Rinse the quinoa and place it in a 2-quart pot with the water, dried tomatoes, and basil. Cover and bring to a boil over high heat. Reduce the heat to low and simmer, without stirring, for 8 to 10 minutes.

2. While the quinoa is cooking, combine all of the Tomato-Walnut Topping ingredients in a medium-sized bowl. Mix well and set aside.

3. Without stirring, add the broccoli to the pot with the quinoa, and replace the lid quickly. Continue to cook for another 8 to 10 minutes, or until the broccoli is tender and the water has been absorbed. Taste the quinoa mixture, and add black pepper as desired. Fluff the quinoa with a fork, and spoon the mixture onto serving plates.

4. Stir the Tomato-Walnut Topping again, and spoon it over the broccoli-quinoa mixture. Serve immediately.

Shepherd's Pie

When you want comfort food that also nourishes the body,
this shepherd's pie will fill the bill.

YIELD: 6 servings

6 medium potatoes, scrubbed and diced (2 pounds)

1/3 cup unsweetened soy milk or cooking water from potatoes

1 tablespoon chickpea miso

1/2 teaspoon ground white pepper

1/3 cup red wine

2 tablespoons coconut aminos

1 cup chopped onion

1 cup chopped celery

1 pound tempeh, sliced and crumbled

4 cups sliced mushrooms (about 10 ounces)

2 teaspoons dried thyme

1 teaspoon dried sage

1/3 cup nutritional yeast

2 cups frozen corn

2 cups frozen peas

1. Place the potatoes in a large pot, and add about 2 inches of cold water. (It's not necessary to entirely cover the potatoes with water.) Cover the pot and bring to a boil over high heat. Then lower the heat to a simmer and cook for 15 minutes, or until done, stirring occasionally and adding a little water if necessary. Drain well, reserving the cooking water if any remains.

2. Mash the potatoes with the soy milk or the reserved cooking water. Stir in the miso and pepper, mixing well. Set aside.

3. Preheat the oven to 350°F. Lightly spray a 3-quart lasagna pan or other rectangular or square baking dish of a similar size with nonstick cooking spray. Set aside.

4. In a large nonstick skillet, combine the wine and coconut aminos. Add the onion and celery, cover, and cook over medium heat, stirring occasionally, for about 4 minutes, or until the celery is almost tender.

5. Add the tempeh to the skillet mixture, cover, and cook for another 5 minutes, stirring occasionally.

6. Add the mushrooms, thyme, and sage to the skillet mixture, and continue to cook and stir until the mushrooms are tender, about 5 minutes. Stir in the nutritional yeast.

7. Transfer the tempeh mixture to the prepared baking dish, spreading it in an even layer. Evenly distribute the corn and peas over the tempeh layer. Then carefully spread the mashed potatoes over the corn and peas. Lightly spray the top of the potatoes with nonstick cooking spray.

8. Bake for about 40 minutes, or until hot and bubbly. If necessary, turn the oven to broil for a minute or two to brown the top. Serve immediately.

Variation

■ Replace some of the potatoes with sweet potatoes.

Golden Pasta and Peas

Although prepared without cheese, Golden Hemp Seed Sauce makes this dish creamy and tasty enough to satisfy any macaroni-and-cheese craving. Prepare the dish using either whole wheat or gluten-free pasta, and add a simple green salad or some steamed vegetables to complete the meal.

YIELD: 5 to 6 servings

3 cups whole wheat macaroni, fusilli, or rotini pasta	1 recipe Golden Hemp Seed Sauce (see page 83), hot
1 cup frozen peas	Minced fresh parsley and paprika for garnish

1. Cook the pasta according to the directions on the package. Place the peas in the colander, and drain the pasta through the colander over the peas to thaw the peas. Return the pasta and peas to the pot.

2. Add the hot, freshly made sauce to the pasta mixture, stirring well to coat. Garnish with parsley and paprika, and serve immediately.

Tex-Mex Quinoa Cakes

Make this quick and easy recipe when you have some leftover quinoa.
It can be doubled to yield more servings, or spiced up or down according to your taste.
These cakes are delicious served plain with a salad or steamed vegetables,
and are even better when topped with salsa or tomato sauce.

YIELD: 4 cakes

1 cup cooked red quinoa	1 teaspoon ground cumin
1/2 cup frozen sweet corn	1 teaspoon smoked paprika
2 tablespoons peanut butter	2 cloves garlic, pressed
1 tablespoon red miso	1/8 teaspoon ground chipotle pepper, or more to taste
1 teaspoon dried basil	

1. Place all of the ingredients in a medium-sized mixing bowl, and mix well, using your hands if necessary.

2. Divide the mixture into 4 equal portions, and shape each portion into a patty that is about 3 inches in diameter and 1 inch thick.

3. Spray a large nonstick skillet with nonstick cooking spray, and heat it over medium heat. Arrange the patties in the skillet and cook for about 4 minutes, or until the bottom is brown. Carefully turn the patties over, and brown on the second side. Serve immediately.

Money-Saving Tips for Following a Whole Food Plant-Based Diet

In general, a plant-based diet is less expensive than a diet that features lots of meat and seafood. But if you find your plant-based food bills too high, try these cost-lowering tips.

■ Whenever possible, cook dried beans instead of using canned. This practice will also eliminate any threats posed by can linings that contain the toxic compound BPA. (See page 21.) If your life is busy, cook the beans in big batches and freeze them for future meals, or invest in a pressure cooker. (See page 24 to learn about pressure cookers.)

Tempeh in Peanut Sauce

Serve this savory mixture over rice and vegetables, over Cauliflower-Leek Mock Mashed Potatoes (see page 170), or—to make an open-faced sandwich—over whole grain toast.

YIELD: 3 to 4 servings

8 ounces tempeh, thinly sliced	1 tablespoon balsamic vinegar
1/2 cup crunchy peanut butter	1 clove garlic, pressed
1 1/2 to 2 cups water, as needed	Pinch of cayenne pepper, to taste
2 tablespoons coconut aminos	

1. Lightly spray a large nonstick skillet with nonstick cooking spray. Add the tempeh and cook over medium-low heat, stirring often, for 5 to 10 minutes, or until the tempeh is golden brown.

2. While the tempeh is cooking, place the peanut butter in a small mixing bowl and slowly stir in the water until 1 1/2 cups of the water have been added, and the water is well mixed with the peanut butter. Stir in the coconut aminos and the vinegar.

3. Pour the sauce mixture over the cooked tempeh in the skillet, and bring to a simmer while stirring constantly. If the sauce is too thick, add all or part of the remaining water.

4. Add the garlic and the cayenne to the skillet, mix well, and serve.

■ Buy grains and beans in bulk. If this means that you end up with more food than you can possibly use, share bulk orders with friends or family.

■ If you have a yard, grow some of your own leafy greens and vegetables. Even if you cultivate only herbs—either outdoors or on a sunny windowsill—you will save a great deal of money.

■ Don't feel that all of your produce has to be organic. While some conventional produce—like strawberries and spinach—is laden with chemicals, other conventional produce—like corn and avocados—contains few if any contaminants. Learn when it's important to buy pricey organic produce and when it's not. (See the discussion on page 7.)

Southwest-Style Black Beans and Vegetables

This flavorful bean and vegetable mixture is especially good over whole wheat pasta, but you can also serve it over rice, grits, polenta, millet, or quinoa. It's easy to make, too, because you can simply use a can of beans and frozen corn if you're in a hurry. You can even replace the chard with prewashed spinach.

YIELD: 4 servings

1 tablespoon coconut aminos

1 tablespoon balsamic vinegar

1 cup chopped onion

4 cups diced yellow summer squash (about 4 medium)

10 ounces Swiss chard, chopped (about 6 lightly packed cups)

$1\frac{1}{2}$ cups fresh or frozen corn

$1\frac{1}{2}$ cups cooked or canned black beans, rinsed and drained

$\frac{1}{3}$ cup sun-dried tomatoes (no oil) cut into small pieces

1 teaspoon ground cumin

1 teaspoon dried basil

1 teaspoon smoked paprika

$\frac{1}{4}$ teaspoon ground chipotle pepper, or more to taste

1. Combine the coconut aminos and vinegar in a large nonstick skillet. Layer the vegetables by placing the onions on the bottom of the skillet followed by the squash and the chard. Do not stir the vegetables together.

2. Cover and cook over medium-high heat until the pan is hot and full of steam. Then reduce the heat to low and cook, without stirring, for about 5 minutes, or until the onions are almost done.

3. Stir the corn and all of the remaining ingredients into the skillet mixture. Cover and continue to cook until the vegetables are tender and the mixture is hot. Serve immediately.

Variation

■ If you are in a hurry, substitute prewashed baby spinach for the chard. Since spinach cooks faster than chard, add it with the corn after the squash is almost done.

Veggie Corn Cakes

These corn cakes are like mini veggie omelets. Enjoy them as a main dish,
a side, a brunch dish, or even an appetizer.

YIELD: About 12 corn cakes

$1\frac{1}{2}$ cups mashed firm tofu (firmly packed) (about 14 ounces)

$\frac{1}{2}$ cup water

1–2 cloves garlic

2 teaspoons baking powder

2 teaspoons chickpea miso

1 cup cornmeal

1 cup firmly packed grated zucchini

$\frac{1}{4}$ cup finely diced red bell pepper

1 teaspoon dried basil

1 teaspoon ground cumin

$\frac{1}{2}$ teaspoon ground turmeric

1. Place the tofu, water, garlic, baking powder, and miso in a blender or food processor, and blend until smooth and creamy.

2. Transfer the tofu mixture to a medium-sized bowl, and add all of the remaining ingredients. Mix well.

3. Spray a large nonstick skillet with nonstick cooking spray, and heat it over medium heat. Drop heaping tablespoons of the batter onto the hot skillet, and cook for 3 to 4 minutes, or just until the bottom is brown. Carefully turn the cakes over, and brown on the second side. Transfer the cakes to a platter, cover to keep warm, and continue to cook the remaining batter. Serve the cakes hot.

Helpful Tip

It may seem like a good idea to make these luscious cakes a little larger, but they must be kept small to allow them to hold their shape. Use no more than a heaping tablespoon of batter for each omelet-like Veggie Corn Cake.

Wild Rice with Carrots and Chestnuts

Chestnuts are so delicious that they should not be reserved for special occasions.
Fortunately, you can now buy them already shelled and cooked, making it easy
to include them even in weekday recipes. This dish is great served alone, topped with
the creamy Hemp Seed Sauce on page 81, or used to stuff a winter squash,
such as acorn or butternut.

YIELD: 4 to 6 servings

1 cup uncooked wild rice, rinsed and drained

3 cups water

1 cup sliced carrots

2 tablespoons coconut aminos

1 tablespoon balsamic vinegar

3/4 cup finely chopped onion

6.5-ounce package cooked chestnuts, halved (1 cup)

2 tablespoons chopped fresh sage, or 1 teaspoon dried

1/2 teaspoon ground white pepper

1. Place the rice in a medium-sized pot along with the water. Cover and bring to a boil over high heat. Reduce the heat to low and simmer, without stirring, for about 40 minutes.

2. Add the carrots to the pot, cover, and continue to cook for 10 additional minutes, or until the carrots are tender. Drain the water through a strainer, reserving it for a sauce or soup. Return the rice and carrot mixture to the pot, cover to keep warm, and set aside.

3. Place the coconut aminos, balsamic vinegar, and onion in a large nonstick skillet, stirring to combine. Cover and cook over medium heat, stirring occasionally, for about 5 minutes, or until the onions are translucent.

4. Stir the chestnuts, sage, and pepper into the skillet mixture. Cover and cook for 3 to 4 minutes to blend the flavors. If the mixture becomes too dry and begins to scorch, add a tablespoon of the reserved cooking water.

5. Add the reserved rice and carrots to the skillet, and stir them into the chestnut mixture. Serve immediately with a green vegetable or a salad.

9.

Hearty Bowls

In both restaurants and home kitchens, health-conscious people who also love good food are turning to bowls—and for good reason. Filled with a combination of vegetables, whole grains or pasta, beans, and other wholesome foods, bowls offer balanced nutrition in one warm and comforting dish. And because all of the ingredients are mixed together, every tempting bite delivers a wonderful blending of flavors.

Bowls are easy to prepare and serve, too, making them ideal for a busy lifestyle. Instead of putting together several different dishes at one time—a salad and a rice and bean dish, for instance—you'll be creating one bowl that combines all of your meal's ingredients. As you'll see when you read through the recipes, bowls are even faster to prepare when you have cooked rice, quinoa, or other grains in your fridge. In fact, these popular dishes are a great reason to do batch cooking whenever you have the time so that you always have some healthy cooked ingredients on hand. Or simply make extra grains whenever you prepare them for a meal. A little planning can pay big dividends, especially on hectic week nights, when time is at a premium.

The following pages present a dozen bowl creations, each offering a perfect blending of textures, flavors, and colors. (Bowls are beautiful, too!) Savory Quinoa Bowl combines high-protein quinoa with onion, garlic, mushrooms, corn, and savory seasonings, and crowns the steaming mixture with crisp chopped vegetables. Eggplant Curry Rice Bowl is a healthy version of a flavorful Indian curry. Creamed Spinach and Mushroom Polenta Bowl is warm, nourishing, and wonderfully creamy. Mama's Soul Bowl is an updated version of an old-time Southern meal that combines collard greens, black-eyed peas, and grits. Or for a super-fast, super-satisfying meal, try the 12-Minute Pasta Bowl.

Although several of our bowl recipes offer variations, you should always feel free to change our recipes by substituting ingredients you prefer or ingredients that you already have on hand for those listed. As long as you include bountiful amounts of veggies along with beans and/or grains; perhaps some tofu or tempeh; and plenty of natural flavorings such as herbs, spices, balsamic vinegar, and coconut aminos, your bowl will provide the nutrition you need as well as the flavors you love.

Eggplant Curry Rice Bowl

*Indian dishes tend to be pretty high in oil and salt, but it's the spices that make them
so delicious. This list of ingredients may look long, but it's mostly common spices,
so don't be afraid to give this recipe a try.*

YIELD: 2 servings

¹/₂ teaspoon mustard seeds	¹/₂ teaspoon ground cumin
¹/₂ teaspoon cumin seeds	2–3 tablespoons water, or as needed
¹/₂ teaspoon fennel seeds	1¹/₂ cups cooked brown basmati rice
2 cups chopped fresh tomato (about 2 medium)	1 cup cooked or canned chickpeas, rinsed and drained
¹/₂ cup chopped onion	2 teaspoons lime juice
1-inch piece ginger root, peeled and sliced	Pinch cayenne pepper (optional)
2 cloves garlic	2 cups chopped leafy lettuce (lightly packed)
2 cups diced eggplant	Fresh cilantro leaves for garnish
2 teaspoons coconut aminos	2–4 tablespoons Taste of India Topping (see page 84) (optional)
1 teaspoon ground turmeric	

1. Heat a heavy medium-sized skillet over medium-high heat. Place the mustard, cumin, and fennel seeds in the skillet and cook for a couple of minutes, or until they start to become fragrant and pop. Remove the pan from the heat, and set aside.

2. Place the tomato, onion, ginger, and garlic in a blender, and blend until coarsely chopped.

3. Place the blended mixture, eggplant, coconut aminos, turmeric, and cumin in the pan with the dry roasted spices. Cover and cook over medium heat, stirring occasionally, for 8 to 10 minutes, or until the eggplant is tender. Add the water, if needed, to keep the sauce from scorching.

4. While the eggplant is cooking, reheat the rice in a medium-sized saucepan: Place the rice in the pan with 2 to 3 tablespoons of water, cover, and cook over medium heat for a couple of minutes, or until the pan is full of steam and the rice is hot.

5. Add the chickpeas to the skillet, and stir and cook just long enough to heat through. Stir in the lime juice and the cayenne, if using.

6. To serve, divide the hot rice between 2 bowls. Top each mound of rice with half of the eggplant curry, scatter the chopped lettuce around the edges of the bowl, and garnish with the cilantro leaves. If you have some Taste of India Topping on hand, sprinkle it over the top of the dish, and serve immediately.

Savory Quinoa Bowl

This easy recipe is a great way to use up some leftover quinoa—and a good reason to make extra whenever you cook this nutritious grain. Since quinoa is a complete protein that's packed with antioxidants and other nutrients, it is a wonderful ingredient in plant-based meals.

YIELD: 2 servings

1/2 cup finely chopped onion	**Toppings**
2–4 cloves garlic, thinly sliced	2/3 cup diced avocado
2 cups sliced mushrooms	2/3 cup quartered cherry or grape tomatoes
2 cups cooked quinoa	
2 cups frozen sweet corn	2/3 cup diced cucumber
2 teaspoons coconut aminos	2/3 cup diced red bell pepper
2 teaspoons balsamic vinegar	Fresh cilantro leaves for garnish
1 teaspoon dried basil	Chipotle Sauce (see page 67, Variation) (optional)
1/2 teaspoon ground cumin	

1. Lightly spray a large nonstick skillet with nonstick cooking spray, and arrange the onion on the bottom of the skillet. Top with the garlic, cover, and cook over medium heat, without stirring, for 2 to 3 minutes.

2. Stir the onions and garlic. Top with the mushrooms (do not stir), cover, and cook for another minute or 2, or until the onions are done and slightly browned. Stir in the remaining ingredients (quinoa through cumin), cover, and cook for another minute or 2, or until the mixture is nice and hot.

3. To serve, divide the steaming hot quinoa mixture between 2 bowls. Scatter the avocado, tomatoes, cucumber, and red bell pepper around the rim of each bowl. Garnish with the cilantro leaves, top with a dollop of Chipotle Sauce if desired, and serve immediately.

Tofu Scramble Rice Bowl

With some leftover rice in hand and some healthy ingredients in the pantry and fridge, you can make this nourishing lunch or dinner in a matter of minutes. Grating the carrots and zucchini allows them to cook in no time!

YIELD: 2 generous servings

1/3 cup finely chopped onion

1/2 cup finely diced bell pepper (any color)

2 cloves garlic, minced

1 tablespoon grated ginger root

1 1/2 cups grated zucchini (about 1 medium)

1 cup grated carrots

2 teaspoons curry powder, mild or hot

1/2 teaspoon ground turmeric

14 ounces firm tofu, crumbled (about 2 cups crumbled)

2 teaspoons coconut aminos

2 cups cooked brown rice or a mix of brown and wild rice

Toppings

1/2 cup chopped tomato

1/4 cup chopped fresh cilantro or parsley

---

1. Spray a large nonstick skillet with nonstick cooking spray. Add the onion, cover, and cook over medium heat for a couple of minutes, or until the onion sizzles. Stir in the bell pepper, garlic, and ginger. Top with the grated zucchini and carrots, cover, and cook without stirring for 2 to 3 minutes.

2. Add the curry powder and turmeric to the skillet mixture, and mix well. Stir in the crumbled tofu and the coconut aminos, cover, and cook for another 2 to 3 minutes, or until the vegetables are done and the tofu is sizzling hot.

3. While the vegetables are cooking, reheat the rice in a medium-sized saucepan: Place the rice in the pan with 2 to 3 tablespoons of water, cover, and cook over medium heat for a couple of minutes, or until the pan is full of steam and the rice is hot.

4. To serve, divide the hot rice between 2 bowls. Top with the tofu scramble, scatter the tomato around the edge of the bowl, and sprinkle the chopped cilantro or parsley over all. Serve immediately.

Variations

■ If you don't like curry, simply leave out the ginger and curry powder. It's a good idea to leave the turmeric in, because it is so good for you and lends the dish a pleasing yellow color. To make sure that the scramble has plenty of flavor, stir in a teaspoon of dried basil, thyme, savory, or another herb that you enjoy.

■ Feel free to add to or replace the carrots and zucchini with other fast-cooking veggies, such as sliced mushrooms, chopped asparagus, snow peas, or frozen peas.

Creamed Spinach and Mushroom Polenta Bowl

Warm, nourishing, and wonderfully creamy, this dish provides a hefty serving of spinach.

YIELD: 2 servings

Polenta

$^{1}/_{2}$ cup uncooked medium- or coarse-ground cornmeal*

$2^{1}/_{2}$ cups water

Spinach Mixture

$^{1}/_{2}$ cup minced onion

10 ounces baby spinach (about 10 cups lightly packed)

2 cups sliced mushrooms

2 teaspoons coconut aminos

1 tablespoon plus 1 teaspoon balsamic vinegar

2 cups water

$^{1}/_{2}$ cup unsalted raw cashews

1 teaspoon dried tarragon

$^{1}/_{4}$ teaspoon white pepper, or to taste

Toppings

$^{2}/_{3}$ cup chopped tomatoes

1 tablespoon minced fresh parsley

---

* Although you can find a product labeled "polenta" in the supermarket, any medium or coarse grind of cornmeal will work well. If you want to avoid GMO corn, buy an organic product.

---

1. To make the polenta, place the cornmeal and water in a medium-sized saucepan. Stirring constantly, bring the mixture to a simmer over medium heat. Reduce the heat to low, cover, and simmer, stirring occasionally, for 10 to 15 minutes, or until the mixture is thick. If the polenta begins to stick to the bottom of the pan, simply turn off the heat and allow to steam with the lid on for a minute or 2 before stirring.

2. While the polenta is cooking, to make the spinach mixture, spray a large nonstick skillet with nonstick cooking spray, and add the onion. Cover and cook over medium heat for a couple of minutes. Add the spinach, mushrooms, coconut aminos, and balsamic vinegar to the skillet. Cover and continue to cook for 2 or 3 additional minutes, or until the spinach and mushrooms are cooked through.

3. While the vegetables are cooking, place the water, cashews, tarragon, and pepper in a blender, and blend until creamy. Pour this mixture over the spinach-mushroom mixture, and continue to cook, stirring constantly, for 1 to 2 minutes, or until the sauce simmers and thickens.

4. To serve, divide the polenta between 2 bowls. In each bowl, make a well in the center of the polenta, and fill with half of the creamed spinach and mushrooms. Top with the tomatoes and parsley, and serve immediately.

Mama's Soul Bowl

Nourish your body and feed your soul with this updated version of an old-time Southern meal. This dish is quick to put together if you have leftover beans and greens. (See the Variations below the recipe.)

YIELD: 2 servings

Greens

3 cups finely chopped collard greens
(about 8 ounces)

1 cup water, or as needed

1 tablespoon balsamic vinegar

1 teaspoon dried tarragon

1 teaspoon liquid smoke

Grits

1/2 cup uncooked coarse- or
medium-ground cornmeal*

2 1/2 cups water

Beans

1 cup cooked unseasoned black-eyed peas
in their cooking liquid, or 1 cup canned
black-eyed peas, rinsed and drained

1 tablespoon coconut aminos

1/2 teaspoon liquid smoke

Toppings

2/3 cup chopped tomatoes

1/4 cup chopped scallions

---

* Although you can find a product labeled "grits"
in the supermarket, any coarse or medium grind
of cornmeal will work well. If you want to avoid
GMO corn, buy an organic product.

---

1. To make the greens, place them in a heavy medium-sized saucepan. Add the water, and bring to a simmer over medium heat. Reduce the heat to low, cover, and cook at a simmer for about 20 minutes.

2. Add the balsamic vinegar, tarragon, and liquid smoke to the greens, and stir. Cover and continue cooking for another 15 minutes, or until the greens are tender, stirring occasionally and adding a little more water if necessary.

3. While the greens are cooking, to make the grits, place the cornmeal in a medium-sized saucepan. Add the water and, stirring constantly, bring to a simmer over medium heat. Reduce the heat to low, cover, and cook at a simmer, stirring occasionally, for 10 to 15 minutes, or until the mixture is thick. If the grits begin to stick to the bottom of the pan, simply turn off the heat and allow to steam with the lid on for a minute or 2 before stirring.

4. Place the beans in a small saucepan, and stir in the coconut aminos and the liquid smoke. Bring to a simmer over low heat, and cover to keep warm.

5. To serve, divide the grits between 2 bowls. In each bowl, make a well in the center of the grits, and fill with half of the hot seasoned beans. Arrange the chopped tomato over the beans and grits, scatter the cooked collard greens around the rim, and distribute the scallions over all. Enjoy immediately.

Variations

■ To make Mama's Soul Bowl with kale instead of collard greens, simply replace the chopped collard greens with chopped kale, and cook as directed above.

■ You can also make this dish using leftover Soul Food Greens (see page 162) and Southern-Style Beans (see page 164). These dishes are already seasoned, so just arrange them in a bowl with the grits, and top with the scallions and tomatoes.

Grits or Polenta: What's the Difference?

Depending on where you live, you may be more familiar with grits than with polenta, or vice versa. What's the difference between these two hearty dishes?

Both grits, a Southern favorite, and polenta, an Italian staple, are prepared with ground dried corn kernels, but traditionally, they are made with two different varieties of corn. Grits are usually made from *dent corn,* while in Italy, polenta is generally made from *flint corn.* This is sort of like making apple pie with two different varieties of apples. The finished dishes are both apple pie, and polenta and grits—for all practical purposes—are both simply cornmeal mush. As long as you have coarse- or medium-ground corn, you can make either dish with success.

Be aware that most of the cornmeal on the market has been genetically modified. If you wish to avoid GMOs, be sure to purchase organic cornmeal.

12-Minute Pasta Bowl

Do you avoid pasta—even though you like it—because you think it's unhealthy? Think again, and use high-quality whole wheat pasta, lots of vegetables, and a plant-based protein such as nuts for a delicious, quick, and balanced meal. The trick to making this dish in twelve minutes is to quickly prep and sauté the veggies while the pasta is cooking. Then everything should be done at around the same time.

YIELD: 2 servings

1 cup uncooked whole wheat penne or rigatoni pasta

4 cups water

$\frac{1}{2}$ cup finely chopped onion

2 cloves garlic, thinly sliced

1 to 2 medium zucchini, quartered and thinly sliced

$1\frac{1}{2}$ cups sliced mushrooms

4 sun-dried tomato halves (no oil), finely chopped

2 teaspoons balsamic vinegar

1 teaspoon dried basil

Toppings

$\frac{1}{2}$ cup quartered grape or cherry tomatoes

$\frac{1}{2}$ cup diced red bell pepper

$1\frac{1}{2}$ cups chopped arugula

$\frac{1}{2}$ cup chopped unsalted raw walnuts or whole pine nuts (pignoli)

---

1. Place the pasta in a 2-quart saucepan and add the water. Turn the heat to high. When the water boils, reduce the heat to medium and cook uncovered for about 10 minutes, or until the pasta is done. (Although this is not the way pasta is usually cooked, it works well and will allow you to focus on prepping the veggies.)

2. As soon as the pasta goes into the pot, quickly chop the onion and garlic. Lightly spray a medium-sized nonstick skillet with nonstick cooking spray, and arrange the onion on the bottom. Top it with the garlic, cover, and cook over medium heat, without stirring, for 2 to 3 minutes while you prep the remaining veggies.

3. When the veggies are prepped, stir the onions and garlic and top them with first the zucchini, then the mushrooms, and then the dried tomatoes. Quickly pour in the vinegar and basil. Do not stir. Cover the saucepan and cook for a couple of minutes. Stir. If the vegetables are starting to dry out or scorch, add 1 tablespoon of the pasta cooking water. Cover quickly, reduce the heat to low, and allow the vegetables to steam for a minute or until done.

4. To serve, drain the pasta and divide it between 2 bowls. Top the pasta with the cooked vegetables, and scatter the tomatoes and bell pepper around the rim of each bowl. Top with the arugula, and sprinkle the walnuts or pine nuts over all. Serve immediately.

Spring Vegetables with Tomato Cashew Cream

This easy, fast, and yummy pasta bowl is chock-full of vegetables and has a creamy blended sauce. As in the 12-Minute Pasta Bowl (see page 142), you can start cooking the pasta in room-temperature water and prep the veggies while the pasta cooks.

YIELD: 2 servings

1 cup uncooked whole wheat penne, medium shell, or rotini pasta

4 cups water

$1/2$ cup chopped onion

2 cups 1-inch pieces asparagus

1 cup sliced mushrooms

$1/2$ cup frozen peas

Sauce

1 cup coarsely diced tomato (1 medium)

$1/2$ cup unsalted raw cashews

1 clove garlic

$1/8$ teaspoon sea salt

Topping

$1/2$ cup chopped radicchio

$1/3$ cup thin strips (chiffonade) fresh basil

2 teaspoons balsamic vinegar

---

1. Place the pasta in a 2-quart saucepan, and add the water. Turn the heat to high. When the water boils, reduce the heat to medium and cook uncovered, stirring occasionally, for about 10 minutes, or until the pasta is done. (Although this is not the way pasta is usually cooked, it works well and will allow you to focus on prepping the vegetables.)

2. When the pasta goes into the pot, lightly spray a medium-sized nonstick skillet with nonstick cooking spray. Add the onion, cover, and cook over medium heat, without stirring, for about 3 minutes, or until the onion is almost tender.

3. Add the asparagus, mushrooms, and peas to the skillet, and stir to mix. Cover and cook for about 2 minutes. Add a tablespoon of pasta cooking water, cover quickly, and steam for about a minute, or until the veggies are tender-crisp.

4. While the vegetables are cooking, to make the sauce, place the tomato, cashews, garlic, and salt in a blender, and blend until very smooth and creamy. (This works well in a high-speed blender. If using an ordinary blender, you may have to add a little more tomato or a tablespoon or 2 of water to make a smooth sauce.) Set aside.

5. To serve, drain the pasta and divide it between 2 bowls. Top the pasta with the vegetables and a big dollop of the sauce. Scatter the radicchio and basil around the rim of the bowl, and drizzle each bowl with a teaspoon of balsamic vinegar. Serve immediately.

Spinach Chickpea Bowl

This flavorful Mediterranean-style dish makes a nourishing lunch or light dinner and can be thrown together quickly if you have some leftover quinoa in the fridge.

YIELD: 2 servings

½ cup finely chopped onion

2 cloves garlic, thinly sliced

1 tablespoon coconut aminos

6 ounces baby spinach
(about 6 cups lightly packed)

1 teaspoon dried thyme

1 cup cooked or canned chickpeas,
rinsed and drained

2 tablespoons lemon juice

2 cups cooked quinoa

Toppings

½ cup finely chopped red or orange
bell pepper

½ cup diced tomato

3 tablespoons chopped fresh parsley

4 green pitted olives, thinly sliced

1. Spray a medium-sized nonstick skillet with nonstick cooking spray, and add the onion. Top with the garlic, cover, and cook over medium heat, without stirring, for 2 to 3 minutes. Stir in the coconut aminos, cover quickly, and cook for another minute.

2. Top the onion mixture with the spinach and thyme (do not stir), cover, and cook for another minute or 2, or until the spinach has wilted.

3. Add the chickpeas to the skillet, cover quickly, and cook for a minute or 2 to heat the chickpeas and blend the flavors. Remove the skillet from the heat and stir in the lemon juice, mixing all the ingredients well.

4. While the veggies are cooking, reheat the quinoa in a medium-sized saucepan: Place the quinoa in the pan with 2 to 3 tablespoons of water, cover, and cook over medium heat for a couple of minutes, or until the pan is full of steam and the quinoa is hot.

5. To serve, divide the steaming hot quinoa between 2 bowls and top with the spinach-chickpea mixture. Scatter the bell pepper and tomato around the rim of each bowl. Top with the parsley and olives, and serve immediately.

Barley Broccoli Bowl

Barley—which is rich in nutrients and relatively low in fat and calories— goes beautifully with mushrooms and walnuts. We added broccoli and a flavorful vinaigrette to make this an especially tasty and nutritious dish.

YIELD: 2 servings

1 pound broccoli, stems peeled and chopped, and tops in bite-sized florets

1 1/2 cups sliced mushrooms

2 cups cooked barley

Vinaigrette

2 teaspoons red miso

1/3 cup water

1/3 cup nutritional yeast

1 tablespoon Dijon-style mustard

1 teaspoon dried tarragon

1 clove garlic, pressed

Toppings

1/2 cup halved cherry tomatoes

1/2 cup roasted unsalted walnuts

1 scallion, chopped

1. Steam the broccoli for 3 to 4 minutes, or until nearly tender. Add the mushrooms, and steam for another couple of minutes, or until the mushrooms and broccoli are cooked. If there is any leftover water in the pot, set it aside to make the vinaigrette.

2. While the vegetables are cooking, reheat the barley in a medium-sized saucepan: Place the barley in the pan with 2 to 3 tablespoons of water, cover, and cook over medium heat for a couple of minutes, or until the pan is full of steam and the barley is hot.

3. To make the vinaigrette, place the miso in a small bowl and slowly stir in the water to dissolve the miso. Add the remaining ingredients, and mix well.

4. To serve, divide the hot barley between 2 bowls, and top the grain with the steamed broccoli and mushroom mixture. Scatter the cherry tomatoes around the rim of the bowl, and sprinkle the walnuts and scallions over all. To complete the dish, spoon a couple of tablespoons of vinaigrette over each bowl, reserving the rest to use over salad or steamed veggies, and serve immediately.

Quinoa and Sweet Potato Bowl

*This hearty, satisfying bowl packs a big nutritional punch, with generous servings
of Swiss chard and walnuts along with nutrient-packed sweet potato. Pay attention
to how you cut the potato, because if the pieces are too small, they will form
a purée, and if they are too large, they won't cook through.*

YIELD: 2 servings

$\frac{1}{2}$ cup uncooked quinoa

1 cup water

1 medium sweet potato, scrubbed and
cut into $1\frac{1}{2}$-inch to 2-inch chunks
(about $2\frac{1}{2}$ cups)

2 bay leaves

2 tablespoons balsamic vinegar

1 tablespoon mirin or white wine

1 tablespoon coconut aminos

$\frac{1}{2}$ cup chopped onion

6 cups coarsely chopped Swiss chard
(about 12 ounces)

$\frac{1}{3}$ cup coarsely chopped unsalted
raw walnuts

1. Rinse the quinoa and place it in a 2-quart pot with the water, sweet potato, and bay leaves.
   Bring to a boil over high heat. Then reduce the heat to low, cover, and cook at a simmer,
   without stirring, for 15 to 20 minutes, or until the sweet potatoes are soft and the water has
   been absorbed. Stir carefully to avoid breaking up the sweet potato. You want chunks of
   potato rather than mashed potato.

2. While the sweet potato is cooking, place the vinegar, mirin or white wine, coconut aminos, and
   onion in a large nonstick or cast-iron skillet. Cover and bring to a sizzle over medium-high
   heat. Stir, reduce the heat to a simmer, and cook covered for a couple of minutes.

3. Add the chard to the skillet, cover, and cook over medium heat, stirring occasionally, for about
   5 minutes, or until the chard is tender.

4. To serve, carefully spoon the quinoa mixture into 2 bowls. Top it with the chard, and scatter the
   walnuts around the rim of the bowl. Enjoy!

Quinoa, Kale, and Carrot Bowl

Health-conscious people often try to sneak small amounts of kale into juices, smoothies, salads, and stir-fries. But if you cook kale well, you will want to eat it in larger amounts—which is great, because kale is so good for you! This dish provides a hearty portion of kale along with quinoa, carrots, and other savory ingredients. Note that the recipe makes use of the vegetable cooking liquid so that you won't lose out on valuable minerals.

YIELD: 2 servings

12 ounces kale, washed and finely chopped (about 5 cups)

1 cup water

2 medium carrots, scrubbed and sliced into $1/_2$-inch rounds

$1^1/_2$ cups cooked quinoa

1 recipe Tahini Yeast Sauce (see page 78), prepared with the vegetable cooking water (see Step 4)

2 tablespoons balsamic vinegar

12 cherry tomatoes, halved

1 scallion, chopped

1. Place the kale in a large heavy pot with a tight-fitting lid. Add the water, and bring to a simmer over high heat.

2. When the pan fills up with steam, turn the heat to low, cover, and cook for about 20 minutes. Add the carrots and continue to cook for about 20 minutes, or until the kale and carrots are tender. The cooking time will vary depending on the age of the kale and how finely it is chopped.

3. While the vegetables are cooking, reheat the quinoa in a medium-sized saucepan: Place the quinoa in a pan with 2 to 3 tablespoons of water, cover, and cook over medium heat for a couple of minutes, or until the pan is full of steam and the quinoa is hot.

4. When the kale is done, drain off and reserve the cooking liquid, and either pour some off or add more water to make $3/_4$ cup liquid. Use this to make the Tahini Yeast Sauce. Stir the balsamic vinegar into the sauce.

5. To serve, divide the hot quinoa between 2 bowls. Top with first the cooked vegetables and then the sauce, reserving any leftover sauce for another purpose. Scatter the tomatoes around the edge of the bowl, top with the chopped scallions, and serve immediately.

Variation

■ To make Quinoa, Kale, and Carrot Bowl more quickly, prepare the vegetables in a pressure cooker. Bring the pressure cooker up to pressure; then let the pressure cool down naturally. This should take less than 10 minutes from start to finish, and the kale will be delicious.

Buckwheat Bowl

One of our favorite bowls, this dish combines toasted buckwheat, potatoes, freshly chopped veggies, and walnuts with a delicious dressing. Deeply satisfying, our Buckwheat Bowl is quick to make and a delight to eat!

YIELD: 2 generous servings

1/2 cup chopped onion

2 cups red potatoes diced into 1/2-inch to 3/4-inch cubes (4 medium-small)

1 teaspoon Herbes de Provence herb blend

1/2 cup uncooked toasted buckwheat groats (also called kasha)

1 cup boiling water

Dressing

1 teaspoon red miso

1/2 teaspoon toasted sesame oil

1/4 cup water

1/4 cup nutritional yeast

1 or 2 cloves garlic, pressed

Topping

2 cups finely chopped curly endive

1 cup cucumber diced into 1/2-inch to 3/4-inch cubes

1 scallion, chopped

1/2 cup chopped unsalted walnuts

1. Spray a large nonstick skillet with nonstick cooking spray. Add the onion and sauté over medium heat for a couple of minutes. Stir in the potatoes and herbs, and cook for another minute or 2, or until the onions start to become translucent.

2. Add the buckwheat groats to the skillet, and stir for another minute or until they are good and hot.

3. Reduce the heat to low, and pour the boiling water into the skillet, being careful not to burn yourself with the steam. Quickly cover; no need to stir.

4. Simmer the buckwheat mixture over low heat without stirring for about 10 minutes. Then remove the skillet from the heat and allow it to sit covered for about 2 minutes. Stir.

5. While the buckwheat is cooking, make the dressing by placing the miso and sesame oil in a small bowl and mixing well. Slowly stir in the water; then add the yeast and garlic. Mix well and set aside.

6. To serve, divide the buckwheat-potato mixture between 2 bowls. Scatter the endive and cucumber around the rim of the bowl, top with the scallions and walnuts, and drizzle the dressing over all. Serve immediately.

10.

Soups and Stews

Soups are truly the ultimate comfort food. Warm and soothing, they fill the house with fabulous aromas as they simmer on the stove, and delight the senses when served steaming in bowls. They also lend themselves beautifully to whole food plant-based cooking. Who doesn't love a thick and smoky split pea soup? If you're worried that your creations will be lacking in flavor because there is no meat or meat stock, worry no more. In addition to veggies, beans, and other naturally tasty foods, our soups are wonderfully seasoned with herbs and spices, miso, balsamic vinegar, and other wholesome ingredients. No one will miss the meat!

In the following pages, you'll find a variety of both soups and stews. Smoky Split Pea and Sweet Potato Soup is hearty fare that owes its distinctive flavor to liquid smoke. Garden Vegetable Soup is chock full of chunky vegetables and brimming with garden-fresh taste. Collard Green Cream is a smooth and creamy dish that provides a wonderful way to eat (and love) your dark leafy greens. For those times when it's just too hot to sit down to a steaming dish of soup, we've included two chilled soups: Avocado Vichyssoise, which we think is even better than the traditional cream-filled soup; and Juicer Gazpacho, a fresh-tasting tomato-based soup. Our stews include Lentil Swiss Chard Stew; and Butternut Squash, Kale, and Black Bean Stew. Serve them in a bowl, or ladle them over your favorite grain. Either way, they will nourish your soul as they feed your body.

You may already know that soup making allows you to be creative—and to clean out the refrigerator. If you don't like one of the vegetables listed in a recipe, feel free to substitute another. If you have some leftover beans, quinoa, or rice on hand, toss it into the soup pot. It's sure to add both flavor and nutrition. If the finished soup isn't quite as thick as you'd prefer, take out some of the veggies and liquid, blend the mixture into a purée, and return it to the pot. Cashews blended until creamy with cooking liquid or vegan milk will also thicken the soup, as will leftover mashed potatoes or butternut squash. The possibilities are both endless and delicious.

Old-Fashioned Bean Soup

Thick and hearty, this soup makes a meal that is both satisfying and inexpensive when paired with a big green salad and Mama's Cornbread (see page 172) or Millet Skillet Bread (see page 171).

YIELD: 6—8 servings

1 pound dried Great Northern beans, picked over and rinsed	1 cup chopped onion (1 medium)
	3 tablespoons balsamic or apple cider vinegar
6 cups water	2 heaping tablespoons chopped fresh rosemary
5 bay leaves	
2 cups sliced carrots (3–4 medium)	1 tablespoon red miso
1¹/₂ cups sliced celery (3 medium)	¹/₄ cup dulse flakes
1¹/₂ cups tomato purée	Pinch of cayenne pepper (optional)

1. Place the beans in a large bowl, and add water to cover by at least 2 inches. Allow to soak at room temperature for 8 to 10 hours. Drain and discard the soaking water.

2. Transfer the soaked beans to a large heavy pot, and add the water and bay leaves. Bring to a boil over high heat. Then reduce the heat to low, cover, and cook at a simmer, stirring occasionally, for about 1 hour.

3. Add the carrots, celery, tomato purée, onion, vinegar, and rosemary to the pot of beans, stirring to combine. Return the mixture to a boil. Then cover the pot, lower the heat, and cook the soup at a simmer, stirring occasionally, for about 30 minutes, or until the beans and vegetables are tender.

4. Ladle a little soup into a cup and add the miso, stirring to dissolve. Return the soup to the pot, and stir in the dulse flakes and cayenne, if using. Ladle into bowls, and serve hot.

Smoky Split Pea and Sweet Potato Soup

Everyone will want to know the secret ingredients in this easy-to-make soup, and they're really so simple: White pepper gives the dish just a bit of heat, and liquid smoke imparts the smoky flavor we like without the carcinogens associated with charbroiling. We enjoy this soup most when the addition of the sweet potatoes is timed so that they cook through but don't break down. Add them too early or dice them too small, and they will become a purée. Then again, if you like purées, additional cooking of the soup will give you the consistency you prefer.

YIELD: 6 servings

2 cups green split peas, picked over and rinsed	2 medium sweet potatoes, peeled and diced into $1\frac{1}{2}$-inch cubes
6 cups water	2 teaspoons liquid smoke
4–5 bay leaves	2 tablespoons chickpea miso
$1\frac{1}{2}$ cups chopped onion (1 large)	$\frac{1}{2}$ teaspoon ground white pepper, or to taste

1. Place the split peas in a large heavy pot. Add the water and bay leaves, and bring to a boil over high heat. Reduce the heat to low, cover, and cook at a simmer, stirring occasionally, for 20 to 25 minutes.

2. Add the onion, sweet potatoes, and liquid smoke to the pot. Return the soup to a boil. Then reduce the heat, cover, and simmer, stirring occasionally, for another 25 minutes, or until the split peas form a purée and the sweet potatoes are tender when pierced with a fork.

3. Ladle a little soup into a cup and add the miso, stirring to dissolve. Return the soup to the pot. Add the white pepper to taste, and ladle into bowls to serve hot.

Helpful Tip

Sometimes, a batch of split peas or other beans remains hard or will not break down no matter how much you cook them. This means that they are old. When this happens, use a blender to turn the peas or beans into a purée.

Garden Vegetable Soup

*This classic vegetable soup is satisfying because it is thick like a stew
and chock full of chunky veggies. Feel free to eat large servings
because it is as good for you as it is delicious!*

YIELD: 8–10 servings

3 cups chopped cabbage	2 tablespoons balsamic vinegar
2 cups diced zucchini or yellow squash	3 stems (6 inches each) fresh rosemary
1½ cups diced potatoes	4 bay leaves
1 cup chopped onion (1 medium)	1 teaspoon dried basil
1 cup 1-inch pieces green beans	1½ cups cooked or canned white or pinto beans, rinsed and drained
1 cup chopped celery (2–3 medium)	
1 cup sliced carrots (1–2 medium)	2 cups fresh or frozen corn kernels
24-ounce jar or can unsalted tomato purée	2 tablespoons white miso
3 cups water	Ground black pepper to taste

1. Combine the cabbage, squash, potatoes, onion, green beans, celery, carrots, tomato purée, water, and vinegar in a large heavy pot. Bring to a boil over high heat. Then reduce the heat to low, cover, and cook at a simmer for about 20 minutes.

2. Add the rosemary sprigs, bay leaves, and basil to the pot, and simmer for about 10 additional minutes. Then add the beans and corn, and cook for another 5 minutes, or until the vegetables are tender.

3. Ladle a little soup into a cup and add the miso, stirring to dissolve. Return the soup to the pot. Add pepper to taste, ladle into bowls, and serve hot.

Helpful Tip

This soup contains a long list of ingredients, but we consider it a clean-out-the-refrigerator kind of recipe, because it is so versatile. The tomatoes, of course, are important, but if you are missing one of the other vegetables or simply don't like it, leave it out or substitute something else. It is also easy to cut the recipe in half if you're feeding only a few people. Another option is to make the full amount and store leftovers in the fridge for 3 to 4 days, or in the freezer for several months.

Butternut Squash, Kale, and Black Bean Stew

Consider this a thick soup to eat from a bowl, or a stew to enjoy over quinoa, rice, or another grain. This hearty dish can also be thinned down with more water and tomato purée to make a "soupier" soup.

YIELD: 6–8 servings

1 medium-large butternut squash (about 2^1/$_2$ pounds)

12 ounces kale, finely chopped (about 5^1/$_2$ cups)

1^1/$_2$ cups chopped onion (1 large)

1^1/$_2$ cups chopped celery (3 medium)

3 cups water

4 bay leaves

1^1/$_2$ cups tomato purée

15-ounce can black beans, rinsed and drained

1 tablespoon smoked paprika

2 teaspoons ground cumin

2 teaspoons dried basil

^{1}/$_4$ teaspoon ground chipotle or a pinch of cayenne, or to taste

1. Preheat the oven to 375°F. While the oven is heating, pierce the squash with a knife and place it on a baking sheet.

2. Bake the squash for 1 hour, or until soft when pierced with a fork. Allow to cool until easy to handle. Then cut the squash in half, scoop out the seeds and stringy parts, remove the peel, and either dice or mash the flesh, depending on how soft it is. Set aside.

3. In a large heavy pot, combine the kale, onion, celery, water, and bay leaves. Bring to a boil over high heat. Reduce the heat to low, cover, and cook at a simmer, stirring occasionally, for 30 to 40 minutes, or until the vegetables are tender.

4. Add the tomato purée, black beans, smoked paprika, cumin, basil, and the reserved squash to the pot, and stir to combine. Simmer for another 10 minutes or so to blend the flavors. Add the chipotle or cayenne, ladle into bowls, and serve hot.

Avocado Vichyssoise

We think this vegan version of vichyssoise is better than the traditional cold soup made with cream! Try it in the summer or whenever you have some leftover potatoes.

YIELD: 4–6 servings

3 cups unsweetened soy, nut, or seed milk	$2/3$ cup chilled water or unsalted vegetable broth, or more as needed
2 cups unseasoned mashed potatoes, chilled	$1/3$ cup minced fresh chives
1 cup mashed avocado (2–3 small)	$1/4$ teaspoon ground white pepper, or more to taste
1 tablespoon chickpea miso	1 medium cucumber, grated

1. Place the milk, potatoes, avocado, and miso in a blender or food processor, and blend until smooth. Do this in two batches, if necessary. Transfer to a large bowl.

2. Stir the chilled water or broth into the potato mixture until you reach the desired consistency. Then stir in the chives and pepper.

3. Ladle the soup into serving bowls, top with the grated cucumber, and serve cold.

Collard Green Cream

Everybody seems to love this easy-to-make soup, and it's such a delicious way to eat your dark green leafy vegetables.

YIELD: 8 servings

6 cups diced potatoes (about 2 pounds)	1 teaspoon dried tarragon
6 cups chopped collard greens (about 1 pound)	$1/2$ teaspoon ground white pepper (optional)
$1^1/2$ cups chopped onion (1 large)	2 cups unsweetened soy, nut, or seed milk
3 cups water or unsalted vegetable broth	2 tablespoons chickpea miso

1. Combine the potatoes, collards, onion, and water or broth in a large heavy pot. Bring to a boil over high heat. Then reduce the heat to low, cover, and cook at a simmer for about 20 minutes.

2. Add the tarragon to the pot, and continue to simmer for another 10 minutes, or until the vegetables are tender.

3. Remove the pot from the heat, and stir in the pepper, if using, and the milk and miso.

4. Transfer the cooked vegetables and liquid to a blender or food processor, and process—in batches, if necessary—until very smooth and creamy. Each time you blend a batch, transfer it to another pot or a serving tureen.

5. Ladle into bowls, and serve immediately. If the soup needs reheating, to preserve the probiotic qualities of the miso, heat it gently and remove it from the heat before it simmers.

Variation

■ Substitute kale for the collard greens.

Juicer Gazpacho

If you have a juicer, it can be used for more than just making beverages. Some people have said that this is the best gazpacho they ever tasted, and that's not surprising because the addition of carrot juice sweetens the tomatoes and gives it a wonderful flavor. The trick is to keep the ingredients chilled and to serve the soup as soon as possible after it's made. For best flavor, use fully ripe in-season tomatoes.

YIELD: 6 servings	
4 medium tomatoes, cored (enough for 2 cups juice)	1/2 green bell pepper, very finely chopped
3 cloves garlic	1 tablespoon red wine vinegar
4 medium-large carrots (enough for 2 cups juice)	1 tablespoon coconut aminos (optional)
1 medium cucumber, grated	2 tablespoons chopped fresh basil, or 1 teaspoon dried

1. Run the tomatoes through the juicer. Transfer both the tomato juice and the pulp to a bowl.

2. Run the garlic through the juicer; then juice the carrots. Add the carrot-garlic juice to the bowl, discarding the pulp.

3. Add all of the remaining ingredients to the bowl, and mix well. Ladle into bowls, and serve cold.

Lentil Swiss Chard Stew

This hearty dish is a stew, to be served either in a bowl or over a bed of your favorite grain. If you want a soup, just add a little more water. Either way, it makes a delicious, warming meal when served with some whole grain bread and a salad.

YIELD: 6 servings

1½ cups uncooked brown or green lentils, picked over and rinsed

4½ cups water

½ cup red wine or water

1½ cups chopped onion (1 large)

1½ cups sliced celery (3 medium))

1½ cups sliced carrots (2–3 medium)

1 pound Swiss chard, coarsely chopped (about 6 cups)

3 tablespoons balsamic vinegar

1 heaping tablespoon chopped fresh rosemary

¼ cup dulse flakes

Freshly ground black pepper to taste

1. Place the lentils, water, and wine in a large heavy pot, stirring to combine. Bring to a boil over high heat. Then reduce the heat to low, cover, and cook at a simmer for about 20 minutes, stirring occasionally.

2. Add the onion, celery, and carrots to the pot, stirring to combine. Return to a boil. Then cover, reduce the heat, and simmer for another 15 minutes. Add the chard, vinegar, and rosemary, and simmer for 10 additional minutes, or until all the vegetables are tender.

3. Stir in the dulse flakes and black pepper to taste, ladle into bowls, and serve hot.

An Onion a Day

Have you ever heard anyone say that an onion a day keeps the doctor away? While you most likely haven't, this statement is not far from the truth. Onions are one of the healthiest foods available. Rich in vitamins and minerals, fiber, sulphuric compounds, and disease-preventive substances known as phytochemicals, onions help improve the health of the beneficial bacteria in your gut, enabling you to better fight infection; improve blood flow; and fight cancer cell growth.

Hearty Potato Kale Soup

This soup provides plenty of comforting nourishment on a cold winter's day.
If you can't find kohlrabi, which may not always be available at your local market,
leave it out or replace it with an equal amount of chopped celery.

YIELD: 6 servings

6 cups diced potatoes (about 2 pounds)

8 ounces kale, finely chopped (about 3 1/2 cups)

3 medium carrots, sliced (about 2 cups)

1 cup chopped onion (1 medium)

1 medium kohlrabi, diced (about 1 1/2 cups) (optional)

1 tablespoon chopped fresh rosemary

1 teaspoon ground turmeric

1 teaspoon dried thyme

1 teaspoon dried basil

4 bay leaves

2 1/2 cups water

3 cups unsweetened soy, nut, or seed milk, divided

1/4 cup whole unsalted raw cashews

1/3 cup dulse flakes

Pinch of cayenne pepper (optional)

Chopped fresh parsley or chives for garnish

1. Place the potatoes, kale, carrots, onion, and kohlrabi, if using, in a large heavy pot. Add the rosemary, turmeric, thyme, basil, and bay leaves, and pour the water over all.

2. Bring the potato-kale mixture to a boil over high heat. Then reduce the heat to low, cover, and cook at a simmer, stirring occasionally, for 15 to 20 minutes, or until the vegetables are tender.

3. Place half of the milk and all of the cashews in a blender. Add a ladle-full of the cooked vegetables, and blend until completely smooth and creamy.

4. Add the rest of the milk, the blended mixture, and the dulse to the pot. Add the cayenne, if desired, and mix well. Ladle into bowls, garnish with the parsley or chives, and serve immediately.

Garlic Miso Soup

We consider this dish a plant-based chicken soup, because it's warming and comforting when you're fighting off a cold. The trick to having delicious results is cooking the soup slowly. Don't omit the teaspoon of toasted sesame seed oil. This tiny bit of oil adds wonderful flavor.

YIELD: 6 servings

1 cup sliced shallots	3½ cups finely chopped kale (about 8 ounces)
2 heads garlic, peeled and thinly sliced (about ⅓ to ½ cup)	5 cups water or unsalted vegetable broth
2 tablespoons water	2 cups diced potatoes (about 12 ounces)
1 tablespoon coconut aminos	1–2 teaspoons dried thyme, or to taste
1 teaspoon toasted sesame oil	1 tablespoon apple cider vinegar
4 bay leaves	1 tablespoon red miso
	Pinch of cayenne pepper, or to taste

1. Combine the shallots, garlic, water, coconut aminos, toasted sesame oil, and bay leaves in a large heavy pot. Cover and cook over low heat, stirring occasionally, for about 15 minutes.

2. Stir the pot. Then add the kale without stirring. The moisture from the kale will keep the shallots and garlic from scorching. Cook covered for another 15 minutes.

3. Add the water or broth, potatoes, and thyme to the pot. Raise the heat to high, and bring to a boil. Reduce the heat to a simmer, cover, and cook until the potatoes and kale are tender. Stir in the vinegar, and remove the pot from the heat.

4. Ladle a little soup into a cup and add the miso, stirring to dissolve. Return the soup to the pot. Add a pinch of cayenne and mix well. Ladle into bowls, and serve hot.

11.

Side Dishes

When they're chosen with care, side dishes complete a whole foods meal, offering not only nutrition but also colors, textures, and flavors that complement the main dish, elevating your fare from mundane to marvelous. Because sides traditionally have been used to add vegetables, grains, legumes, and other plant-based foods to the diet, they naturally lend themselves to your healthy new eating plan, giving you an endless number of ways to add nourishing foods and great taste to your meals.

This chapter provides a diverse collection of delectable side dishes based on whole grains, dark greens, luscious legumes, and vibrant vegetables. No boring sides here; these dishes add not just nutrition but also pizzazz to your meals. Yes, you'll find healthier ways to make old favorites, but you're also likely to find taste combinations that are new to you and your family. Butternut squash is often prepared with sweeteners and sweet spices, but Baked Butternut Squash with Garlic and Miso offers a savory take on this popular vegetable, providing a very different—and truly delicious—flavor. You may have enjoyed Brussels sprouts steamed or sautéed, but did you ever have them simmered with fresh tomato, onion, garlic, and herbs? We think you'll approve. In Rutabaga and Sweet Potato Casserole, the rutabaga holds its shape while the sweet potato cooks into a luscious purée, providing a marvelous contrast of textures. And Broiled Endives takes a vegetable usually served in raw form and, with very little effort, transforms it into a tempting cooked dish. Other options include Baked Italian Rice with Garlic and Herbs, BBQ Beans, Soul Food Greens, Mirin-Braised Zucchini and Peppers, Cauliflower-Leek Mock Mashed Potatoes, and more. We even present two easy-to-prepare breads—Millet Skillet Bread, and Mama's Cornbread—that will be more than welcome at your dining table. Throughout this chapter, we offer tips on pairing sides with plant-based main dishes and on varying both ingredients and cooking methods to suit your tastes and your available time.

Sides are an essential part of any balanced diet. We know that our sensational sides will help you make all of your meals healthier, tastier, and wonderfully satisfying.

BBQ Beans

It always pays to make a couple of sauces or toppings and have them on hand for speedy meal preparation. If you have Oven-Caramelized Onions (see page 86) and Easy BBQ Sauce (see page 78) in your fridge, you can stir them into a can of beans for a fast dish of comfort food that won't blow your diet. Try BBQ Beans with a green salad and some rice or cornbread for a "down home" kind of meal.

YIELD: 3 servings

1¹/₂ cups cooked or canned Great Northern beans, rinsed and drained

¹/₄ cup Easy BBQ Sauce (see page 78)

¹/₄ cup Oven-Caramelized Onions (see page 86)

1. Place the beans, sauce, and onions in a medium-sized saucepan, stirring to combine.
2. Cook the beans over medium heat, stirring often to prevent sticking, until hot. If the mixture gets too dry, add a tablespoon or 2 of water. Serve immediately.

Baked Italian Rice with Garlic and Herbs

If you want something that has a little more pizzazz than plain rice but is still easy to make, try this. It is delicious served with Dandelion Greens with White Beans (see page 125).

YIELD: 4 servings

1 cup uncooked brown rice, rinsed and drained

3 tablespoons sun-dried tomatoes (no oil) cut into small pieces

6 cloves garlic, cut into slivers

3 bay leaves

1 teaspoon dried basil

¹/₂ teaspoon dried thyme

¹/₂ teaspoon dried oregano

Pinch saffron (optional)

2 cups boiling water

¹/₂ cup diced fresh tomato

Chopped fresh parsley or chives for garnish

1. Preheat the oven to 375°F.

2. Combine the rice, sun-dried tomatoes, garlic, bay leaves, basil, thyme, oregano, and saffron, if using, in a 2-quart baking dish. Stir to mix.

3. Pour the boiling water over the rice and herb mixture. Cover immediately and place on the middle rack of the oven. Bake for 30 minutes without stirring.

4. Quickly remove the cover of the baking dish, and top the rice mixture with the fresh tomato. Cover and bake for another 15 minutes, or until the water has been absorbed. Fluff the rice, garnish with the chopped parsley or chives, and serve hot.

Beets with Tops

When you can find beets with fresh and abundant tops, cook them together in one pot. The liquid from the tops will cook the beets without adding extra water, which makes the dish tastier and more nutritious because you don't end up draining off the nutrients and flavor along with the water.

YIELD: 4 to 6 servings

2 pounds beets with tops	1 tablespoon coconut aminos
2 tablespoons balsamic vinegar	1 teaspoon dried tarragon

1. Wash and coarsely chop the tops of the beets. Scrub and thinly slice the bulbs.

2. Place the vinegar and coconut aminos in a large heavy pot with a well-fitting lid. Place the chopped beet tops on the bottom of the pan, and arrange the sliced beet root over the tops. Do not stir. Sprinkle with the tarragon.

3. Cover the pot and place it over medium heat. When it gets hot and full of steam, usually after 3 or 4 minutes, turn the heat to low. Cook at a simmer without stirring for about 25 minutes, or until the beets are tender. You can quickly remove the cover to check the beets after 15 to 20 minutes to make sure they do not need liquid. If they appear to be scorching, add a couple of tablespoons water, but this probably will not be necessary. Mix the greens and sliced beets together before serving hot.

Soul Food Greens

Kale, collard greens, mustard greens, and turnip greens have always been a staple in Southern cooking because they are easy to grow and so nutritious. Traditionally, they are prepared with loads of pork fat and salt—not a healthy option. Instead, we cook them just until tender with onion, balsamic vinegar, and other flavorful ingredients. The result is a thoroughly enjoyable side dish that provides a bounty of vitamins and minerals.

YIELD: 4 servings

1 pound greens (collard, kale, turnip, or mustard)	1 teaspoon liquid smoke
1 large onion, chopped	1 cup stemmed, thinly sliced shiitake mushrooms
2 tablespoons balsamic vinegar	1 teaspoon dried tarragon
1 tablespoon coconut aminos	

1. Wash the greens by filling up a sink with water. Immerse the greens, swish them around, remove them from the water, and place them in a colander. Do this one to three times, until the water that remains in the sink is clear. (The number of rinses needed will depend on the type of greens and how dirty they are. Turnip greens seem to need the most rinsing, and can benefit from 5 minutes of soaking before draining.)

2. Remove the stems from large collard, turnip, and kale greens only. To chop the greens, stack 4 or 5 washed leaves and roll them up lengthwise. Make a slit lengthwise down the middle; then chop crosswise. If you are using the stems, chop them finely. Set aside. (See the inset on page 163.)

3. Spray a large heavy pan with nonstick cooking spray, and place the onions in the pan. Add the vinegar, coconut aminos, liquid smoke, and reserved chopped greens without stirring. Cover and cook over low heat for about 30 minutes. If at any time it starts to smell as if the onions are scorching, add about 1/2 cup water and stir. (If the pan is heavy and the lid is tight-fitting, you will probably not need to add water, especially when cooking mustard greens. Do not stir unless the vegetables begin to scorch.)

4. Stir the greens, and add the mushrooms and tarragon. Cover and continue to cook, stirring occasionally, until tender. This can take anywhere from 5 to 15 minutes, depending on the age of the greens. Serve with Mama's Cornbread (see page 172) and beans while you listen to the Delta blues. Store any leftovers in a covered container for 3 or 4 days.

Variations

■ Instead of slow-cooking the greens in a covered pan, try pressure-cooking them. Simply follow this recipe by combining all the ingredients except for the tarragon and mushrooms in a pressure cooker. Bring the pressure cooker up to pressure; then let the pressure cool down naturally. Add the tarragon and mushrooms, cover, and cook for another minute or so, just long enough to cook the mushrooms and soften the tarragon.

■ Instead of slow-cooking the greens in a pan, steam them. Most recipes steam greens for such a short time that they are leathery. Be sure to cook yours until they are tender, from 30 to 45 minutes, depending on the greens. Then toss them with a vinaigrette and serve.

Helpful Tip

Turnip greens rival kale in most nutrients, and are even higher in calcium. Seasonally, they are available at farmers markets and can often be purchased at a bargain because today, few people know how to use them. Turnip roots can be added to their tops and cooked together. Just wash the roots well, slice them, and place them on top of the onions in Step 3 of the recipe.

Cleaning and Cutting Leafy Greens

It is important to wash leafy greens—kale, collards, mustard greens, spinach, Swiss chard, beet tops, and turnip greens, as well as all lettuce varieties—to remove any dirt, grit, or sand. Place the greens in a bowl or the sink, fill with cool water, then swish them around. Remove the leaves, drain the water, and repeat. Three washing like this should clean even the grittiest of greens.

When chopping coarse large-leafed greens like collards and mustard greens, I usually stack four or five of the washed leaves and roll them up lengthwise. I then cut through the bunch vertically down the center, slice the leaves crosswise (usually at 1/4– to 1-inch intervals), and finely chop the stems. If the stems are very large and tough, which does not happen often, I remove and discard them. Keep in mind that the finer you cut coarse greens, such as collard and kale, the quicker they will cook. It is also important to remember that they will dramatically reduce in volume as they cook, so be sure to make enough!

Chopping Large-Leafed Greens

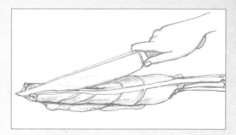

1. Cut the rolled-up leaves down the center.

2. Slice the leaves crosswise.

Southern-Style Beans

Beans and greens paired with cornbread, grits, or rice make a wonderfully nutritious meal. The trick to preparing delicious beans is to cook them slowly, until a thick gravy forms from their cooking water. In the American South, they use pinto beans, Great Northern beans, or black-eyed peas, but if you go a little further south to Cuba, black beans are cooked in a similar manner with great results. Cooking a strip of kombu seaweed in the pot is said to enhance not only the digestibility and flavor of the beans, but also their nutrient value.

YIELD: 6 servings

2 cups dried pinto beans, picked over and rinsed

6 cups water, or as needed

6-inch strip kombu seaweed

1 medium onion, chopped

6 bay leaves

2 tablespoons coconut aminos

1–2 tablespoons balsamic vinegar, or to taste

2 teaspoons ground cumin

2–3 cloves garlic, pressed

Freshly ground black, chipotle, or cayenne pepper to taste

1 teaspoon liquid smoke, or 2 teaspoons smoked paprika (optional)

Chopped scallions for garnish

1. Place the beans in a large bowl, and add water to cover by at least 2 inches. Allow to soak at room temperature for 8 to 10 hours. Drain and discard the soaking water.

2. Place the beans, the 6 cups water, and the kombu in a large heavy pot. Bring to a boil over high heat. Then cover, reduce the heat to low, and cook at a simmer, stirring occasionally, for about 1 hour.

3. Add the onion, bay leaves, coconut aminos, vinegar, and cumin to the pot, and continue to cook, stirring occasionally, for another 30 minutes, or until the beans are very tender and the water has turned into a thick gravy. If the beans become too dry, add more water.

4. Once the beans are tender, add the garlic, the pepper of your choice, and liquid smoke or paprika. Transfer the beans to a serving bowl, top with the scallions, and serve hot.

Variations

■ Substitute black-eyed peas, black beans, Great Northern beans, or kidney beans for the pinto beans.

■ Shorten cooking time by using a pressure cooker for Step 2. Just bring the machine up to pressure and let it cool down on its own. You may want to reduce the water by a cup so that the dish is not too watery. When the pressure drops, check to see if the beans are done. Most varieties will be if they are fresh. If the beans are not soft, either bring the cooker back to pressure or cook the beans in the usual way. Finish the recipe as written.

Helpful Tip

Try to always buy fresh dried beans. When dried beans get old, you can cook them for what seems like forever without them getting tender. If you buy bagged beans, check the expiration date on the package to make sure the sell-by date hasn't passed. If you buy beans from bins, choose a store with a high turnover rate so that the bins are replenished often.

Baked Butternut Squash with Garlic and Miso

Usually, butternut squash is served with sweetener and sweet spices, but once you taste this savory take on squash, you may prefer it.

YIELD: 4 servings

1 medium to large butternut or other winter squash	2 teaspoons yellow or white miso 1–2 cloves garlic, pressed

---

1. Preheat the oven to 350°F.

2. Pierce the squash with a knife and place it on a baking sheet. Place the sheet on the middle rack of the oven, and bake for about 1 hour, or until the squash is soft and a knife can be easily inserted through the flesh. Allow to cool until easy to handle.

3. Cut the squash in half and discard the seeds and stringy parts. Scrape the flesh out into a large bowl, add the miso and garlic, and mix well. The squash will probably break down into a purée when mixed. If not, mash it with a potato masher until smooth.

4. Serve immediately or, if necessary, reheat in a covered ovenproof dish for 10 to 15 minutes, or until warm. To preserve the probiotic properties of the miso, avoid heating the squash more than necessary.

Helpful Tip

If you end up with leftover squash, stir it into a soup or freeze it for later use.

Rosemary Millet Purée

Think of this mildly flavored grain dish as a sort of soft polenta, but made with millet instead of corn. Top it with vegetables, beans, sauce, or just about anything you like.

YIELD: 2 to 3 servings

½ cup uncooked millet, rinsed and drained

1½ cups water

2 teaspoons coconut aminos

1 tablespoon chopped fresh rosemary

Finely minced fresh parsley for garnish

1. Place all of the ingredients except the parsley in a blender, and blend until smooth.

2. Transfer the blended mixture to a medium-sized saucepan, and bring to a boil while stirring constantly. Cover, reduce the heat to very low, and cook at a simmer, stirring occasionally, for 10 minutes, or until the mixture is thick. Remove the pot from the heat, leaving the cover on. Allow the purée to sit and steam for 3 minutes to prevent it from sticking to the bottom of the saucepan.

3. Transfer the purée to a serving bowl, sprinkle with parsley, and enjoy.

Mirin-Braised Zucchini and Peppers

Here is a fast and colorful side that goes well with any grain, bean, tofu, or tempeh dish.

YIELD: 4 servings

1½ cups sliced onion

2–3 cloves garlic, thinly sliced

2 tablespoons mirin

1 tablespoon rice or cider vinegar

1 tablespoon coconut aminos

2 medium zucchini (about 1¼ pounds), halved lengthwise and sliced

1 medium red bell pepper, sliced in lengthwise strips

1 medium yellow or orange bell pepper, sliced in lengthwise strips

2 teaspoons dried basil

1. Heat a large nonstick skillet over medium heat and spray with nonstick cooking spray. Add the onion, cover, and cook for 2 to 3 minutes, or until the onion begins to sizzle and turn translucent.

2. Stir the onions. Then add the garlic, mirin, vinegar, coconut aminos, zucchini, bell peppers, and basil without stirring. Cover and cook for 3 to 4 minutes over medium-low heat.

3. Stir the vegetables and cook uncovered for another couple of minutes, or until the squash and peppers are done and some of the liquid has reduced. Serve the vegetables hot along with any liquid that remains in the skillet.

Helpful Tip

Mirin is a traditional Japanese sweet cooking wine and a staple of Japanese cuisine. Make sure to buy real mirin, which does not contain sugar or additives. If you don't want to invest in a bottle of mirin, you can use white wine or vegetable broth instead.

Summer Squash with Tomatoes

Prepare this dish with any type of yellow squash, zucchini, or pattypan squash you prefer. Use it as a side or as a topping for pasta, quinoa, or another grain.

YIELD: 4 to 6 servings

1 cup chopped onion	1 tablespoon balsamic vinegar
6 cloves garlic, minced	2 pounds yellow summer squash, pattypan squash, or zucchini, quartered lengthwise and sliced
3–4 bay leaves	
1 teaspoon dried basil	
1 cup chopped ripe tomatoes	$1/3$ cup small pieces sun-dried tomatoes (no oil)

1. Place the onion, garlic, bay leaves, and basil in a large nonstick skillet. Add the chopped tomatoes and vinegar, and top with the squash. Layer the ingredients without stirring.

2. Cover the pan and cook over medium heat for about 5 minutes, or until the pan fills with steam and the vegetables begin to cook.

3. Quickly remove the lid, add the sun-dried tomatoes, and replace the lid. Continue to cook for about 3 more minutes, or until the vegetables are tender. Mix and serve hot.

Rutabaga and Sweet Potato Casserole

*In this dish, the sweet potato breaks down and becomes a purée, while the
rutabaga holds its shape. It is a perfect winter dish, because it's warming
and satisfying and goes beautifully with bean and grain dishes.*

YIELD: 4 servings

1 medium rutabaga, peeled and
cut into 1/2-inch cubes

1 large sweet potato, peeled and
cut into 1-inch cubes

1 cup chopped sweet onion

1 teaspoon dried tarragon

1 cup water

1 tablespoon yellow miso

1. Preheat the oven to 350°F.

2. Place the rutabaga, sweet potato, and onion in a 2-quart casserole dish. Sprinkle with tarragon and add the water.

3. Cover and bake for 45 minutes. Stir the vegetables, then continue to bake, covered, for another 15 to 30 minutes, or until the rutabaga is tender.

4. Remove from the oven and add the miso. Stir until the miso dissolves and the sweet potato becomes puréed. Serve hot.

Broiled Endives

*Belgian endives are delicious raw in salads, but they are also wonderful
when quickly cooked and browned in the oven.*

YIELD: 4 servings

4 medium-sized heads Belgian endives,
halved lengthwise

About 1/2 cup water

1. Preheat the oven to 500°F.

2. Place the endive halves cut side up in a shallow baking dish. Add about ¼ inch water and cover the dish with aluminum foil. Bake for 5 minutes, or until tender.

3. Turn the oven to broil. Remove the foil from the dish, and broil the endives for 3 to 4 minutes, or until the tops are lightly browned. Serve plain or with a little dressing, such as Hempannaise (see page 67).

Brussels Sprouts Simmered with Tomato

This is a wonderfully tasty way to cook Brussels sprouts so that every member of your family will happily benefit from the many nutrients provided by this vegetable, including fiber; vitamins B_1, B_6, C, and K; minerals such as folate, manganese, choline, and copper; and more.

YIELD: 4 servings

1 cup chopped onion	3 bay leaves
3 cloves garlic, minced	1 teaspoon dried basil
1 tablespoon balsamic vinegar	1 large ripe tomato, chopped, or
2 teaspoons coconut aminos	1¼ cups canned tomatoes with juice
	1 pound Brussels sprouts, trimmed

1. Spray a heavy medium-sized pot with a tight-fitting lid with nonstick cooking spray. Add the onion, garlic, vinegar, coconut aminos, bay leaves, basil, tomato, and Brussels sprouts, layering the ingredients without stirring. (Note that you don't have to cut up the tomatoes because they'll break down during cooking.)

2. Cover and cook over medium-low heat without stirring for about 15 minutes, or until the Brussels sprouts are tender. Check the liquid during cooking, and add about ¼ cup water if necessary to keep the vegetables from scorching.

3. Mix the vegetables together, and serve hot.

Cauliflower-Leek Mock Mashed Potatoes

This purée will satisfy any mashed potato craving and is delicious as is or topped with Walnut Gravy (see page 79). The millet gives it a potato-like consistency, so even people who claim not to like cauliflower usually enjoy this creamy dish.

YIELD: 6 servings

1 large cauliflower (1½ to 2 pounds), cut into florets

3 medium leeks, cleaned and chopped (about 6 cups)

½ cup millet, rinsed and drained

2 cups water

1 teaspoon ground turmeric

1 tablespoon chickpea miso

½ teaspoon ground white pepper

Minced fresh parsley or ground paprika for garnish

1. Place the cauliflower, leeks, millet, water, and turmeric in a large heavy pot. Bring to a boil over high heat. Then reduce the heat to low, cover, and cook at a simmer for about 25 minutes, or until the water has been absorbed.

2. Add the miso and pepper to the vegetable mixture, and blend with an immersion blender, in a food processor, or in a high-speed blender to form a purée.

3. Transfer the purée to a serving bowl, sprinkle with parsley or paprika, and enjoy either as is or topped with gravy.

Can Children Thrive on a Whole Food Plant-Based Diet?

Children of all ages can learn to enjoy plant-based meals. Just as important, children thrive on this health-promoting diet. Research has shown that youngsters raised on fruits, vegetables, whole grains, and legumes tend to be slimmer and healthier than those raised on standard western fare, which is usually loaded with fat, sugar, and salt. They have stronger immune systems and get sick less often, have more normal blood sugar levels, live longer, and may actually score better on tests in school. Girls raised on a plant-based diet have a reduced risk of estrogen-sensitive cancers. And as long as children enjoy a varied diet of many different whole foods, they will get all the nutrients they need for proper growth and development. In fact, the American Dietetic Association has confirmed that an appropriately planned plant-based diet is healthful for individuals during all stages of the life cycle, including infancy, childhood, and adolescence.

Millet Skillet Bread

You need a well-seasoned cast-iron skillet for this recipe. This gluten-free bread bakes quickly and has a mild flavor and cornbread-like texture. If you're lucky enough to have leftovers, store them in the refrigerator or freezer and toast before serving.

YIELD: 6 servings

1¼ cups uncooked millet, divided	½ teaspoon baking soda
½ cup garbanzo flour	1 cup unsweetened soy, nut, or seed milk
1 teaspoon baking powder	2 tablespoons apple cider vinegar

1. Preheat the oven to 375°F. Spray the sides and bottom of a well-seasoned 11-inch cast-iron skillet lightly with nonstick cooking spray.

2. Place ¼ cup millet in a blender, and blend the grain to a flour-like consistency. Generously sprinkle the millet flour over the sides and bottom of the skillet to coat.

3. Place the remaining cup of millet in a blender, and blend to a flour-like consistency. Transfer the flour to a large mixing bowl, and stir in the garbanzo flour, baking powder, and baking soda. Be sure to mix well.

4. In a measuring cup or small bowl, combine the milk and vinegar, mixing well. Add the milk mixture to the millet mixture, and combine the ingredients by stirring from the bottom to the top with a folding motion to form a batter. Do not overmix.

5. Spread the batter in the prepared skillet, and bake for 13 to 15 minutes, or until the bread is firm and a toothpick inserted in the center comes out clean. Do not overbake. Slice into wedges and serve hot from the oven.

The Dangers of Dairy

A growing body of research shows an association between the consumption of dairy products—including milk, cheese, butter, and sour cream—and the occurrence of a number of disorders, including irritable bowel syndrome, constipation, acne, breast and ovarian cancer in women, and prostate cancer in men. Soy, nut, and seed milks, as well as the products made from them, are delicious alternatives that come packaged with antioxidants and phytochemicals. (For a discussion of nondairy milk options, see page 18.)

Mama's Cornbread

*Actually better than mama's because it's so much healthier, this cornbread is chock full
of kernels of sweet corn, and doesn't contain any sugar, salt, or fat. Mama would approve!
The garbanzo flour lightens it up, helps it slice without crumbling, and provides protein.
The trick to creating a crisp crust is using a well-seasoned cast-iron skillet
and sprinkling it generously with cornmeal. Leftovers can be sliced,
stored in the refrigerator or freezer, and toasted before serving.*

YIELD: 8 servings

$1\frac{1}{4}$ cups cornmeal, divided

1 cup garbanzo flour

1 teaspoon baking powder

1 teaspoon baking soda

1 cup frozen sweet corn kernels

$1\frac{1}{2}$ cups unsweetened soy, nut, or seed milk

2 tablespoons apple cider vinegar

1. Preheat the oven to 350°F. Spray the sides and bottom of a well-seasoned 11-inch cast-iron skillet lightly with nonstick cooking spray. Then generously sprinkle the skillet with $\frac{1}{4}$ cup cornmeal to coat.

2. Place the remaining cup of cornmeal in a large mixing bowl, and stir in the garbanzo flour, baking powder, and baking soda. Be sure to mix well. Add the corn kernels, and mix again. Set aside.

3. Place the skillet on one of the large burners of the stove, and heat it over medium-low heat.

4. In a measuring cup or small mixing bowl, combine the milk and vinegar, mixing well. Add the milk mixture to the cornmeal mixture, mix just enough to form a batter, and quickly pour it into the heated skillet.

5. Cook the batter on top of the stove for 4 to 5 minutes, or until bubbles start to appear on the surface of the batter. Then transfer the skillet to the top rack of the oven and bake for about 25 minutes, or until the cornbread is firm and a toothpick inserted in the center comes out clean. Slice into wedges and serve hot from the oven, turning the pieces over so that the crispy bottom is on top.

12.

Desserts

Although all of us love dessert, we know that most sweet treats are loaded with fat, sugar, and other ingredients that pose a danger to our health. Although sweet to the tongue, they're bitter to the body. But desserts don't have to be prepared with cream, oils, refined sugar, and the like. They don't have to be unhealthy. In the following pages, we offer over a dozen delights that are nutritionally superior to any that you're likely to find in stores and restaurants, but are still delectable and utterly satisfying.

How do we make desserts so wholesome and yet so yummy? Most of our creations feature whole fruit, complete with all its nutrients, in a starring role. Other ingredients include whole grains like oatmeal; nuts; soy, nut, or seed milk; silken tofu; unsweetened applesauce; and butternut squash; as well as natural flavorings like pure vanilla and cinnamon. Our desserts are sweetened with dates, with raisins, or with small amounts of pure monk fruit powder—just enough to enhance the natural sweetness of the other ingredients. The result is a wide range of offerings, including rich Chocolate Avocado Pudding, Chocolate Walnut Drop

Cookies, refreshing Fruit Sorbet, Iris's Delicious Apple Crisp, Stuffed Figs, Orange Apricot Squares, Better Than Pumpkin Pie, Wholesome Banana Bread, and much more. No one will feel deprived when they dig into these desserts. They are truly luscious.

Although every one of our creations makes a wonderful end-of-meal treat, many can do double duty. Top a slice of Wholesome Banana Bread with nut butter and enjoy it for breakfast, or use Erica's Oatmeal-Raisin Cookies to satisfy midday hunger. These are not "forbidden" pleasures, but real food that you can enjoy—in moderation—without guilt.

We hope that the following collection will inspire experimentation. Our icy Fruit Sorbet can be made with many varieties of fruit, including melon, strawberries, blueberries, papaya, mangos, peas, and peaches. By substituting bananas, you can create Nice Cream, which rivals any soft-serve ice cream. Kanten Fruit Jell can be prepared with your favorite fruit juice, with lemonade, or with hibiscus tea. And our versatile Pecan Pie Crust can be used to hold many different fillings. Be bold, keep your emphasis on healthful ingredients, and enjoy!

Chocolate Avocado Pudding

This rich and creamy pudding makes a delectable special-occasion dessert when spooned into a pretty dish, topped with berries, and garnished with fresh mint leaves. To serve six people rather than four, use more berries per serving. Be sure to choose ripe avocados when preparing this luscious dessert!

YIELD: 4 to 6 servings

1/2 cup firmly packed pitted dates	1/8 teaspoon pure monk fruit powder
3 tablespoons water, if needed	1/3 cup cocoa or cacao powder
2 cups diced avocado (2–3 avocados)	1/4–1 cup sliced fresh strawberries
2 teaspoons vanilla extract	4–6 sprigs mint

1. Place the dates and water in a small saucepan. Cover and cook for 3 to 4 minutes, or until the water is absorbed. If the dates are nice and soft, you can skip this step.

2. Place the cooked dates or soft raw dates in a blender or food processor along with the avocado and vanilla extract, and blend until smooth and creamy. Transfer the blended mixture to a medium-sized bowl.

3. Stir the monk fruit powder and the cocoa or cacao powder into the avocado mixture, mixing well. To serve, divide the pudding evenly among 4 to 6 dessert dishes or stemmed glasses. Top with the strawberries and garnish each dish with a sprig of mint before serving.

Variation

■ To make a lower-glycemic version of Chocolate Avocado Pudding, omit the dates and add an additional 1/8 to 1/4 teaspoon of pure monk fruit powder.

Chocolate Walnut Drop Cookies

These cookies taste a lot like brownies, but they are not too sweet or gooey, and each one is topped with a crunchy walnut half.

YIELD: 40 cookies

1 cup unsalted raw walnut halves

1 cup garbanzo flour

$1/3$ cup cocoa or cacao powder

1 teaspoon baking powder

$1/2$ teaspoon baking soda

$1/2$ teaspoon pure monk fruit powder, or to taste

1 cup firmly packed soft pitted Medjool dates

1 cup unsweetened soy, nut, or seed milk

1 teaspoon vanilla extract

40 unsalted raw walnut halves

---

1. Preheat the oven to 350°F. Prepare two cookie sheets by spraying them lightly with nonstick cooking spray and sprinkling them generously with flour. Set aside.

2. Place the cup of walnuts in a blender or food processor and grind to a flour. Transfer to a mixing bowl. (Make sure to grind the nuts first so the blender or food processor is not wet. If you are using a food processor and the quantity of nuts is not large enough to easily grind, add the flour to the food processor for more bulk.)

3. Add the garbanzo flour, cocoa or cacao powder, baking powder, baking soda, and monk fruit powder to the ground walnuts. Mix well and set aside.

4. In a blender or food processor, combine the dates, milk, and vanilla extract. Blend until smooth, and transfer to a large mixing bowl.

5. Add the flour mixture to the date mixture, and stir to make a thick batter.

6. Using a teaspoon, drop 20 mounds of batter on each prepared cookie sheet, leaving about an inch between drops. Press a walnut half into each mound.

7. Bake for 12 to 14 minutes, or until the cookies are firm but not dried out. Remove the cookies from the baking sheet with a spatula and allow to cool completely before storing in an airtight container.

Erica's
Oatmeal-Raisin Cookies

These cookies are both delicious and versatile. Serve them as a healthful dessert with a nice mug of tea, pair them with vegan yogurt and berries for a nutritious snack, or use them as on on-the-go breakfast. They're best when eaten the day they're baked, but leftover cookies can be frozen and reheated in a toaster oven whenever you're in the mood for a wholesome treat.

YIELD: 12 cookies

1 cup mashed ripe bananas (about 3 medium)

½ cup unsweetened applesauce

½ cup raisins

½ cup shredded unsweetened coconut

¼ cup unsweetened soy, nut, or seed milk

1 teaspoon vanilla extract

1 teaspoon ground cinnamon

2 cups uncooked quick-cooking rolled oats

1. Preheat the oven to 350°F, and line a baking sheet with parchment paper. Set aside.

2. Place the bananas, applesauce, raisins, coconut, milk, vanilla extract, and cinnamon in a large mixing bowl, and stir to combine. Stir in the oats, mixing well.

3. Drop the dough by the heaping tablespoon into mounds on the prepared baking sheet. You can smooth out the mounds a bit, but don't flatten them. Bake for 25 minutes, or until firm and lightly browned.

4. Serve warm or at room temperature, preferably the day they are baked. These cookies do not last long because they are high in moisture and do not contain added sugar. Therefore, it is best to freeze them in an airtight container after the first day and take them out as needed. Remove them from the freezer an hour or 2 before you use them. To reheat, wrap them in aluminum foil and bake in a toaster oven for about 5 minutes at 350°F.

Delicious
Apple Orchard Crisp

This easy-to-make and wholesome dessert, perfect for fall or winter, is wonderful when served warm from the oven, but is also good chilled the next day—if you're lucky enough to have any leftovers.

YIELD: 5 to 6 servings

1 cup unsalted raw pecans, divided

$1/2$ cup uncooked old-fashioned rolled oats

1 teaspoon ground cinnamon

$3/4$ cup firmly packed pitted Medjool dates

1 cup water

1 teaspoon vanilla extract

1 teaspoon minced tangerine zest

5 small apples such as Pink Lady (about $1^1/4$ pounds), washed, cored, and sliced (peel if not organic)

1. Preheat the oven to 350°F. Lightly spray an $8^1/2$ by $4^1/2$ by 3-inch loaf pan with nonstick cooking spray. Set aside.

2. In a blender, grind $3/4$ cup of the pecans to a meal-like consistency. Transfer the meal to a medium-sized mixing bowl. Coarsely grind or chop the remaining $1/4$ cup of nuts, and add them to the mixing bowl.

3. In a blender, grind the rolled oats to a flour or meal-like consistency, and add the meal to the mixing bowl. Add the cinnamon, and mix well.

4. In a blender, combine the dates, water, vanilla extract, and tangerine zest. Blend to a paste.

5. Evenly distribute the sliced apples in the prepared pan. Spread the date paste over the apples, and sprinkle the pecan mixture evenly over the top, pressing it in slightly. Cover with a piece of aluminum foil.

6. Bake for 20 to 30 minutes. Remove the foil and continue baking for about 20 minutes, or until the top is browned and the apples are tender and bubbly. Serve warm or chilled.

Fruit Sorbet

You can make Fruit Sorbet in a food processor, a Champion or Omega juicer, an ice cream maker, or a high-speed blender such as a Vitamix. It makes an elegantly light and luscious dessert. Melon, strawberries, blueberries, papaya, mangos, pears, and peaches are all delicious choices. If you want to make creamy Nice Cream, try the Variation found at the end of the recipe.

YIELD: 4 servings

4 cups bite-sized pieces fruit	$1/8$ teaspoon pure monk fruit powder, if desired
1–2 tablespoons lemon juice, if desired	Mint leaves or fresh fruit for garnish

---

1. Place the fruit of your choice in a plastic freezer bag, and freeze for 6 hours or until solid.

2. Remove the bag from the freezer and hit it against the countertop to separate the frozen chunks.

3. Process the frozen fruit in your choice of machine, adding lemon juice and/or monk fruit powder to taste. (See the inset on page 179 for specific directions.) Transfer immediately to serving bowls, or store it in the freezer for up two hours, or until ready to serve. If either Sorbet or Nice Cream (below) is stored in the freezer for too long, it will freeze solid and have to be broken up and processed again.

Variation

■ To create a super-creamy soft serve ice cream-type dessert known as Nice Cream, follow the directions for Fruit Sorbet, but use mostly frozen bananas instead of other frozen fruit, and omit the lemon juice and monk fruit powder.

Using Your Kitchen Appliance to Make Sorbet or Nice Cream

As explained on page 178, a variety of kitchen appliances can be used to prepare either Fruit Sorbet or Nice Cream. The technique, though, is a little different for each machine. To create a light and delicious frozen treat, follow the directions below.

In a Food Processor: Fill the bowl of the food processor about two-thirds full with frozen fruit. Add a pinch of monk fruit powder, if using. Pulse the machine to get it going, and then process until the fruit is blended, scraping the sides of the bowl as needed. A tablespoon or two of water or lemon juice will help to get the blending process started. Don't over-blend.

In a High-Speed Blender: Place the frozen fruit and a pinch of monk fruit powder and/or lemon juice, if using, in the machine. Start processing the fruit on slow speed, using the tamper to push the fruit down into the blades. Then turn the speed higher until the fruit is blended. Don't over-blend.

In a Juicer: Use the blank plate suggested in the manufacturer's instructions for making ice cream and nut butter. Push the frozen fruit through the hopper. Then quickly stir in a pinch of monk fruit powder/and or lemon juice if using.

In an Ice Cream Machine: Don't freeze the fruit first. Instead, blend the fruit into a slurry in a blender or food processor, mixing in the lemon juice and monk fruit powder, if using. Then pour the mixture into the machine and process it according to the manufacturer's directions.

Kristen's
Kanten Fruit Jell

Kanten is a Japanese jelled dessert made from agar-agar, which is a type of seaweed. Agar-agar is very low in calories, flavorless, and colorless, and can be cooked with fruit juice to create a delicious molded dessert. Unlike a gelatin-thickened dessert, this fruit jell will stay firm at room temperature.

YIELD: 6 servings

4 cups unsweetened fruit juice,   1/4 cup agar-agar flakes
fresh or bottled

1. Place the fruit juice in a 2-quart saucepan, and sprinkle the agar-agar flakes over the juice. Bring the mixture to a boil over high heat while stirring constantly. Reduce the heat to low and simmer, stirring occasionally, for about 5 minutes, or until the agar has completely dissolved in the juice.

2. Pour the mixture into an 11 by 7-inch baking dish. Place the dish in the refrigerator and chill for about 2 hours, or until the kanten is firm.

3. Cut the fruit jell into squares, remove with a spatula, and serve. Store any leftovers in a covered container in the refrigerator.

Variations

■ After the kanten has cooled slightly, fold in nuts or slices of fresh or dried fruit.

■ Replace part or all of the fruit juice with lemonade or hibiscus tea sweetened with a little monk fruit powder.

■ Add mint leaves or spices to the juice while it's simmering. Strain out the herbs and spices before chilling.

Orange Apricot Squares

*Dried apricots make these little treats sweet
and provide a nice change from date and fig bars.*

YIELD: 16 (1-inch) squares

2 cups chopped unsulphured dried
Turkish apricots

$3/4$ cup orange juice or water

1 teaspoon ground ginger

1 teaspoon ground cardamom

$1/2$ teaspoon ground coriander

$1/4$ teaspoon ground nutmeg

2 teaspoons vanilla extract

1 cup unsalted raw walnuts or pecans

$1/2$ cup uncooked old-fashioned
rolled oats

$1/4$ teaspoon pure monk fruit powder

1. Preheat the oven to 350°F. Lightly spray the sides and bottom of an 8 by 8-inch square baking dish with nonstick cooking spray. Set aside.

2. Place the apricots, juice or water, and spices (ginger through nutmeg) in a medium-sized saucepan. Cover and bring to a boil over medium heat. Reduce the heat to low and cook for about 5 minutes, or until the liquid is absorbed, stirring occasionally. Stir in the vanilla extract and set aside.

3. In a blender or food processor, combine the nuts, rolled oats, and monk fruit powder. Grind to a coarse meal.

4. Sprinkle a little less than half the walnut mixture evenly over the bottom of the prepared baking dish. Distribute the apricot filling over the nut mixture by dropping it by the spoonful over the mixture and then spreading it out in an even layer.

5. Sprinkle the rest of the nut mixture over the top of the apricots, and firmly and evenly press it into the apricot mixture, using your hands or a spatula.

6. Bake for about 25 minutes, or until the top is light browned and firm to the touch. Allow to cool for at least 10 minutes before cutting into squares and serving.

Pecan Pie Crust

This is a quick and easy crust for a sweet pie. Unlike a crust that has to be carefully mixed and painstakingly rolled out, this press-in crust does not require any special skills to make, yet it is quite good. Fill the crust with a pumpkin-like filling, as in the recipe for Better Than Pumpkin Pie on page 183; use a fruit filling; or prebake it and spoon in Teff Chocolate Pudding (see page 185).

YIELD: 1 (9-inch) crust

2 tablespoons flaxseeds

$\frac{1}{2}$ cup uncooked old-fashioned rolled oats

1 cup unsalted raw pecans

2 soft pitted Medjool dates

2 tablespoons water, as needed

1. In a blender or coffee mill, grind the flaxseeds to a powder. Transfer the ground flax to a medium-sized mixing bowl.

2. In a blender or food processor, grind the old-fashioned oats to a flour. Transfer to the bowl with the flax.

3. In a blender or food processor, combine the pecans and dates and grind to a coarse meal. Transfer to the bowl with the other ingredients and mix well. While stirring with a fork, sprinkle in the water until the mixture is just moist enough to stick together. Do not add more water than is needed.

4. Lightly spray a 9-inch pie pan with nonstick cooking spray. Transfer the crust mixture to the pie pan, and press it over the sides and bottom of the pan to form an even crust. Press firmly around the edges so they are neat and hold together.

5. For a pre-baked crust, bake at 350°F for 15 minutes, or until crisp and brown, and allow the crust to cool before spooning in the filling. For pies that don't need a pre-baked crust, such as Better Than Pumpkin Pie (see page 183), follow the directions that are presented in the pie recipe.

Better Than Pumpkin Pie

You will probably find this as good as any pumpkin pie you have ever eaten.
Actually, it's made from butternut squash. Any other large, dense, sweet winter squash,
such as Hubbard or kabocha, would also work. You can prepare this dessert with canned
pumpkin in a pinch, but fresh squash has the best flavor and is very easy to use.

YIELD: 9-inch pie

1 medium butternut or other winter squash	3 teaspoons pumpkin pie spice
1 cup firm silken tofu, mashed	1/4 teaspoon pure monk fruit powder, or to taste
1 cup firmly packed soft pitted Medjool dates	1 recipe Pecan Pie Crust, unbaked (see page 182)
1 teaspoon vanilla extract	1/4 cup chopped unsalted raw pecans

1. Pierce the squash with a knife and place it in on a baking sheet in the oven at 375°F. (It's not necessary to preheat the oven.) Bake for about 1 hour, or until soft. Cut the squash in half, discard the seeds and stringy parts, and scoop out enough flesh to make 2 cups of mashed squash, reserving the rest for a soup or side dish.

2. In a high-speed blender or food processor, blend together the baked squash, tofu, dates, vanilla extract, pumpkin pie spice, and monk fruit powder until smooth and creamy.

3. Fill the crust with the squash mixture, spreading it out evenly. Sprinkle the chopped pecans on top, pressing them slightly into the filling.

4. Bake at 350°F for about 50 minutes, or until firm to the touch. Allow the pie to set for at least 20 minutes before slicing. (The filling will firm up more as it cools.)

Helpful Tip

Be sure to use *silken* tofu—the type sold in aseptic containers—when making Better Than Pumpkin Pie. This product has a mild flavor and a good texture for desserts.

Stewed Rhubarb

*Using raisins instead of sugar makes rhubarb plenty sweet
and a lot more nutritious than a sugar-sweetened dish.*

YIELD: 6 servings

5 cups rhubarb, cut into $1/2$-pieces (stalks only)

1 cup raisins

2 tablespoons grated orange zest

1 cinnamon stick

1 teaspoon vanilla extract

$1/4$ cup water or apple juice

$1/8$ teaspoon pure monk fruit powder, or to taste, if desired

1. Place all of the ingredients except for the monk fruit powder in a heavy medium-sized pot over low heat. Cover and bring to a simmer. Reduce the heat to low and cook, stirring occasionally, for 10 to 15 minutes, or until the rhubarb is tender. If the rhubarb begins to stick to the bottom of the pot, add a little more water—but just enough to keep it from sticking.

2. Taste, and stir in the monk fruit powder, if desired. Chill before serving.

Strawberry Pie

*This refreshing pie is as pretty as it is flavorful when it is made with fresh in-season
strawberries. It's easy to prepare, too! Dress it up with Basic Cashew Cream or Cashew
Cream with Vanilla (see page 71), or serve as is. If the strawberries are nice
and sweet, you will not have to add the monk fruit powder or stevia.*

YIELD: 9-inch pie

1 recipe Pecan Pie Crust (see page 182), pre-baked and cooled to room temperature

3 cups sliced strawberries (about $1 1/2$ pints)

$2 1/2$ cups unsweetened berry juice blend

$2 1/2$ tablespoons agar-agar flakes

$1/4$ teaspoon pure monk fruit powder, or a few drops of stevia extract (optional)

1. Fill the baked pie shell with the strawberries. Place the pie in the refrigerator, and chill for about an hour.

2. Place the juice and agar-agar flakes in a medium-sized saucepan, stirring to mix. Bring to a boil over high heat. Then reduce the heat to a simmer and cook, stirring occasionally, for about 5 minutes, or until the agar flakes have completely dissolved. Transfer the mixture to a bowl and allow to cool for 3 to 5 minutes. Taste, and if additional sweetness is desired, stir in the monk fruit powder or stevia.

3. Pour the fruit juice mixture over the strawberries, and return the pie to the refrigerator. Chill for a couple of hours, or until firm. Slice and serve.

Teff Chocolate Pudding

Teff is a tiny chocolate-colored grain from Ethiopia, with a subtly sweet flavor. It is gluten-free and high in fiber, and makes a wonderful base for this chocolate pudding.

YIELD: 6 servings

$1/2$ cup teff, rinsed and drained	2 teaspoons vanilla extract
2 cups water	$1/4$ cup cocoa or cacao powder
1 cup firmly packed soft pitted Medjool dates	$1/8$ teaspoon pure monk fruit powder to taste, if desired

1. Combine the teff and water in a medium-sized pot, and bring to a boil. Reduce the heat to low, cover, and cook, stirring occasionally, for 15 to 20 minutes, or until the water is absorbed.

2. Transfer the cooked teff to a food processor or high-speed blender along with the dates and vanilla extract. Blend until very smooth.

3. Transfer the blended mixture to a bowl, and stir in the cocoa or cacao powder. Stir in the monk fruit powder, if using.

4. Spoon the pudding into individual dessert bowls or stemmed glasses and serve warm.

Stuffed Figs

Make this in late fall or winter when you can find freshly dried figs that are still nice and soft. You can wrap them up to throw in a backpack for a hike, but they are pretty enough to serve to guests as part of an elegant buffet.

YIELD: 18 to 20 figs

18–20 large brown dried figs	1 teaspoon ground cardamom
1¼ cups unsalted raw pecans	18–20 pecan halves

1. Cut off the very tip of the stem end of the figs and, using your fingers, open up each fig to form a little pouch. Set aside.

2. Place the pecans and cardamom in a blender or food processor, and coarsely grind the nuts.

3. Stuff the figs with the nut mixture and top each one with a pecan half, pressing it into a filling. Store in an airtight container in the refrigerator until ready to serve.

Strawberries in Rose Water Sauce

Rose water lends an exotic touch to this simple dessert. Try these delectable strawberries alone, or spoon some over Teff Chocolate Pudding (see page 185). Kudzu is available in most health food stores and is sold with Japanese foods. Rose water is available in stores that sell Middle Eastern foods.

YIELD: 8 servings

¼ cup kudzu root powder	4 cups sliced strawberries
¼ cup plus 1 tablespoon water	1 teaspoon rose water
4 cups unsweetened mixed berry juice	

1. Place the kudzu and water in a small bowl, and stir to dissolve.

2. Combine the juice and dissolved kudzu in a medium-sized pot. While stirring constantly, bring the mixture to a rolling boil and cook for 1 to 2 minutes, or until the mixture thickens. Transfer to a serving bowl and allow to cool.

3. Stir the strawberries and rose water into the cooled juice mixture, and chill before serving.

Wholesome Banana Bread

Make this delicious treat when you have too many ripe bananas.
Or just buy too many ripe bananas as an excuse to make it.

YIELD: 1 loaf

1½ cups whole grain spelt flour	½ teaspoon ground nutmeg
½ cup garbanzo flour	½ cup chopped dates
1½ teaspoons baking powder	½ cup chopped unsalted raw pecans
1 teaspoon baking soda	1½ cups mashed bananas
2 teaspoons ground ginger	1 cup unsweetened soy, nut, or seed milk
1 teaspoon ground cinnamon	2 tablespoons cider vinegar

1. Preheat the oven to 350°F. Spray a 8½ by 4½ by 3–inch loaf pan with nonstick cooking spray, and dust it generously with flour. Set aside.

2. In a mixing bowl, combine the spelt flour, garbanzo flour, baking powder, baking soda, ginger, cinnamon, and nutmeg, mixing well. Stir in the chopped dates and pecans. Set aside.

3. In a separate mixing bowl, combine the mashed bananas, milk, and vinegar, mixing well.

4. Add the flour mixture to the wet mixture, and stir with a folding motion just enough to combine the ingredients and make a batter. Do not overmix.

5. Transfer the batter to the prepared loaf pan, and bake for 35 to 40 minutes, or just until the loaf is firm to the touch and a toothpick inserted in the center comes out clean.

6. Run a knife around the edges of the pan to loosen the loaf and remove it from the pan. Allow to cool for at least 5 minutes before slicing and serving.

Helpful Tip

When your loaf of Wholesome Banana Bread has cooled completely, you can slice it and place it in a bag in the freezer. This will allow you to take out slices as needed and enjoy them for dessert, toast them for a delicious treat, or serve them for breakfast with nut butter and fresh fruit.

Metric Conversion Tables

COMMON LIQUID CONVERSIONS

Measurement	=	Milliliters
1/4 teaspoon	=	1.25 milliliters
1/2 teaspoon	=	2.50 milliliters
3/4 teaspoon	=	3.75 milliliters
1 teaspoon	=	5.00 milliliters
1 1/4 teaspoons	=	6.25 milliliters
1 1/2 teaspoons	=	7.50 milliliters
1 3/4 teaspoons	=	8.75 milliliters
2 teaspoons	=	10.0 milliliters
1 tablespoon	=	15.0 milliliters
2 tablespoons	=	30.0 milliliters

Measurement	=	Milliliters
1/4 cup	=	0.06 liters
1/2 cup	=	0.12 liters
3/4 cup	=	0.18 liters
1 cup	=	0.24 liters
1 1/4 cups	=	0.30 liters
1 1/2 cups	=	0.36 liters
2 cups	=	0.48 liters
2 1/2 cups	=	0.60 liters
3 cups	=	0.72 liters
3 1/2 cups	=	0.84 liters
4 cups	=	0.96 liters
4 1/2 cups	=	1.08 liters
5 cups	=	1.20 liters
5 1/2 cups	=	1.32 liters

CONVERTING FAHRENHEIT TO CELSIUS

Fahrenheit	=	Celsius
200–205	=	95
220–225	=	105
245–250	=	120
275	=	135
300–305	=	150
325–330	=	165
345–350	=	175
370–375	=	190
400–405	=	205
425–430	=	220
445–450	=	230
470–475	=	245
500	=	260

CONVERSION FORMULAS

LIQUID

When You Know	Multiply By	To Determine
teaspoons	5.0	milliliters
tablespoons	15.0	milliliters
fluid ounces	30.0	milliliters
cups	0.24	liters
pints	0.47	liters
quarts	0.95	liters

WEIGHT

When You Know	Multiply By	To Determine
ounces	28.0	grams
pounds	0.45	kilograms

Index

"EMPOWERING"

Joel Fuhrman, MD, *New York Times* **Best-selling Author**
President, Nutritional Research Foundation

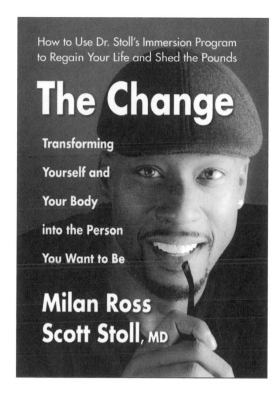

How to Use Dr. Stoll's Immersion Program to Regain Your Life and Shed the Pounds

The Change

Transforming Yourself and Your Body into the Person You Want to Be

Milan Ross Scott Stoll, MD

THE CHANGE
Transforming Yourself and Your Body into the Person You Want to Be
Milan Ross and Scott Stoll, MD

Working at Whole Foods had been good to Milan Ross. It not only allowed him to earn a decent living but also provided the medical insurance his family so desperately needed. But it wasn't until Milan was offered the opportunity to attend Dr. Stoll's Immersion program that his life totally changed. This is the story of how Milan Ross lost two hundred and twenty-five pounds of excess weight and found the passion his life had been missing.

Since 2010, Dr. Scott Stoll, a medical doctor and past Olympic athlete, has conducted a week-long intensive health program. The seven-day course provides the most up-to-date information on nutrition, achievable exercise, and culinary education, as well as encouragement, coaching, and vision casting. While food is the centerpiece of the program, it is meant to be a transformational experience that forever changes the attitudes, habits, and lives of those who attend the program—all in just one week. It was to this program that Whole Foods sent Milan Ross.

The Change not only tells the personal story of Milan Ross and what he experienced during that crucial week of his life but also provides the voice of Dr. Stoll, who takes the reader through the very same program Milan experienced. Unlike weight-loss books that offer quick fixes to lose the pounds, *The Change* is designed to look within each individual and see what is driving him or her to eat food that is known to be unhealthy. Based on science and inner strength, which is the true seed of change, this book is meant to have its readers lose weight and be healthy not for just a month or a year but for a lifetime.

$24.95 • 240 pages • 6 x 9-inch hardback • ISBN 978-0-7570-0432-2

LIVE FOODS LIVE BODIES!
Recipes for Life
Jay and Linda Kordich

Through years of healthful living, Jay and Linda Kordich have learned that abundant energy, enhanced mental clarity, and a sense of well-being are easily within reach. In *Live Foods Live Bodies!,* they reveal all their secrets, including juice therapy and a living foods diet. This powerful book—lavishly illustrated with beautiful full-color photos—was designed to help you transform the person you are into the person you want to become, and features over 100 kitchen-tested recipes for delectable juices, salad dressings, soups, and much more.

$18.95 US • 240 pages • 7.5 x 9-inch quality paperback • ISBN 978-0-7570-0385-1

JUICE ALIVE, SECOND EDITION
The Ultimate Guide to Juicing Remedies
Steven Bailey, ND, and Larry Trivieri, Jr.

Fresh juices offer a powerhouse of antioxidants, vitamins, minerals, and enzymes. In this easy-to-use guide, two health experts tell you everything you need to know to maximize the benefits and tastes of juice. They explore the history of juicing, examine the healthful components of juice, and offer practical advice about the types of juices available, as well as buying and storing tips for produce. A chart matches up common ailments with the most appropriate juices, and 100 recipes make good nutrition completely delicious.

$14.95 US • 288 pages • 6 x 9-inch quality paperback • ISBN 978-0-7570-0266-3

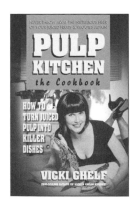

PULP KITCHEN
How to Turn Juiced Pulp into Inspired Dishes
Vicki Chelf

"What can I do with all that pulp?" If you juice, you've probably asked yourself this question more than once. It seems like such a waste . . . and it is! Leftover pulp from juiced produce can improve the texture of many foods and also add flavor, color, dietary fiber, and nutrients.

In *Pulp Kitchen,* noted cook and best-selling author Vicki Chelf shares the many uses for this unique and often overlooked ingredient. She offers helpful preparation and storage guidelines, plus a handy chart of pulp and juice yields for various types of produce. Next come dozens of kitchen-tested recipes highlighting pulp's goodness and versatility. Great food can be made even better—and better for you—through the simple addition of pulp.

$14.95 US • 144 pages • 6 x 9-inch quality paperback • ISBN 978-0-7570-0396-7

THE WORLD GOES RAW COOKBOOK
An International Collection of Raw Vegetarian Recipes
Lisa Mann

People everywhere know that meals prepared without heat can taste great and improve their overall health. Yet raw cuisine cookbooks have always offered little variety—until now. In *The World Goes Raw Cookbook,* raw food chef Lisa Mann provides a fresh approach to (un)cooking with recipes that have an international twist.

After discussing the healthfulness of a raw food diet, *The World Goes Raw Cookbook* tells you how to stock your kitchen with the tools and ingredients that make it easy to prepare raw meals. What follows are six recipe chapters, each focused on a different ethnic cuisine, including Italian, Mexican, Middle Eastern, Asian, Caribbean, and South American dishes. Whether you are already interested in raw food or are exploring it for the first time, the taste-tempting recipes in *The World Goes Raw Cookbook* can add variety to your life while helping you feel healthier and more energized than ever before.

$16.95 • 176 pages • 7.5 x 9-inch quality paperback • ISBN 978-0-7570-0320-2

EAT SMART, EAT RAW
Creative Vegetarian Recipes for a Healthier Life
Kate Wood

As the popularity of raw vegetarian cuisine continues to soar, so does the evidence that uncooked food is amazingly good for you. From lowering cholesterol to eliminating excess weight, the health benefits of this diet are too important to ignore. Now there is another reason to go raw—taste! In *Eat Smart, Eat Raw,* cook and health writer Kate Wood not only explains how to get started, but also provides kitchen-tested recipes guaranteed to delight even the fussiest of eaters.

Eat Smart, Eat Raw begins by discussing the basics of cooking without heat. This is followed by twelve chapters offering 150 recipes for truly exceptional dishes, including hearty breakfasts, savory soups, satisfying entrées, and luscious desserts. There's even a chapter on the "almost raw." Whether you are an ardent vegetarian or just someone in search of a great meal, *Eat Smart, Eat Raw* may forever change the way you look at an oven.

$15.95 • 184 pages • 7.5 x 9-inch quality paperback • ISBN 978-0-7570-0261-8

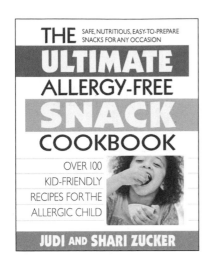

THE ULTIMATE ALLERGY-FREE SNACK COOKBOOK
Over 100 Kid-Friendly Recipes for the Allergic Child
Judi and Shari Zucker

If you have kids, you know how hard it is to find healthy snacks. And if your kids have food allergies, it's even more challenging. Commercially made crackers, chips, and other snack foods tend to be highly processed and loaded with sugar, trans fats, preservatives, and other undesirable ingredients. So what's the solution? How can you provide your child with safe snacks that are not only appealing, but also nutritionally sound?

The Ultimate Allergy-Free Snack Cookbook is designed to help. It provides over 100 vegetarian recipes that are free of eggs, cow's milk, soy, wheat, peanuts, tree nuts, fish, and shellfish. They are also free of gluten and refined white sugar. Best of all, the snacks are wholesome and nutritious—rich in whole grains and fiber, and low in calories. Of course, even the most nutritious foods won't benefit your kids unless they eat them. So the chapters are jam packed with kid-favorite choices—cookies, brownies, chips, pizza, burgers, sorbets, smoothies, and more. But this book is not just about recipes. It also offers helpful tips and support for anyone with an allergic family. This really is the ultimate snack cookbook!

$15.95 • 144 pages • 7.5 x 9-inch quality paperback • ISBN 978-0-7570-0346-2

VICKI'S VEGAN KITCHEN
Eating with Sanity, Compassion & Taste
Vicki Chelf

Welcome to *Vicki's Vegan Kitchen!* Come on in. There's always room for anyone who wants to experience the pleasures of vegan cooking. After all, it's no secret that dishes made with fresh local ingredients that are properly prepared are absolutely delicious . . . and the healthiest that the planet has to offer. As Dr. T. Colin Campbell's comprehensive China Study has shown, there is an undeniable link between a vegan diet and the prevention of serious health conditions, including heart disease, cancer, type II diabetes, and autoimmune diseases. And as you are about to discover, *Vicki's Vegan Kitchen* is the perfect cookbook to support this healthy dietary lifestyle. In it, author Vicki Chelf—cooking teacher and decades-long follower of the vegan diet—shows you just how easy it is to prepare divinely delicious plant-based foods.

Once you step into *Vicki's Vegan Kitchen*, you won't want to leave. Along with enjoying the delicious, satisfying food it offers, you will ultimately enjoy the radiant health that it brings.

$17.95 US • 320 pages • 7.5 x 9-inch quality paperback • ISBN 978-0-7570-0251-9

THE ULTIMATE ALLERGY-FREE COOKBOOK
Over 150 Easy-to-Make Recipes That Contain No Milk, Eggs, Wheat, Peanuts, Tree Nuts, Soy, Fish, or Shellfish
Judi and Shari Zucker

For too many people, the term "allergy-free cooking" conjures images of bland and boring meals—dishes that seem to be "missing something." But the fact is that meals can be made flavorful, satisfying, and healthful, and still eliminate common allergenic foods. Best-selling authors Judi and Shari Zucker have created a cookbook that will guide you in doing just that. *The Ultimate Allergy-Free Cookbook* is an exciting collection of over 150 delectable dishes that contain absolutely no eggs, cow's milk, soy, wheat, peanuts, tree nuts, fish, or shellfish--the eight foods most likely to cause allergic reactions. It offers valuable information on the dangers of cross-contamination of allergens in packaged foods, and helps you understand food labels. You'll even learn how to stock a safe allergen-free kitchen.

$15.95 • 192 pages • 7.5 x 9-inch quality paperback • ISBN 978-0-7570-0397-4

GOING WILD IN THE KITCHEN
The Fresh & Sassy Tastes of Vegetarian Cooking
Leslie Cerier

Go wild in the kitchen! Venture beyond the usual beans, grains, and vegetables to include an exciting variety of organic vegetarian fare in your meals. *Going Wild in the Kitchen,* written by expert chef Leslie Cerier, shows you how. In addition to providing helpful cooking tips and techniques, this book offers over 150 kitchen-tested recipes for taste-tempting dishes that contain such unique ingredients as edible flowers; tasty sea vegetables; wild mushrooms, berries, and herbs; and exotic ancient grains like teff, quinoa, and Chinese "forbidden" black rice. The author encourages the creative instincts of novice and seasoned cooks alike, prompting them to "go wild" in the kitchen by adding, changing, or substituting ingredients in existing recipes. To help, an extensive ingredient glossary is included, along with a wealth of helpful cooking guidelines. Lively illustrations and a complete resource list for finding organic foods completes this user-friendly cookbook.

Going Wild in the Kitchen is more than a unique cookbook—it's a recipe for inspiration. Excite your palate with this treasure-trove of distinctive, healthy, and taste-tempting recipe creations.

$16.95 • 240 pages • 7.5 x 9-inch quality paperback • ISBN 978-0-7570-0091-1

**For more information about our books,
visit our website at www.squareonepublishers.com**

About the Authors

Milan Ross was born and raised in Saint Louis, Missouri, and graduated from Central Visual and Performing Arts High School. After pursuing a career in the music industry and getting married, his family was faced with a health crisis, which required him to find a job that provided health insurance to cover mounting medical bills. In 2012, Milan walked away from his career in music and took a position with Whole Foods Market. This fateful decision changed not only Milan's life but also the life of each member of his family.

As an overweight individual, Milan was intrigued by the health retreat offered by Whole Foods to its employees in need. He soon applied and was accepted. After attending Dr. Stoll's Immersion program in 2013, Milan lost over two hundred and twenty-five pounds. He has since made it his life's mission to help people attain optimal health and change their lives, conducting speaking engagements across the United States. In addition, Milan has developed his own organic health food line, Full Flavor Vegan.

Scott Stoll, MD, received his medical degree from the University of Colorado. He is board certified by the American Board of Physical Medicine and Rehabilitation and specializes in regenerative medicine, utilizing natural treatments, diet, and lifestyle to aid the body in healing chronic disease and injuries.

Prior to receiving his MD, Dr. Stoll was a member of the 1994 US Olympic Bobsled team, and he currently serves as a physician for USA Bobsled & Skeleton. He is cofounder of the Plantrician Project and the International Plant-Based Nutrition Healthcare Conference; has served as a member of the Whole Foods scientific and medical advisory board; is athletic team physician for Lehigh University; and is department chairman of Physical Medicine and Rehabilitation at Coordinated Health.